GOVERNMENT IN ACTION
IN THE UNITED KINGDOM

By the Same Author

THE NORMAN CONQUEST AND THE COMMON LAW
THE PASSING OF PARLIAMENT

Government in Action

in the United Kingdom

GEORGE W. KEETON

LONDON · ERNEST BENN LIMITED

NEW YORK · BARNES & NOBLE · INC

First published by Ernest Benn Limited 1970
Bouverie House · Fleet Street · London · EC4
and Barnes & Noble Inc
105 Fifth Avenue · New York 10003

© George W. Keeton 1970

Distributed in Canada by
The General Publishing Company Limited · Toronto

Printed in Great Britain

ISBN 0–510–27611–3
SBN 389–03998–5 (USA)

Contents

Introduction

EVER SINCE 1945, the United Kingdom has been attempting, without apparent success, to adjust herself to a changed world, and to a changed status in it. When the United Kingdom went to war in 1939, with the Commonwealth in support, she was still a leading world power, the centre of a worldwide financial system, who, with France, had dominated European affairs, and had exercised a major influence upon world affairs, throughout the inter-war period. When, after the fall of France, Winston Churchill appealed to the United States in memorable terms 'Give us the tools and we will finish the job', few in Britain doubted that it was possible, and in this they were in accord with the predominant opinion in the United States. Yet, as later events have shown, the task was too great, and only the attack by Hitler upon Russia, and the Japanese attack upon Pearl Harbor, made it possible to build the great coalition which brought about the overthrow of those two ruthless dictatorships. When, at a later stage in the war, with victory already in sight, Churchill was asked what his reaction to the worldwide revolt against 'colonialism' would be, he replied that he had not become Prime Minister to preside over the liquidation of the British Empire. A quarter of a century later, practically nothing remains of that formerly worldwide system. Scarcely a year has passed without one or more additions to the lengthy list of independence acts, and the zeal of Whitehall administrators, inspired by ideas to which their predecessors were total strangers, has given independence in season and out of season to areas in all continents, without waiting for evidence that the independence so achieved could be maintained, or even that the entity so emancipated had an internal coherence that would ensure its future prosperity. Some areas have been given independence almost in spite of themselves. Others such as the Falkland Islands and Gibraltar, have remained obstinately British, in spite of the thinly veiled desire of the government of the day to barter them, in one case certainly, for transitory commercial advantages. The rapidity with which the British, French, and Dutch colonial empires have disappeared has no counterpart in history, and it is therefore not surprising that economic and political instability, dictatorships, and even civil wars, as in Nigeria and the Congo, have followed swiftly upon it. Into the vacuum thus created, the United States has slipped, with aid almost prodigally poured out. This aid has been given upon the hypothesis that many of the ills with which emergent nations are afflicted spring from poverty, disease, and ignorance, and that stability and prosperity will follow upon the eradication of them. The history of the emergent nations shows little to support such an optimistic diagnosis, and today, in the United States, it has been substantially abandoned.

In the United Kingdom, too, there has been a more realistic assessment of the relations between the British and the emancipated territories than was expressed in the early years of independence. The idea that Commonwealth unity could be preserved has been abandoned in face of a variety of conflicting interests within the Commonwealth itself; immigrants into the United Kingdom; apartheid in South Africa (now no longer a Commonwealth member); white domination in Rhodesia, with the consequential assertion of independence; the question of the entry of the United Kingdom into the Common Market; the Suez crisis; and Kashmir – all these, and numerous other problems, political and economic, are milestones in Commonwealth disintegration, not because they existed, but because the Commonwealth link was too shadowy for any agreed solution to be attempted. The idea that common interest in remaining together would prove more durable than formal institutions, or even definite commitments, has proved a complete failure, and its obituary was probably written by Michael Stewart, as Foreign Minister, on his visit to India in December 1968, when he explained that what was desired by the United Kingdom was a more 'mature' relationship between the two countries. By this he was understood to mean a relationship which recognised that the outlooks and policies of the two countries differed widely, that Britain's primary interest was now in Europe, and that her interest in the Indian subcontinent was minimal. Whatever regrets may be felt for the passing of a great era of Anglo-Indian association, it is at least refreshing for a responsible British Minister to recognise that the inconsistencies and vagueness with which the Commonwealth ideas have always hitherto been enveloped have failed to supply a useful purpose, and ought therefore to be discarded. At long last, and with many pauses and digressions along the way, the United Kingdom has assumed a freedom to decide and act in the international sphere to which she has been a stranger since the Napoleonic Wars. From this point of view, the joining of the Foreign and Commonwealth Offices, together with the disappearance of the Colonial and India Offices at an earlier date, is symbolic. What is of interest is that these far-reaching changes in the national outlook have taken place without protest, and almost without comment. Even the decision of the Labour government to restrict, and ultimately to end, its activities east of Suez have evoked only formal cries of dissent from the Opposition. No one really believes that at any future date the British can decisively influence events east of Suez again. After the fall of France in 1940, a mood almost of gaiety took possession of Britain, which was summed up in the phrase: 'At last we are on our own.' A somewhat similar mood has been the result of an almost undignified scramble to shed the last of her colonial responsibilities.

What the British people have unfortunately failed to appreciate is that these vast and worldwide changes have profound secondary consequences for them, even if one ignores (as is now the fashion) the possible harmful effects upon the emancipated territories themselves. The last are unfortunately not hypothetical. Without exception, these territories, on achieving independence, have obtained financial, economic, and other aid, from Britain, the United States, and the United Nations. This has concealed the severity of the operation which has occurred. No country (not even a so-called 'underdeveloped' country) can live indefinitely upon this aid. Whilst much of very great value has been done in a very short space of time through its instrumentality, much also has been done which is of very doubtful value, sometimes at the cost of laying waste the country's material resources, and of provoking a drift from the countryside into the towns. If the African nations, for example, care to study in detail the economic and social history of India, Pakistan, Burma, and Ceylon since independence, they will find much to disturb them, as they will also in the more lengthy history of the countries of South America. Independence, in fact, is simply the starting-point for a list of new problems, to be faced in a fiercely competitive world, under conditions which steadily become more difficult.

These, however, are no longer the problems of the United Kingdom, which has problems of her own in abundance. One which
rises directly from this vast and continuous transfer of power
arises from the fact that, for the first time since the reign of Queen
Elizabeth I, the British, except for a small minority, are now compelled to concentrate their efforts within the islands which make
up the United Kingdom, and that they are already experiencing
the cramping effects of this constriction. It is difficult to assess
with accuracy the numbers of British subjects who went abroad to
settle permanently in the two centuries which preceded 1939, but
the populations of British Canada, of the United States, of Australia, New Zealand, South Africa, and even of South America,
are evidence of the scale of that emigration, which, far from depriving the United Kingdom of initiative and skill, actually stimulated it in those who remained, and who increased startlingly in
numbers in the century which separated Waterloo from the outbreak of the First World War. Some evidence of this is that all
parts of the United Kingdom contributed to a race of overseas administrators, engineers, doctors, lawyers, and others who governed
vast areas which were being opened up to development, and that
others furnished the manpower in the armed forces, military and
naval; who secured the internal order, and protected these vast
areas from external attack, so making their peaceful development
possible. Migration to the 'white' nations of the Commonwealth
is still proceeding, and remains possible because, as yet, it is still
possible to transfer one's assets there; but the race of administrators and specialists which worldwide responsibilities demanded has
vanished almost without trace, and the classes from which they
have been drawn have been progressively submerged by ruinous
taxation, allied to a changed social outlook.

Problems of many kinds, to which the British people have long
been strangers, have pressed upon them continuously since 1945.
For example, there has been the exceedingly difficult problem of
adjustment in the international sphere to the status of a second-rate
power. The lesson has been learnt slowly, and not without serious
inroads upon national pride. The Suez fiasco brought home, as
nothing else could have done, the realisation that it was no longer
open to Britain to dictate the course of events in the Middle
East, and that British foreign policy inescapably depends upon the
approval of the United States. It also demonstrated the futility
of dreams of a 'third force', which might retain freedom of action

in a world dominated by two super-powers, the U.S.S.R. and the U.S.A.; of continental size, and alone possessing the resources to wage a full-scale nuclear war. In similar fashion, it has been demonstrated that it is vain for any Western European state to seek to pursue a defence policy which can compete, either in man-power or weaponry, with the programmes of the two super-powers. They can exist only within some larger framework in which the United States is the dominant partner, and which is, in the last resort, an element in a worldwide defensive system. Western Euro-pean states can, and do, influence the formation of American de-fensive policies, although not decisively, but it is only within such a framework that particular foreign policies can now operate. Even were the American dream of a United Western Europe to be achieved, it would be with the intention that such a unit should assume a greater responsibility for local defence, again within a worldwide framework, designed to assure the security of the non-communist world.

There is no need to multiply instances of these overriding condi-tions in the conduct of foreign relations. They are generally under-stood, and they explain, to an important degree, the failure of the Commonwealth concept. Even for its members, the centre of gravity is now not in London, but in Washington. This is true, not only in the political sphere, but in those of finance and economic development also. The impoverished condition of the United Kingdom since 1945 has disabled her from furnishing the resources for rapid advance which all Commonwealth members have re-quired. Increasingly they have been supplied by the United States, and more recently by Germany and France, and even by the U.S.S.R. There is, of course, the World Bank, which finances development schemes advanced by the underdeveloped nations themselves; the United States contributes half of her capital, and her President is always an American. This change has exercised a marked influence upon the outlooks of the recipients, who have increasingly come to regard the Commonwealth as something lacking in reality, especially as the division between members upon such questions as Suez, the restriction of coloured immigra-tion into the United Kingdom, the independence of Rhodesia, and the Civil War in Nigeria has become apparent. Even in the United Kingdom, interest in the Commonwealth as a link has practically ceased.

The external changes which have been briefly touched upon

have profoundly affected the national outlook. The disappearance of colonial and overseas responsibilities has been accepted almost with relief. The problems of the new nations have appeared to have little relevance, and there have been expressions of irritation that they should appear to complicate the solution of Britain's own. In the negotiations which accompanied the United Kingdom's first application to join the Common Market, the position of the Commonwealth was a factor which received extended attention. This was much less apparent on the second application, and if the time should arrive when the United Kingdom's entry became an accomplished fact, the effect upon the Commonwealth would be considerably less than it would have been in 1963 or 1964. The first application, in fact, served notice upon members that the traditional relationship with the United Kingdom was about to be profoundly modified, and Commonwealth nations have modified their external relationships progressively since that date. The result is that the Commonwealth nations are less dependent upon British support than before.

The purpose of this book is to examine how far the constitutional machinery and political organisation of the United Kingdom is adequate for the tasks which lie ahead, and also how far, in the changed context, democratic government and personal freedom can still be regarded as the basic assumptions upon which English public life is based.

Public life, and the constitutional system in which it operates, has changed profoundly since World War II, and it is still in the process of change. Old-fashioned political machinery has been examined and, where possible, adapted to fit the needs of an overwhelmingly urban society, committed to a technological culture. This far-reaching reorganisation is not peculiar to the United Kingdom. It is shared by other Western European nations and by the United States. In 1968, Louis Heren drew attention in *The Times* to some observations of Mark Acuff, one of Senator Eugene McCarthy's campaign managers in his unsuccessful bid for the Presidency. After stressing the difficulty of adapting democracy to a technological culture, he added: 'Today, it is not only the black and the poor and the young who feel powerless to affect the machinations of the system. In the last half of the twentieth century, the smog-bound, tax-hounded, and radar-trapped suburbanite also feels cast adrift in a sea of technocracy where no one cares and, worse, no one listens.'

It is not without significance that the particular appeal of Senator McCarthy was exactly to the classes whom Mr Acuff mentioned. In the United Kingdom, the problem is a similar one, and the reaction is the same. There is, however, a major difference. In the United States, clear limits to the encroachments of government upon individual liberty are set by the constitution. The citizen of the United Kingdom is exposed to a greater degree because of the lack of any formal constitutional document. As a direct result, invasion of personal liberty, the growth of bureaucracy, and an increasing authoritarianism in government have proceeded a good deal further. In the following chapters, the main features of that encroachment are examined, and the final chapter contains some suggestions for improvement.

I

The Problem

THE BASIC fact of life with which all British governments since 1945 have grappled, so far with only very limited success, is that 50 million people, rising possibly to 65 million by the end of the century, are crowded into Britain with a high standard of living. There is no possibility that they can feed themselves, and accordingly, they must export to live, in a world where competition becomes steadily keener; where many more nations than before, having industrialised to a significant extent, seek to compete both within the domestic market and abroad; and finally, where there is no association – no dependent Commonwealth – whose resources can be developed on favourable terms, and whose economies are geared to the needs of Britain. For some years after the end of World War II, there existed the comforting assumption that a high degree of technical skill, developed in a community where educational standards were already high, and which were planned to become still higher, allied with the experience and initiative of British manufacturers, would produce a steady and continuous growth in industry and exports, sufficient to preserve and improve the British standard of living. From this point of view, the end of the colonial era in the world as a whole, with the emergence of many new nations, seeking to transform themselves almost overnight by the development of their resources and industrialisation, offered many new opportunities, from which British industry, in competition with others, could benefit. Emancipation and economic development were to go hand in hand for the national benefit of the participants.

Side by side with the technological revolution, upon which Britain's future prosperity was to depend, marched two other major changes: (1) The establishment of the Welfare State, and (2) the nationalisation of the coal industry, of transport, and finally, of the steel industry. To discuss the wisdom or otherwise of undertaking such far-reaching changes when so much of the future was at risk would be inappropriate here. There have clearly been very great benefits. There have also been very serious disadvantages, more especially in connection with the nationalisation, de-nationalisation, and re-nationalisation of steel. From first to last, this has been treated as a party question, to which the welfare of the industry itself must take second place. This was inevitable, once the nationalisation of certain key industries had become part of the dogma of one of the major political parties. Yet it has become increasingly irrelevant to Britain's interests, in an age when the distinction between an industry which is nationalised and one which is controlled from Whitehall tends to become blurred, and when any major industry exists only within a framework of regulations, controls, orders, directives, incentives, and taxation designed to control its growth, the price of its products, and even of the markets to which its products are dispatched.

These changes have not only transformed society. They have produced the greatest concentration of power in the government of the day that Britain has known, certainly since the Cromwellian dictatorship. They have also involved the regulation of individual lives from cradle to grave by the departments of government. They have subjected people to the direction of a growing army of civil servants, and to the jurisdiction of innumerable boards, tribunals, and officials, making decisions which daily affect everyone, and against which there is usually no redress by the ordinary processes of law, a development against which lawyers and judges have frequently protested, but which continues unabated. Speaking at the Annual Dinner of the High Court Journalists' Association on 28 November 1968, both Sir Leslie Scarman and Lord Justice Danckwerts drew attention to the dangers inherent in this, and Lord Justice Danckwerts said with characteristic vigour:

> 'It does not belong to the history of any particular parliamentary party – although the Socialist party believed in regulating everything in life. It goes back to the Education Act, 1944, and various Acts since then. You will find that instead of the Courts investigating cases and making an order to protect the subject, the matter is decided irrevocably by some Minister, or worse – some bloody-minded civil servant.'[1]

In *The Passing of Parliament*, published very appropriately on 5 November 1952, these ominous features of Britain's national life were discussed at length. Briefly, the theme of that book was

[1] *The Times*, 29 November 1968.

that Parliament was progressively failing in its historic functions, that much governmental power had passed to the department of state, that there were few remaining checks on the power of the Cabinet, and especially of the Prime Minister, and that, unless the process was arrested, Britain was in danger of finding herself under the control of a dictatorship, however soothingly disguised. The primary reason for these evils, I suggested, was the lack of a written constitution – a situation which was a source of weakness, and not of strength. In the final paragraph of that book I wrote:

'It is the very existence of a formally unfettered Parliamentary sovereignty that is the main source of weakness in Britain's existing institutions, when the legal sovereign has shown itself so willing to delegate its powers as Parliament has done during the past half century. If the temper of the times remains favourable to increasing interference with the lives of citizens, towards the destruction of individual initiative, and towards the concentration of economic wealth in the State, then any safeguards which legal and political ingenuity may devise will remain as ineffective as Consumers' Councils within state monopolies are today. Behind the high-sounding generalisations of present-day politics, the issue is really a very simple one. It is whether Britain should accustom herself to the ant-like existence of the fully-integrated and planned state, or whether she believes that individual initiative and increased opportunity are more likely to produce more tolerable conditions of life for the bulk of her citizens. In the long run, it is impossible to preserve freedom of the mind when the power to choose has been removed from the citizen in more and more areas of his daily life. In the end, there will have been produced something like the planned stagnation of the Chinese Empire. That would be an odd fate for a people who built the Common Law, and who were responsible for Magna Carta, *habeas corpus*, and dominion status. Yet the threat is real and the hour late. Britain's present predicament presents a challenge which it is impossible to ignore.'

Unfortunately, although the warning contained in that book received full attention and discussion in the press, the political parties remained completely unaffected by it, and in the intervening years, the situation has deteriorated, so far as personal freedom of choice is concerned, to a degree which would not have been regarded as possible in 1952. Encroachments have been continuous and steadily more direct, and the views expressed in *The Passing of Parliament* in 1952 are now the underlying assumptions of public discussion of present political insecurity. For example, a leading article in *The Times* of 21 September 1968, under the title *The British Constitution*, after taking comfort from the statement that, as yet, there are no signs either of Caesarism or of the one-party state in Britain, continues that there will have to be constitutional changes in response to the sudden rise of Scottish and Welsh nationalism, and that a new revising chamber in Parliament, as a substitute for the Lords, will have to be devised. It then adds:

'The political power of the State to oppress its own citizens is greater now than it has ever been in the past and it is still growing rapidly. It is no longer reasonable to assume that we can do without formal safeguards.'

The writer continues by pointing out that a modern government could (1) prolong the life of Parliament, probably indefinitely, and (2) govern by decree. Against these threats, he argues, there are no effective safeguards, and he continues that there should be a written constitution, providing self-governing assemblies for Scotland, Wales, and other areas. There should be a limitation of the power of the Prime Minister to dissolve Parliament, and a Supreme Court to interpret the constitution. He concludes:

'Too much power is centralised in Westminster and, of that power, too much is centralised in the Prime Minister, who is subject to too few restrictions on his freedom of action so long as he can maintain the support of his own party. The existence of general elections, of a free press and television, and of free judges and of free law still makes this a democratic system of government, and in many ways an admirable one – but there is an urgent need to change some parts of our constitution, and these reforms ought to include stronger safeguards for the liberties we possess and a greater opportunity for local and democratic action.'

Every point made in this leading article was discussed in *The Passing of Parliament* over sixteen years earlier, since which time the position has deteriorated a good deal further. Both the major political parties have enjoyed the power and the freedom from responsibility which the modern distortion of the constitution has

B

given them, although with variations in emphasis; and until recently
their response to suggestions for change to a more balanced, and less
arbitrary, system of government has been tepid, if not completely
negative. Meanwhile, the shadows lengthen. For example, in a
letter to *The Times*, dated 10 September 1968, discussing nationalisation and denationalisation, John Lee, M.P. for Reading, wrote:

> 'The crux of the matter is not simply that denationalisation is
> a retrogade policy, it is that it challenges the very existence of a
> two-party democracy. For, if a political party in Government
> cannot introduce legislation, confident that once passed it will
> become a permanent feature of the political system, that party
> must sooner or later become reluctant to share power, and the
> prospect of power, with its opponents.'

This clearly expressed first intimation of a one-party dictatorship failed to evoke any reply in the correspondence columns of
The Times.

Shortly before the publication of the leading article already mentioned, there appeared in *The Times* an article by Cecil H. King,
in which he discussed the declining reputation of parliamentary
democracy, not only in the United Kingdom, but in the Western
world generally, and sharply criticised the complacency with
which Ministers and Members of Parliament envelop themselves.
This followed a searching analysis by Ian Trethowan in *The
Times* of 30 May 1968, under the title, *Parliament's Corridors of
Chaos*, showing the ineffectiveness of the House of Commons in
attempting to control that chaos. At about the same time, Professor
Hood Phillips, discussing Parliamentary reform, argued that four
years should be the maximum life of a Parliament, that there
should be a second chamber with effective powers to delay, or
even to reject, legislation, and that the time had come for a written
constitution. Few would now maintain that Parliament is an efficient
mode of government, or even that it commands the respect which
it has enjoyed in the past. It has become the fashion to defend it by
arguing that any other system is likely to be worse, or by suggesting
that an overhaul of the committee procedure of the House of
Commons is likely to produce an improvement. This last suggestion
would leave the overriding problem of the over-concentration of
power in a few hands quite untouched. It is this fact which is responsible for so many of our present discontents, and which has
produced the present vogue for public demonstrations.

Two recent examples will illustrate this over-concentration of power in action. The decisions of Mr Justice Donaldson in *Lee* v. *Enfield B.C.*[1]; and *Lee* v. *Department of Education and Science*[2] record two stages of a controversy in which a Minister of State attempted to act *ultra vires*, after a local education authority had sought to implement a scheme of education for a school, which had been prepared in defiance of the school's articles of government, and in opposition to the plainly expressed preferences of the parents of the pupils at the school. The issue, as may be imagined, was whether the school, a grammar school, should be incorporated into a comprehensive school. This is an issue upon which conflicting opinions are strongly held, but the point of principle in these two decisions was that both the local authority and the department of state in support attempted to override (in this case, so far as the law was concerned, unsuccessfully) the legal limitations which the Education Act, 1944, had imposed upon the exercise of their very wide powers. Unfortunately, the check received by the department in these two decisions was only a temporary one, since it immediately proceeded to amend the school's articles of government, to render any further opposition futile. One point should be stressed in respect of problems such as these. In times of rapid change, such as the present, any government must make a number of decisions which will be unwelcome to particular groups of people. National and local interests will frequently be found to conflict. The root of public dissatisfaction is to be found in the rapidly increasing number of such decisions affecting an individual's occupation, the place where he lives, and almost every aspect of his daily life; coupled with the feeling of powerlessness to influence these decisions to any noticeable extent.

There exists in the House of Commons a committee which scrutinises delegated legislation, mainly with the object of discovering excessive assumptions of governmental power by the departments of state, and in its discussion of this problem, *The Times* noted that:

'Mr Page, the Chairman of the Statutory Instruments Committee since Labour came to power in 1964, together with his nine colleagues from all three parties, meet about once a fortnight to examine the flood of Whitehall orders to see whether

[1] (1967) 66 L.G.R. 19.
[2] (1967) 66 L.G.R. 211.

departments are exceeding the authority they have been granted
by Parliament, and to demand explanations if they have any
doubts. When Mr Page came back after the summer recess more
than 500 orders were waiting for examination by this committee
– a task which it was demonstrably impossible for them to carry
out effectively within a limited time.'

It is only too clear that the legislation which appears in the
Annual Statutes has long ceased to be a guide to the laws by which
the United Kingdom is governed, and that the departments of
state have taken over from Parliament a very wide area of its
former legislative functions. Untroubled by the external conflict
of the political parties they increasingly extend their control of all
aspects of public life.

Recently, there has been a hint of governmental control of
broadcasting and television in a speech by Anthony Wedgwood
Benn and a lecture by Richard Crossman in October 1968. Both
were cabinet Ministers; whilst the kite-flying address of Wedgwood Benn was mainly polemical, and contained the remarkable
observation that 'broadcasting is too important to be left to
broadcasters', the lecture by Crossman purported to be a measured
contribution. Whether either of these declarations was seen or
approved, either by the Prime Minister or the Cabinet, has not
been stated, and what today remains of the collective responsibility of the Cabinet is an interesting speculation. *The Times* of
27 October 1968 devoted six full columns to a report of Crossman's lecture (entitled *The Politics of Television*). There is much in
it that is interesting and acute, but there was a general complaint
of the triviality of much of television, a plea for more time to be
given to current affairs, to be treated seriously and in depth, and
there was an underlying assumption that someone (whose identity
was not specified) knew better than the programme arrangers or
the public what was good for the public. Possibly the most vital
part of Crossman's lecture, however, was that in which he
lucidly analysed recent developments in government, the decline
of Parliamentary democracy, and its progressive replacement by
'plebiscitary democracy', by which he apparently meant public
demonstrations and marches. Crossman regretted this development, and repudiated the idea that the decline of Parliament
was inevitable. 'We can halt the process of alienation,' he said,
'and restore the vitality of parliamentary democracy. But in order

to do so we must be prepared to use the new media of mass communication rightly, and it is because I believe this that I am so alarmed by what I see of the impact of television on our politics.' Without in any way doubting Crossman's sincerity, it may perhaps be pointed out that much depends upon who decides that the media of mass communication are used 'rightly'. The experiences of Soviet Russia and China, more recently of France, and most recently of all, of Czechoslovakia, have not been entirely reassuring upon this point. If the idea is pursued further, what happens if broadcasting and television are used 'rightly', and the Press 'wrongly' – or is some means to be found to enable the Press also to decide 'rightly'?

Crossman's lecture has much to say, as one would expect, upon participation in political life, but very little, apart from his suggestions about broadcasting, upon how this is to be achieved. Have those who gave evidence at the Stansted inquiry 'participated'? If so, what has been the result? A similar question might be asked about the Enfield parents. 'Participation' would often appear to be a right to be guided, as indeed Crossman's lecture plainly implies. One is reminded of the remark of Mr Justice Henn-Collins in *Franklin* v. *Minister of Town and Country Planning*[1] that if he had not power under the New Towns Act, 1946, to quash an order of the Minister, made in face of strong local opposition and in respect of which the Minister had acted with bias, then 'the subject had a right to fulminate, and nothing more'. Stevenage, in respect of which this order was made, is not far from Stansted, and both are not too distant from Enfield. Doubtless inhabitants of all three are reflecting, or have reflected, upon the joys (and cost) of 'participation' and 'fulmination'.

It is not open to question, and Crossman does not question it, that discussion of 'participation' has grown in strength with the increasing alienation of ordinary citizens from the process of government. Such alienation is not the peculiar characteristic of young persons, even if they are apt to demonstrate it more colourfully than others. A feeling of frustration and aimlessness is not confined to the young, and it may be remarked that it has grown in direct proportion to the increase of governmental 'participation' in the life of every citizen. Summing up nineteenth-century developments in local government, Maitland remarked at the end of his *Constitutional History*: 'We are becoming a much governed

[1] [1948] A.C. 87.

nation.' Today Britain is an overgoverned nation, and alienation from the processes of government has now extended to the local government organs whose progressive development Maitland had described with his customary insight. A recent writer[1] has pointed out that one important reason for the increasing reluctance of candidates of the desired quality to offer themselves for election is the degree of control now exercised by the central government, enforced by financial sanctions, over local authorities who now are for many purposes little more than the agents of Whitehall. Recognition of this fact by the public at large has been in part responsible also for the apathy of local electorates, which now see local elections primarily as a means of testing public opinion upon the activities of the central government. On this point, the writer was emphasising the conclusions reached by the Committee upon the Management of Local Government in 1967, which stated:

'The trend of recent legislation and the practice of government departments have been steadily reducing the discretion of local authorities and converting them into agents of Ministers and Whitehall. This tendency must be arrested and reversed; otherwise persons of the calibre required for effective local democracy will not offer themselves for election.'[2]

It is apparent that today there is a deep and ever-widening gap between those who govern and those who are governed, and at this point it is pertinent to ask how this has come about. The classical political scientists of the nineteenth century were wont to describe the primary functions of government as the preservation of public order internally, the protection of its citizens and their interests externally, the administration of justice, and the raising of taxation sufficient to discharge these functions. There might be subordinate functions, but these were limited, and expenditure upon them always required justification. Gladstone, it may be recalled, was sometimes derided for his budgeting for candle-ends. That was almost a century ago, and this conception of government was already obsolescent by the outbreak of World War I. From 1870 onwards, as both Maitland and Dicey noticed, there was a decisive change in the functions of government, in response to ever-widening conceptions of social responsibility. It reached its most complete expression in the years following 1945, in the conception

---

[1] J. P. Mackintosh, *The Devolution of Power*, Ch. 1.
[2] Ibid, pp. 28–9.

of the total Welfare State, to which both the major political parties have given unqualified adherence. It is this change which has been overwhelmingly responsible for the vast growth both of legislation by Parliament, and even more of delegated legislation, together with the elaboration of administrative tribunals of many kinds, without which such social legislation cannot be effective. To sum up, Parliament has changed from the deliberative body which it was for so long, and which was probably seen to best advantage in the nineteenth century when the freedom of members to decide upon issues placed before it had not yet become a fiction, to an instrument by means of which the dominant party can implement policies of social change to which its members are pledged at party conferences, and which they have announced in anticipation of a general election to an electorate comprising the sum total of the adult population. In such an environment the view of the individual, as distinct from his vote, is significant only when it is embodied in the view of some pressure group distinct from a political party.

It was only to be anticipated that such a great change in the conception of popular government should involve also far-reaching changes in the structure of Parliament itself. Primarily, it has produced an intensification of party discipline, in order that the programme of the dominant party may be achieved, if possible, within the lifetime of a single Parliament. Coincidentally, except where a general election has resulted almost in stalemate, there has been a marked tendency for each Parliament to endure for approximately its full legal term of five years. But above all, there has been an acceptance by all three major parties of the principle that the policies of the government of the day, when implemented by the House of Commons, should not be obstructed, or even noticeably impeded, by a second chamber whose fundamental weakness was that it was not popularly elected. This was clearly expressed at the time of the debates upon the first Parliament Act in 1911, and it has been repeated in later curtailments of the power of the House of Lords. More recently, there have been significant additions of life peers, by government nomination, but it has not been suggested that this dilution has affected the principle, although the hope has been expressed that the addition of successive groups of nominees would make for better informed and more evenly balanced debates. Whether these aspirations have been satisfied is not altogether clear.

It must also be stressed that, although opinions may have varied upon the details of changes, there has been tacit agreement between the major political parties that the House of Lords should cease to be an effective political force. They have differed only upon the degree of emphasis which they have placed upon this view. The preamble to the Parliament Act of 1911 expressly stated that it was a temporary measure only, until a more democratic second chamber should be created. The Conservative Party was in power, with only brief intervals, during the entire inter-war period, yet the reform of the powers and composition of the House of Lords remained a dead letter. Conservatives, it would seem, were as little enamoured of an effective check upon the legislative dominance of the House of Commons as Liberal or Labour governments, even though the stock complaint, first of Liberal, and later of Labour, governments has been that Conservatives are in a permanent substantial majority in the second chamber. Although this may be true, and although the tempo of social change under post-war Labour governments has been greater than anything previously experienced, the House of Lords has felt too weak, or has deemed it constitutionally improper, to attempt even a temporary check to the flood of legislation which is presented to it, not infrequently too late in the session for adequate consideration by the second chamber to be possible. We are left, therefore, with an unwritten constitution (under which, so far as power is concerned, a single chamber has unlimited competence) which is the instrument by virtue of which the government, who are the leaders of the dominant party in the House of Commons, may over a period of approximately four years make legislative changes of unlimited extent. These changes, increasingly comprehensive in scope, can, and do, affect the lives and livelihoods of every citizen to an increasing extent, with the object of establishing patterns of social conduct, the detailed regulation of which is committed to the departments of state, by increasingly wide delegations of governmental power. So extensive has been the encroachment of the governmental juggernaut upon the freedom of the ordinary citizen that it has been necessary to establish both a Council on Tribunals and an Ombudsman. These measures although they have achieved some modest success, have left the underlying problem untouched; and their creation has not in any way brought about an abatement of the frustration which the ordinary citizen feels when he is compelled to recognise his powerlessness in face of one of the innumerable manifestations of governmental influence.

Still more recently, the situation in the United Kingdom has been aggravated even further by repeated financial crises, devaluation, and a stubborn balance of payments problem, necessitating rigid control of many aspects of economic life, where the classic nineteenth-century conception of freedom of contract has been, for many purposes, replaced by governmental planning of the economy, involving also a control of incomes and prices, unknown in England since the Middle Ages, and to which trade unions, industry, and commerce must conform. If a descriptive name were to be applied to the second half of the twentieth century, the most appropriate would be *The Age of Interference*.

Over-government and over-administration are not attributable to the activities of one government alone, still less to one particular party, although there are differences in emphasis. They are visible in many developed countries, and the reactions which they produce are evident in the United States, Canada, France, Italy, and doubtless elsewhere. In Italy, France, and Canada they have produced strong movements for its limitation. These may be expressed in a variety of ways, and they are naturally influenced by local conditions, and by history. In Canada, for example, the special problem of Quebec is the product of Canada's history, although it has acquired a new urgency with the steady extension of the functions of the Dominion Government in Canada's economic development. This development has also been responsible for a more general demand for an extension of the powers of the provinces, in opposition to what is felt to be an encroachment by the Dominion Government. In France also, the constitution is being studied afresh, with the object of securing a substantial measure of decentralisation, although it is scarcely to be expected that such measures will satisfy the aspirations of Breton nationalists. There have been similar developments in Italy, where again there exists a special regional problem in Sicily, which already possesses considerable local autonomy.

It is against this background that the particular stresses and strains to which the United Kingdom is subject must be considered. Here too there are particular local problems as well as general reactions. Probably the greatest paradox of our own time is that Ulster, whose almost violent loyalty in the past was a contributory factor to the Irish difficulties of the nineteenth century, has now, on the threat of interference from Whitehall, produced a separatist movement of its own. But the British Isles today contain more centrifugal forces than at any time since the personal union of England and Scotland in 1603. There are Scottish Nationalists, Welsh Nationalists, possibly Cornish and Manx Nationalists, and even these may not be the end. The constitutional inquiry under Lord Crowther, established by the government in December 1968, includes all except Cornwall, but with the addition of the Channel Islands, within its purview. All the movements have grown in direct proportion to the increase of interference and direction from Whitehall and Westminster. It is against over-government and over-administration that these movements are directed and not against peoples, and whilst, because of history, language, and culture, the frustration of these groups may be expressed in a specialist form, they do not differ in essence from the frustrations experienced by the masses of English men and women whose dissociation from the party game is now total. Louis Heren, analysing the British political and constitutional problem, doubted (in a contribution to *The Times* of 17 December 1968) whether a British federal system was possible, and he stressed particularly the collusion which exists between the two major parties, so far as the concentration of power at the centre is concerned. At the same time he recognised the dangers of the alternative. 'One must assume,' he observes, 'that government power will continue to increase because of the growing complexity of the modern world. There are dangers, especially for the liberties of the individual.' These observations are of general application, and they imply that even in the United States, where personal rights have been written into federal and state constitutions, the threat to personal freedom has been recognised. In the United Kingdom, the threat is more direct, because the individual has no similar guarantees, in respect of which superior courts can exercise an independent function. The threat to personal liberty today is incessant, insidious, and increasing. For this reason, the feeling of frustration is apparently more widespread. As yet, no modern state, and certainly not the United Kingdom, has succeeded in solving the problem which is posed by planned development, which step by step removes from the individual the power to make decisions, whether good or bad, for himself.

II

What is the British Constitution?

EVERY MODERN state, with the exception of the United Kingdom, possesses a constitution – that is to say, a framework of government, embodied in a comprehensive document, formally adopted, and operating as the fundamental law governing the state's existence and its mode of government, and for that reason, capable of alteration only by some solemn act, of a special and occasional nature, which is distinct from the processes applicable to ordinary legislation. In the Western world, the adoption of such a constitution is sometimes the consequence of a revolution, but usually it is the result of prolonged discussion and general agreement. Sometimes both factors are present. The classic example of such a constitution is that of the United States. When the thirteen American colonies achieved their independence in 1783, they had already a long tradition of separate government, in which the colonists had participated, through representative assemblies, in varying degrees, and in the last paragraph of the Declaration of Independence, their independent sovereignties were emphatically affirmed. The same principle of the sovereignty of each of the thirteen states was reaffirmed in the Articles of Confederation, adopted at the Continental Congress in 1777, following which, a confederation of loosely associated states came into existence. This encountered a succession of practical difficulties, arising from the differing outlooks and policies of the members, and in 1787 a general convention of delegates from all thirteen states met at Philadelphia, and hammered out, after full debate, the essentials of a federal union, which was ultimately embodied in the present constitution of the United States. In doing so, the delegates had sought to achieve a balance between states' rights and the powers of the central government, by a division of sovereignty between them; they had attempted to confine the legislative and the judiciary to their respective spheres, and over against both they had established the Supreme Court, as the interpreter and guardian of the constitution. Further, they had provided the ordinary citizen with a

27

number of constitutional rights, embodied in the constitution, and once again protected by the Supreme Court. Finally, they had directed that the constitution could only be changed by a complicated process, which required two-thirds majorities in both houses of Congress, and ratification by the legislatures or conventions in three-quarters of the states. Not unnaturally, constitutional amendments have been rare – only twenty – in the entire history of the federal constitution. It would be quite wrong to assume, however, that during this long history, the American constitution has remained static. There have been vast developments of the activities of the federal government, to meet a variety of emergencies – for example, wars, the nationwide depression of the thirties, the spread of organised crime across state boundaries, and above all, in response to ever-broadening conceptions of social responsibility. This, as in the United Kingdom and elsewhere, has produced an increasing growth of executive power. All this, however, has taken place within the framework of the original constitution which, though frequently subject to intense strains, has never been overthrown. Further, the ordinary citizen has continued to regard the Supreme Court as the ultimate power for the protection of those rights which are guaranteed by the constitution, and which received an emphatic vindication when the Supreme Court invalidated as unconstitutional important sections of President Franklin Roosevelt's New Deal legislation. Whilst there may be varying views even today of the wisdom of what the Supreme Court then did, no one, and least of all the judges of that court, has questioned the principles upon which their decisions were based. They are repeated again and again in the judgments which that court has delivered. To quote only two of the great judges who have expounded those principles, Chief Justice Warren said in *Trop* v. *Dulles*[1] 'The provisions of the Constitution are not time-worn adages or hollow shibboleths. They are vital living principles that authorize and limit governmental powers in our Nation. They are the rules of government.'

Of the Bill of Rights embodied in it, Mr Justice Frankfurter said:

'Man being what he is cannot be safely trusted with complete unanimity from outward responsibility in depriving others of

[1] 356 U.S. 86, 103.

their rights. At least such is the conviction underlying our Bill of Rights.'[1]

And again:

'When we are dealing with the Constitution of the United States, and more particularly with the great safeguards of the Bill of Rights, we are dealing with principles of liberty and justice "so rooted in the traditions and conscience of our people as to be ranked as fundamental" – something without which "a fair and enlightened system of justice would be impossible".'[2]

The force of these observations, delivered by such high judicial authority would in any case be great; but when delivered, as in the United States Supreme Court, with authority to hold unconstitutional any legislation or executive action which infringes them, they are irresistible. No English court has any comparable power.

The contrast is the more remarkable when it is remembered that the Parliament of the United Kingdom has an unrivalled experience in enacting constitutions, some of them federal, by virtue of which the judiciary enjoy similar powers. Following a conference of delegates of the Canadian provinces at Quebec in 1865, a number of resolutions were adopted defining the principles which would govern the establishment of a federation of the provinces in British North America. Upon these, and upon subsequent debates in the provincial legislatures, was based the British North America Act, 1867, uniting Canada (i.e. Quebec and Ontario), Nova Scotia, and New Brunswick, in a federal union which has since been joined by the newly formed prairie states, by Prince Edward Island, British Columbia, and (in more recent days) by Newfoundland. That Act defines with precision the functions of central and provincial governments, the division of powers between them, the composition of their legislatures, the mode in which executive power is exercised, taxation, and many other matters. The Act constituting the Commonwealth of Australia is equally comprehensive. In both Constituent Acts, the interpretation of the constitution was entrusted to the Supreme Court of the Federation, subject to an ultimate appeal to the Judicial Committee of the Privy Council – an ultimate appeal which has only recently been abolished.

---

[1] *Joint Anti-Fascist Ref.* v. *McGrath* 341 U.S. 125, 171.
[2] *West Virginia Board of Education* v *Barntte* 319 U.S. 624, 652.

These were not the only occasions when the British Parliament enacted a constitution for a Dominion. The Union of South Africa was created in 1909. New Zealand was granted responsible government in 1852 and, on a smaller scale, an Act of 1871 established the Federation of the Leeward Islands, which was dissolved in the year 1956.

There is no need to multiply examples of institution-making by the British Parliament, nor to discuss them in detail. It is sufficient to observe that Parliament has experienced no difficulty at all in providing constitutions for others – nor has it ever questioned the wisdom of such a proceeding. It has nevertheless refused to recognise that the process had any relevance to the United Kingdom, and accordingly, the United Kingdom remains in lonely isolation, the only considerable state in the modern world without a written constitution.

If we turn to the constitutional lawyers, and more especially to Dicey, whose *Law of the Constitution* has influenced so greatly the thinking of successive generations of English lawyers, we find that the oddities of the English system are really attributable (in Dicey's view) to the peculiarities of the Englishman and the supremacy of the Common Law. In his acute analysis of the nature of Parliamentary sovereignty, he points out that the French constitution, as it was known to him, as well as other continental constitutions, had defined and limited the competence of the legislature, without at the same time investing the judiciary with the power to declare void legislation which exceeded the limits set by the constitution. It is only in the United States, he says, that the constitution has given such a power to the judiciary and this, he concludes, 'provides the only adequate safeguard which has hitherto been invented against unconstitutional legislation'. Oddly, this conclusion fails to take into account the constitutions of Canada (which existed before Dicey first delivered his lectures) or of Australia (which had been created eight years before he prepared the seventh edition of his work). This failure is not without significance. Whilst restraining himself from describing the English constitution in the extravagant language of eighteenth-century writers, Dicey was nevertheless at pains to explain that the absence of a formal constitution was, on the whole, a good thing. This is the more remarkable since, in his introductory chapter, discussing the nature of constitutional law, he points out:

1. That it is made up of a miscellaneous collection of statutes, such as the Bill of Rights, 1689, the Bill of Settlement, sundry Habeas Corpus Acts, and various Acts affecting the franchise, together with a number of decisions of the courts upon the rights of the individual, which are capable of modification by the ordinary processes of legislation, and which (as Dicey had previously explained) were mixed up with other rules of law upon many other topics;

2. That the theory of the constitution was often completely at variance with facts; for example, in the enumeration of the practice and extent of the royal prerogative by Blackstone, which, says Dicey, is the exact opposite of the truth. Indeed, throughout Blackstone's account of the powers of the Crown, he says, 'we are in the midst of unrealities and fictions'; and:

3. That the actual laws which are termed constitutional are meaningless without linking them with innumerable political understandings, of every degree of importance and unimportance, which Dicey termed the conventions of the constitution. These have no legal validity and have varied from one age to another, and are, in any case, he concludes, not the province of the lawyer, but of the student of politics. All this is the more extraordinary when it is remembered that the entire edifice of cabinet government rests upon convention, and not upon law.

Dicey is inclined to make merry at the expense of the constitutional historian. 'Historians,' he remarks, 'in their devotion to the earliest phases of ascertainable history are infected with a love which, in the eyes of a lawyer, appears inordinate, for the origins of our institutions, and seem to care little about their later developments.' The truth of the matter is that unless one has constantly to refer to Britain's political history, much of that which now exists appears to be inexplicable. For example, how or why has it happened that Britain possesses so extraordinary and so absurd a legislative chamber as the House of Lords has now become? How did it come about that a nation which, in the past, has set some store upon the separation of powers, possesses the office of Lord Chancellor, which today has no direct contact with the Court of Chancery, which carries a seat in the Cabinet, whilst at the same time conferring upon its occupant the control of the judiciary? Examples could be multiplied indefinitely, but these will be sufficient to illustrate the proposition that, without a knowledge of the past, Britain's present system of government is meaningless.

At the opening of his prefatory essay upon 'The True Nature of Constitutional Law', Dicey quotes from Hallam's *Middle Ages* a passage extolling the perfections of the English constitution in unmeasured terms. Hallam wrote in 1818, when the dangers of the French Revolution and the Napoleonic Empire had been overcome and when England (ironically) had entered upon a period of repression which terminated with the passing of the first Reform Bill in 1832. It is valuable, therefore, to compare Hallam's extravagances with the shrewd assessment of de Lolme, a Swiss, who came to England about the year 1768, to make a close study of her institutions, and who published an Essay upon the Constitution of England in 1770. After discussing the political upheavals which had afflicted England in the past, he writes:

'However, as what has not happened at one time may happen at another, future revolutions (events which no form of government can totally prevent) may perhaps end in a different manner from that in which past ones have terminated. New combinations may possibly take place among the then ruling powers of the State, of such a nature as to prevent the constitution, when peace shall be restored to the nation, from settling again upon its ancient and genuine foundations, and it would certainly be a very bold assertion to affirm, that both the outward form, and the true spirit of the English government, would again be preserved from destruction, if the same dangers to which they have in former times been exposed should again happen to take place.

'Nay, such fatal changes as these we mention may be introduced even in quiet times, or, at best, by means in appearance peaceable and constitutional. Advantage, for instance, may be taken by particular actions, either of the capacity, or of the misconduct of some future king. Temporary prepossessions of the people may be so artfully managed as to make them concur in doing what will prove afterwards the ruin of their own liberty. Plans of apparent improvement in the constitution, forwarded by men who, though with good intentions, shall proceed without a due knowledge of the true principles and foundations of government, may produce effects quite contrary to those which were intended, and in reality pave the way to its ruin.'

It is only in our own day that the extreme cogency of this last paragraph can be fully appreciated; and de Lolme is virtually the only writer who has appreciated that Britain has never had a constitution, only a government.

The reasons for this are inevitably historical, as are also the reasons for the inordinate complacency of so many eighteenth- and nineteenth-century writers upon the English constitution. Government, so far as the United Kingdom is concerned, has for centuries meant Parliamentary government, and this was only secured after a lengthy civil war and a dynastic change. Not unnaturally, therefore, writers have regarded Parliamentary government, erected upon the rock of Parliamentary sovereignty, with the same veneration as American writers have regarded the American constitution, with its guarantee of indissoluble association. There was ample justification for this. England had created a balanced constitution at the moment when other European countries had moved, and were still moving, towards absolute forms. These, in some cases, as the eighteenth century progressed, were 'enlightened', but could not be a substitute for the Parliamentary system, buttressed by Common Law protection for personal liberty. The Revolution of 1688, increased prosperity, spreading widely through the community, the creation of a flourishing colonial empire, and victory in long and taxing wars, all suggested that a constitutional monarchy had greater potentiality than the régimes to which it was opposed. In the nineteenth century, Palmerston's somewhat naïve assumption that the difficulties which European nations periodically experienced could be cured by the adoption of institutions modelled on those of Britain, seemed to be founded on both experience and logic. Few, if any, remembered the reservations expressed by de Lolme in the passage which has been cited. De Lolme, after all, it might be suggested, was a foreigner, born in a country which possessed a written federal constitution, and his remarks could have little application to the stable, but ever-developing, institutions of a country which was an example to the world, with an instinctive dislike of formal instruments of government, which the brief and unhappy interlude of the Commonwealth has done nothing to abate.

This may perhaps explain why the Revolution of 1688, unlike other European revolutions, produced no formal constitutional document. The Civil War in the middle of the seventeenth century had settled that Parliament, and not the King, ruled. James II had directly challenged this, and both the political parties (with few dissidents) had agreed that he should be replaced by rulers whose

c

title was plainly Parliamentary. Once this had been settled, things could go on as before. In order to emphasise the continuity in English institutions, the change of régimes was disguised by fiction. When James II abruptly departed, no Parliament was in existence. Accordingly, the members of the only Parliament of James's reign were reconvened as a Convention. It could not be a Parliament, since there was no sovereign to summon it. The Convention agreed that William and Mary should be joint sovereigns, and once they had accepted the invitation, the Convention neatly transformed itself into a Parliament, and proceeded to enact, with the sovereigns of their choice, measures which declared illegal the most hated part of James II's exercises of royal prerogative, together with a Bill of Rights, placing a number of rights of the citizen, which the Whigs had asserted against the Crown, upon a statutory basis. Nothing more was thought to be necessary. Parliament had vindicated its supremacy, and the precise position of the sovereign in such a settlement was left for the future to establish.

Behind these changes, and providing theoretical justification for them, lay a body of political doctrine which derived from both the Whigs and the moderate Tories. Clarendon, the first Chancellor of Charles II, had been opposed to Charles I's attempt to establish personal rule, but when compelled to make a choice at the outbreak of the Civil War, he had reluctantly declared himself a Royalist. Nevertheless, for him, the lesson of history was that the English political system was a constitutional monarchy, with built-in checks and balances, and this is what he regarded as having been re-established in 1660. Had he lived to see the Revolution of 1688, he would have regarded it as a further exemplification of his theories of government, even though the first decade of Charles II's reign furnished numerous examples of the limitations of the checks and balances theory.

'The King,' says Trevelyan,[1] 'was indeed put by the Cavalier Parliament on an absurdly short allowance, which hampered all branches of the administration and ere long tempted him to sell the control of his foreign policy to Louis XIV of France. But the shortage was a natural result of the return to "the just balance of the constitution", which Clarendon believed to be the last word in political wisdom. Till Parliament could control policy and expenditure it would not consent to open wide the public purse. When the Commons insisted on searching the royal account books to trace

---

[1] *History of England*, p. 453.

the actual use made of money voted for the maritime war with Holland, Clarendon and the courtiers were scandalized at such an invasion of the province of the executive by the legislature. Yet this was a first step on the road to that Parliamentary control of expenditure, which alone could secure for the King's government the liberal and continuous supplies from the taxpayers essential to a great nation in modern times.'

In other words, Clarendon's balance was always precarious, if not altogether illusory, and in the eventful three years 1678–81 the Whigs almost completely overturned it. Few, indeed, whether Tory or Whig, could agree upon the point at which a balance might be maintained.

The Revolution of 1688 found its philosophic justification in the works of John Locke. Government, in his view, was founded upon a social contract, of members of a group, to establish order, and the preservation of natural rights, and in the last instance, it is to the public will of that society to which its members owe obedience. This, it will be apparent, has two major consequences. It will, in the first place, justify the Revolution of 1688, since the popular will is entitled to express itself by the exercise of its sovereignty against a ruler who has violated his trust. Secondly, it provides that the legislative branch of government, through which the popular will is habitually expressed, is supreme for this very reason. Although the executive is distinct, and may have separate functions, nevertheless it must yield to the will of Parliament in the exercise of power. Thus, although there is the germ of a theory of separation of powers to be found in Locke, the checks and balances of Clarendon have disappeared. Parliament reigns supreme. It is one of the curiosities of political theory that French and American writers, on the eve of their own revolutions, imagined that they derived their own theories of the separation of powers from Locke, the High Priest of the English Revolution, when they were more closely related to those of Bolingbroke, a Tory, and of Hume, who can scarcely be identified with either political party. To both of them, the constitution which was fashioned in the Revolution of 1688 was the most perfect example of a 'mixed' form of government that the mind of man could devise. In the language of the eighteenth century, it blended the monarchic, the aristocratic, and the popular elements in government, and equilibrium was maintained by the checks which each could exercise upon the other. For the checks to be successful, however, it was necessary that the balance between the three elements should be maintained, and this, even in the eighteenth century, was not invariably the case. For example, Walpole governed and maintained himself in office for longer (1721–42) than any other Prime Minister by a system of Parliamentary corruption. This was attacked by Bolingbroke, on the ground that this was upsetting the balance in the Crown's favour. Hume, on the other hand, justified Walpole's corruption on the ground that it preserved the power of the Crown against the encroachments of the House of Commons. A little later in the century, Whig writers were to use this same theory of 'checks and balances' as the basis for an onslaught upon George III and his Ministers, during their prolonged struggle with the Whig oligarchy, and at the end of the century, Burke eloquently explained the excellence of this system, in denouncing the excesses of the French Revolution.

The impact of that Revolution upon Europe was responsible for the evolution of nineteenth-century theories of government which were at variance with traditional thought. When the Revolutionary and Napoleonic system was eventually destroyed, the countries of the continent were faced with the necessity of establishing, or re-establishing, their political life, and although a very wide variety of political systems was projected, they had some features in common. They all accepted the necessity for the fundamental law of the state to be embodied in a constitutional code. Secondly, they all accepted the necessity for a constitutional guarantee for the rights of the individual, and finally, there was general acceptance of the theory of the separation of powers, as a means of establishing checks and balances between the legislative, executive, and judicial powers. These principles did not necessarily find expression in the régimes which were set up immediately after the Congress of Vienna, but as the century progressed, they found ever-clearer expression in the revolutionary movements which swept Europe at regular intervals during the nineteenth century. By the end of the century, they had won virtually universal acceptance, outside Russia.

This contrast between English and continental experience was frequently discussed by English writers in abstract terms, which often ignored the historical reasons for the divergence. It was precisely because continental nations had so frequently been exposed to the peril of an overthrown régime, and to arbitrary rule, that they attempted, when peace and independence were restored, to achieve security and to buttress personal security by written constitutions and constitutional guarantees of personal liberty. The United Kingdom, which had escaped invasion, and whose institutions had continued to function, although under increasing strain, during a quarter of a century of revolution and continental conquest, experienced no similar need. Pride in such institutions was natural, and it was strengthened when constitutionalism survived, although with far-reaching changes, in the era of continental revolutions, in which many countries were involved, and from which they eventually emerged, all with new written constitutions. From these upheavals, English writers concluded that flexible, unwritten constitutions were best, often without adding the necessary qualification that they were best in the particular circumstances of evolution which prevailed in the British Isles.

Trevelyan, with historical insight, gives the true explanation of the deep-rooted aversion of Englishmen to a written constitution:[1]

'It was well for England that the Revolution Settlement did not supply her with a brand new, water-tight, unalterable, written constitution. A sacrosanct written constitution was necessary to achieve the federal union of the States of North America after they had cut themselves adrift from the old Empire. For England it was not at all necessary, and it would certainly have proved inconvenient. If England had been given a rigid constitution when James II was deposed, the Crown would have had assigned to it, in perpetuity, powers which within thirty years of the coronation of William and Mary it handed over to be exercised by its Parliamentary advisers. It is probable, also, that a rigid constitution, drawn up according to the Rights of 1689, would have excluded the King's Ministers from sitting in the House of Commons.

'A written constitution, as distinct from the sum of ordinary law and custom, is alien to the English political genius. One of the worst signs of the straits to which Cromwell was driven by his inability to find a basis of national agreement, was the fact that he promulgated written resolutions dividing up by an absolute line – never to be altered – the powers of Protector and Parliament respectively. These expedients were contrary to the real method of English progress. The London fog which decently

[1] *History of England*, p. 511.

conceals from view the exact relations of executive and legislature at Westminster, has enabled the constitution to adapt itself
unobserved to the requirements of each passing year.'

But Cromwell was, after all, the product of a revolution, and his
position necessitated definition; and Trevelyan's commendation of
the London fog would find few supporters at the present time.

Dislike for formal documents, acceptance of the supremacy of
the Common Law, and a willingness to compromise were the hall-
marks of nineteenth-century constitutional doctrine in England.
Very great changes, social and political, were taking place, and
although it was assumed that the constitution was sufficiently
flexible to assimilate them, it was apparent to shrewd observers that
much had changed, and was changing, and that there was ground
for considerable apprehension. From this point of view, Walter
Bagehot's political classic, *The English Constitution*, first published
in 1865, and its second edition, published shortly after the Reform
Act of 1867, is very revealing. Into the second edition, which retains the acute analysis of the first, there has been introduced a note
of apprehension. Compared with later changes in the franchise,
the Reform Act of 1867, which conferred the vote mainly on skilled
artisans, may not seem to be a cause for misgiving. Nevertheless, the
second edition is preceded by a lengthy introduction in which even
so detached a critic as Bagehot explains that the two political parties
must henceforth shape their programmes in order that the working
classes now enfranchised may not combine together in order to
extract natural benefits as the price of their support. Bagehot, it is
plain, regards this possibility as a serious one, attended by unknown
dangers, since he is acute enough to perceive that the power of the
House of Commons has been greatly enhanced by the two extensions of the franchise in 1832 and 1867, and that in future it will be
impolitic for the House of Lords to attempt directly to thwart the
popular will, when clearly expressed. With similar clarity, he perceived the ever growing power of the Cabinet, although even he
could not foresee the extent to which it has come to dominate the
political scene today.

Following along the line of earlier writers, Bagehot devotes a
chapter to 'checks and balances', and this chapter reads strangely
a century later. After discussing American federalism, and reaching
the anticipated conclusion favouring a unitary system, with a sovereign Parliament with the House of Commons as the dominant

partner, Bagehot considered whether the King could restrain the caprice of an erratic ministry, and reached the conclusion that he could not. He then reached the surprising conclusion that 'the regulator, as I venture to call it, of one single sovereignty is the power of dissolving the otherwise sovereign chamber confided to the chief executive'. Since Bagehot's day, it has become too obvious for discussion that the Prime Minister's power to advise a dissolution is one of the principal factors in his control of his party in the House of Commons. Bagehot's regulator is no regulator at all, but simply the principal method (another being the discretion to appoint peers without limit) whereby the Cabinet enforces its absolute rule.

Even in Bagehot's day, therefore, it was already apparent that the 'checks and balances' of the settlement of 1689 had virtually disappeared, for reasons which will be discussed more fully in the next chapter. The political centre of gravity had changed, and was continuing to change. As it did so, the factors which had served as controls in the past had been shown to be ineffective, and this has become even more apparent in recent times. Much of Bagehot's acute analysis has no application at all to the constitutional system which now exists – for example, his chapters on the King and the House of Lords – and throughout his book the modern reader is conscious that the emphasis is continually at fault. Bagehot, equally with Burke and Hume, belongs to the history of political theory, not to present-day political life.

Perhaps no writer has influenced thinking upon the constitution more profoundly than Dicey. Successive generations of lawyers, judges, and statesmen have been familiar with the successive editions of his *Law of the Constitution*. His critics have been very numerous, but they have all paid tribute to the vigour and clarity of his argument. Dicey wrote as a lawyer, distinguished alike as a practitioner and as a teacher. For him, the law of the constitution was supported by the twin pillars, the sovereignty of Parliament and the Rule of Law. These, as the historians have pointed out, were exactly the pillars upon which the Settlement of 1689 was based. History and law on that point, therefore, were at one. For Dicey, any suggestion of 'checks and balances' was unthinkable. Parliament was the legal sovereign, and that was the end of the matter. If there were any limits upon its omnipotence, they were limits, not of law, but of expediency. When he first wrote, Dicey was also untroubled by the thought that there were limits to the

Rule of Law which, with considerable satisfaction, he contrasted with what he thought to be the *droit administratif* of France and the continent. By the time he came to prepare the edition of 1908 (the last for which he was responsible), he had been assailed by many doubts. Something very like *droit administratif* was growing up in England, and its limits were indefinite. It was ominous, he thought, but the ordinary courts can deal with any actual or probable breach of law committed by a servant of the Crown, and this, he thought, distinguished what was growing up in England from 'true *droit administratif*'. Dicey, it will be evident, left the argument in the air. There was no introduction of 'true *droit administratif*' into the British political and constitutional system. What, then, was it that was being introduced? And what (he might have added) would be its effect upon the two fundamental norms upon which his exposition of constitutional law was based?

Dicey naturally confined his exposition of the nature of Parliamentary sovereignty to its legal implications, but it is to be noticed that the term itself is regularly used in different senses. Historians are apt to use it to describe the triumph of Parliament over Stuart notions of Divine Right and their extra-legal activities in 1688. Political writers sometimes use it (as Bagehot did) to denote that it is Parliament – or rather the House of Commons – which supports, or brings about, the fall of governments. In Bagehot's day, this still had considerable elements of truth in it. Today, it is only in extreme circumstances, such as the expectation of invasion in 1940, that such a potentiality can be realised. At other times, the most notable feature of the system is the power of the Cabinet.

Consideration of the works of Bagehot, Dicey, and many others, shows that it is extremely difficult to say what the English constitution is. It is one thing to a historian, another to a political scientist, and still another to a lawyer. Much depends upon the significance which a writer attaches to particular episodes in the past, or to the day-to-day procedure of Parliament and government. For this reason, as well as for others, the nature, extent, and binding force of constitutional conventions have been much debated in the past, and may be so again in the future. There is also another factor of major importance. Where there are no fundamental rules, the constitution is always in process of change. It was one thing in the eighteenth century, something quite different in the nineteenth, and something totally different again today. At the outset of his introduction to the second edition of *The English Constitution*, Bagehot says:

> 'There is great difficulty in the way of a writer who attempts to sketch a living Constitution – a Constitution that is in actual work and power. The difficulty is that the object is in constant change. An historical writer does not feel this difficulty; he deals only with the past; he can say definitely, the Constitution worked in such and such a manner in the year at which he begins, and in such and such respects different in the year at which he ends; he begins with a definite point of time and ends with one also. But a contemporary writer who tries to paint what is before him is puzzled and perplexed; what he sees is changing daily. He must paint it as it stood at some one time, or else he will be putting side by side in his representations things which never were contemporaneous in reality. The difficulty is the greater because a writer who deals with a living Government naturally compares it with the most important other living Governments, and these are changing too; what he illustrates is altered in one way, and his sources of illustration are altered probably in a different way.'

Of course, all constitutions, since they govern the lives and public conduct of large communities, are constantly changing. The difference between the United Kingdom and other states is that there are no limits to change in the United Kingdom, and that the players can, and do, alter the rules of the game as they go along. The English constitution, in fact, is no more than the product of past political experience, with a number of legally binding rules which can be changed at any time by the ordinary processes of legislation, as interpreted by politicians and writers at any particular moment. The eighteenth-century view of the perfection and commendability of the constitution has long since been abandoned, in the face of increasing change, not only in the rules, but in sources of political power. Such extreme flexibility has been of benefit in the past. Can we be certain that it is working satisfactorily at the present time?

III

Parliament

IN THE penetrating *Introduction* to his account of the Stuart era in his *History of England*, Trevelyan remarks:

> 'In the Stuart era the English developed for themselves, without foreign participation or example, a system of Parliamentary government, local administration and freedom of speech and person, clean contrary to the prevailing tendencies on the continent, which was moving fast towards regal absolutism, centralized bureaucracy, and the subjection of the individual to the State. While the Estates General of France and the Cortes of Aragon and of Castile were ceasing to exercise even their mediaeval functions, while the political life of Germany was atrophied in the mosaic of petty Princedoms that constituted the Empire, the House of Commons, under the leadership of the squires and in alliance with the merchants and the Common lawyers, made itself the governing organ of a modern nation. This it achieved by developing inside itself an elaborate system of committee procedure, and by striking down the royal power in a series of quarrels of which the chief motive was religious, and the chief result political.'

He points out that England was able to bring about these changes because of the absorption of Europe in the Thirty Years' War, and also that the strength of the system was fully and successfully tested in the long struggle with France which followed the accession of William III, and which extended to Waterloo. During the eighteenth century, he adds, English institutions, though imperfectly understood, became an example (and also an object of envy) to the world. It was the Revolution of 1688 which guaranteed the permanence and efficiency of England's political institutions. Thenceforward 'there was agreement in general policy between executive and legislature, between King and Parliament, as formerly under the Tudors; but this time it was Parliament that led the King who had to follow.'

The Revolution of 1688 was indeed as decisive an event in the development of English political institutions as the Norman Conquest, but the victory of Parliament was only possible because of much that had happened before. The foundations of Parliamentary sovereignty had been firmly laid before the close of the Middle Ages. It needed only the ineptitude of the Stuarts, and the resolution of the Commons, for the building to come into existence.

Already in the fifteenth century Sir John Fortescue, the Lancastrian Chief Justice, had written that the King of England was no absolute monarch, with arbitrary power, but the ruler of a kingdom governed by law, to which the King himself was subject; a kingdom, moreover, in which the royal will was limited by the existence of Parliament.

At no time after the Norman Conquest had an English King exercised absolute power, and when Richard II tried to do so, he was deposed (1399). Parliament came into existence in the reigns of Henry III and Edward I, as a means of securing the assent of the kingdom to legislative changes, and especially to taxation which exceeded the customary dues to which the King was entitled as of right. It originated, as Trevelyan points out, at a time when similar assemblies were coming into existence elsewhere in Europe, and when even the Papacy temporarily found it expedient to make a response to the prevailing fashion for representative assemblies. In the countries of Western Europe, this development was a consequence of the growing inadequacy of feudalism as a system of government. Feudalism was founded on long-established custom, and was tenacious of customary rights and duties. If the ruler wished to deviate from custom, or to secure additional resources for government, he must secure the consent of those affected by his measures. For a time, he secured those consents separately – from barons, from merchants, from clergy – but in the thirteenth century, the process was simplified by convening national assemblies of the estates of the realm. Everywhere else but in England, these remained extraordinary assemblies, with few, if any, common interests between the various orders of the community and as the power of the rulers grew, the importance of these national assemblies declined. In some cases, they practically ceased to exist. Even where they preserved a shadowy existence, they failed to have any noticeable influence upon the conduct of public affairs. The French States-General, for example, did not meet between

1614 and 1788. Its assembly in the latter year was the immediate prelude to the French Revolution.

The reasons for the different evolution of Parliamentary institutions in England were various. One was the extraordinary cohesiveness of the English people, and their sense of national unity, at a time when the rest of Europe thought in terms of a society dominated by feudal conceptions. Even the Church of England, though organised as a separate estate since the Norman Conquest, played an important part in the national development. Stephen Langton, Archbishop of Canterbury, had led the national resistance to John, and the list of mediaeval clerics with a conception of national solidarity is an impressive one. Much also is attributable to the behaviour of members of Parliament when they met. At first, Parliament preserved the form in which it had originally been summoned; a form which reflected the desire of the King to secure general consent to measures of extraordinary taxation. The tenants-in-chief with territorial titles sat as one body, and their assembly included the bishops and greater abbots who were present also as territorial magnates. The clergy also sat as a separate estate, being represented by proctors and others from each diocese. Finally, the commons, at first representing almost exclusively the more important towns, sat as a 'third estate', and were summoned rather to assent than to debate. Gradually, important structural changes occurred. The lesser clergy, unlike their leading dignitaries, had little interest in secular matters in general, and accordingly they progressively stayed away from meetings of Parliament, preferring to vote their taxes (which were often a matter of negotiation) separately in Convocation – a practice which was only finally abandoned at the time of the Civil War. So far as tenants-in-chief (who, by the fourteenth century, included the vast majority of freeholders, holding in knight-service) were concerned, there had long been a distinction, which is reflected in Magna Carta, between *majores barones* and *minores barones*. It has been plausibly suggested that the *majores barones* were assessed individually by the Exchequer, whilst the *minores barones* were assessed through the sheriff of the county. If this is so, the distinction is still further emphasised by the mode of summons to early Parliaments. The greater barons were summoned individually by writ, and such a personal summons, followed by the taking of a seat in Parliament, ultimately became the test by which it was determined whether or not a person was a Peer of the Realm, and therefore was entitled to membership of the House of Lords. The *minores barones*, or Knights of the Shire, as they came to be called, were from the first summoned through the sheriffs, but because of their numbers, they were not summoned as a body, but were directed to send two representatives for each shire. By the reign of Edward III, they habitually sat with the burgesses from the towns, and accordingly the Commons quickly acquired the character of a coherent national assembly, with the Knights of the Shire acting as a link between the merchants and the barons. This link was to prove of cardinal importance in early Stuart times, when the leaders of the Parliamentary party were either peers or country gentlemen. In the reign of Henry VI, the franchise governing the election of Knights of the Shire was restricted to 40/- freeholders, thus excluding leaseholders and tenants of copyhold land; but as the value of money declined, a measure which originally was restrictive in intention became a means whereby the collective opinion of the landed interest could express itself in Parliament, and Kings and Parliamentarians in turn attempted to dominate the elections. In the eighteenth century, the creation of 40/- freeholds by great territorial magnates was one of the principal instruments by means of which the great aristocratic houses maintained their ascendancy over the House of Commons.

For two centuries after the establishment of Parliamentary government, the function of the Commons was a subordinate one. It was the privilege of the peers, as the successors of the King's great tenants-in-chief, to advise and consent to legislation, whilst the Commons were summoned only to consent. In the first centuries after the Norman Conquest, Kings had governed, with the aid of their Council, by means of ordinances. Gradually, statutes, passed by the King in Parliament, took their place by the side of ordinances, but it was not until the Revolution of 1688 that it was finally settled that the King had no legislative power, independent of Parliament. The change in emphasis had been gradual, for all the mediaeval Kings had issued ordinances, and although the Tudors for the most part preferred to legislate through the instrumentality of Parliaments which they carefully schooled and led, it was not doubted that the King had *some* independent powers of legislation, although a theory was developing that major changes should only be brought about by legislation, ordinances or proclamations issued by the King in Council being reserved for matters of lesser or temporary importance. When James I, early in his reign, sought to challenge this developing theory, Chief Justice

Coke boldly affirmed in the *Case of Proclamations*[1] that the King could not by proclamation create any offence not previously known to law, but the King may by proclamation admonish his subjects to keep the laws, and upon neglect of such an admonition, an offender could be punished, but by the ordinary processes of law: that is to say, failure to observe the proclamation would not of itself make the offence punishable in the Star Chamber – a court which at that date was coming to be regarded as an instrument of the Royal Prerogative.

Following this emphatic denial of an independent legislative competence to the Crown, the dispute until 1688 turned upon the question whether the King had power to dispense with the laws in favour of particular individuals, or to suspend them altogether, either permanently or for a particular period. Both Charles II and James II attempted to do this, and by these means James II sought to remove, without Parliamentary concurrence, the disabilities on Roman Catholics. In *Godden* v. *Hales*,[2] James II was able to secure a judgment from compliant Judges of the Court of King's Bench, upholding the legality of the dispensing power. The Bill of Rights, which received statutory force in the first year of William and Mary's reign, declared illegal the asserted suspending power and also the dispensing power 'as it has been exercised of late.' From this date, therefore, it has been impossible to assert that the King, or Queen, has any independent legislative function, leaving the sovereignty of Parliament in the legislative sphere unchallenged.

Until the fifteenth century, it was still the right of the King to accept or reject proposals for legislation which originated in either House of Parliament. Technically, such proposals arose by way of petition only. In Henry VI's reign, however, there was a far-reaching change of form. The legislative changes proposed by Parliament, as agreed by the two Houses, were placed before the King in the form of a bill, to which the King assented or which he rejected. From this time onwards any influence exercised by the sovereign over the form or content of legislation must be indirect, through the control which the Crown exercised over the actual members of either House of Parliament. Such control probably reached its highest point during the Tudor period, although restiveness became increasingly apparent during the later years of

[1] (1610) 2 St Tr 723
[2] (1686) 11 St Tr 1165

Elizabeth's reign. Had it not been for such effective control, the sweeping changes in Church and State which accompanied the Reformation in England could never have been carried out.

Originally, Parliament was regarded as the supreme court of the realm; and indeed, it was styled 'the high court of Parliament' until recent times. Some writers have regarded the proceedings in Parliament in respect of legislation as having some of the characteristics of a trial, or at least of a disputation, in which the King's servants stated the case for the Crown, upon which Parliament ultimately gave its decision. There were many other occasions, however, when the judicial character of Parliament was apparent. Parliament, for example, was the tribunal which adjudicated upon the thirty-three articles of accusation against Richard II, and pronounced the sentence of deposition. It was to Parliament again that the Duke of York appealed, in the reign of Henry VI, when he asserted his claim to the throne in opposition to the House of Lancaster. These were dynastic conflicts; and exceptional, and greater, constitutional significance therefore attaches to the attempts by Parliament to control the King's Ministers, and to punish them for misgovernment, by impeachment – a procedure by means of which great offenders were accused by the Commons before the House of Lords. Clumsy as this procedure was, it had the effect of bringing those who flouted Parliament to trial and punishment, in the centuries before cabinet government was evolved. As cabinet government developed, impeachments gradually became obsolete, the last two occurring at the end of the eighteenth century and the dawn of the nineteenth, in the impeachments of Warren Hastings and Lord Melville.

Mediaeval Parliaments invariably responded to the influence of the great barons. When the King and his barons were in accord, there was tranquillity. When, as in the reigns of Edward II and Richard II, the King and his barons were in conflict, the barons strove to embody their demands in legislation. In the long drawn-out struggle between the Houses of York and Lancaster, each faction in turn, as it gained ascendancy, packed Parliament, in order to destroy its opponents by acts of attainder; and to secure obedience to the régime. During the reigns of the first two Tudors, there were far-reaching changes. Few of the great mediaeval baronial families had survived, and those which had, no longer disposed of armies of retainers. Until the Reformation, the greater abbots and bishops regularly outnumbered the lay peers in the House of Lords.

Afterwards, the abbots had disappeared, and the bishops no longer enjoyed the semi-independent status which they had enjoyed in an earlier age. Gradually, the number of peers increased, and like their predecessors, they sought to support their dignities by the ownership of land, but they no longer lived in gloomy castles, nor supported hordes of retainers. Elizabeth I was extremely niggardly in the creation of new peers, and when she did create one, she sought to attach the holder to her by public service and attendance at court. This close association had the consequence that throughout her reign, the House of Lords was substantially conformist, so that the initiative in respect of Parliament's place in the constitution passed increasingly to the House of Commons.

As yet, there was no theory that Parliament was sovereign, or that its legislative competence was unlimited. This, in any case, would have been repugnant to orthodox sixteenth-century theories of an ideal commonwealth, in which each group within a society had its place and function, and contributed to the welfare of the whole. In such a society the privileges and duties of the ruler were absolute, having been determined by Natural Law, and no person or group could invade them. Sir Edward Coke, a very great Common Lawyer, expressed this point of view exactly when he said that a statute which infringed Natural Law was void. Until the Reformation, Parliament had not sought to legislate upon matters of religion or in violation of the royal prerogative. Throughout Elizabeth's reign she stubbornly restrained Parliament from legislating to modify the religious compromise which had been achieved at the outset or, later, upon the question of succession to the throne. To do so, she considered, would have been to trespass upon the royal prerogative.

It will be evident that there would in any case have been matters of great constitutional importance to be settled after the Queen's death. They were made more difficult of solution by the unfamiliarity of the Stuarts with the character of English political life. The Scottish Parliament was not a national assembly, as its English counterpart was. It was the temporary meeting place of hostile factions, some of which from time to time threatened by armed force the King himself. In retaliation the ruler sought to rally support by extreme assertions of the royal prerogative, which, when extended to England, could not fail to provoke strong resistance. Prior to the accession of James I, the English constitutional system worked largely because important areas of it could not be precisely defined. In the hands of a strong king, the royal prerogative could be a powerful weapon: in the hands of a weak King, it could not protect him from the strength of a united Parliamentary opposition. Able rulers, such as the Tudors, preferred to leave it like that. Primarily, they would work through Parliament. If it was necessary to use the prerogative, then circumstances would decide whether the language should be that of command or of cajolery. The implication, in any event, was that the sovereign was acting for the general good, with the support, express or tacit, of the most politically significant part of his subjects. By and large, this assumption was generally correct, so long as the Tudors ruled.

Both Parliament and wide classes in the nation were quick to react to the pretensions of the Stuarts, and in doing so, they found strong and able allies in the Common Lawyers. Basically, the first two Stuarts regarded Parliament as a national assembly, summoned to carry out policy which the King had settled, independently of them. If Parliament refused to comply with the royal will, then it could be dissolved, and other ways of enforcing the King's policy must be evolved. It was for this reason that the functions of the prerogative courts were very greatly extended, and that new ones were established. Of these, the most important were the Court of Star Chamber, in which persons opposing the royal policy were punished, and the Court of High Commission, which enforced the royal policy in matters of religion. The prerogative courts were regarded with great hostility by the judges and practitioners in the Common Law courts. If pursued to its logical conclusion, Stuart policy involved the subordination both of Parliament and the courts to the royal will, and their united opposition could therefore be predicted with certainty. When Chief Justice Coke was dismissed by James I in 1616, he was shortly afterwards returned to the House of Commons, and entered upon a second career as one of the leaders of the Parliamentary opposition. Thenceforward Parliament and Common Lawyers were united in their insistence upon the supremacy of Parliament over the royal administration, and in the supremacy of the Common Law over all rival jurisdictions and, in particular, over the prerogative courts. The two most generally hated, the Star Chamber and the Court of High Commission, were abolished on the meeting of the Long Parliament in 1640; and although James II briefly recreated the High Commission under the title of the Court of Ecclesiastical Commission, it did not survive the collapse of his reign, brought on by the birth of a Roman Catholic Prince of Wales and the acquittal of the Seven Bishops earlier in 1688.

During the prolonged constitutional conflicts of the seventeenth century, England experimented with many varieties of government – with absolute monarchy, with military despotism, with several forms of republican government during the Commonwealth, and finally, with constitutional monarchy. The restoration of Charles II in 1660 established that England preferred constitutional monarchy to republicanism, and still more emphatically, to the hated military government of the major-generals; and the Revolution of 1688 reaffirmed this decision as against the personal rule of a King, who made no secret of his determination to be as absolute as Louis XIV. The Revolution of 1688 reflected the final triumph of Parliamentary sovereignty within a monarchical framework. From that date onwards, Parliamentary sovereignty has been the accepted basic principle upon which English political life is founded. In legal terms it has meant that there are no limits to the legislative competence of Parliament. It can make laws upon any topic – even upon its own composition and functions – and there is no body which can deny their validity. The courts can interpret those laws, but they cannot, as in the United States, challenge their constitutionality. A further consequence of this fundamental principle is that Parliament could not limit its own omnicompetence, or limit that of any succeeding Parliament. Parliament can, and has, disfranchised individuals and groups from time to time. It has extended its own life, even though the duration of Parliaments has been fixed by statute. The life of the Parliament elected in 1910 was extended to 1918, because of World War I, and that of the Parliament elected in 1935 was extended until 1945 because of World War II. There is nothing in law to prevent further extensions for other reasons, and sometimes there have been irresponsible suggestions that this should be done.

In spite of this omnicompetence, Parliament does not, and cannot, govern. Whilst it can do many things, and can debate any topic which is placed before it, its chief function is to clothe in legal form the proposals which the government places before it. If it failed to do so, the 'government' could not continue, and it must then either resign or there must be a general election. The maintenance of government therefore depends upon an effective accord between Parliament and government. Before this is examined, however, it is first necessary to explain what is meant by Parliament.

If one turns to the language of a statute one finds that the enacting formula which used to precede the actual text of an Act of Parliament read as follows:

> 'May it please your Majesty that it may be enacted, and be it enacted by the King's most Excellent Majesty, by and with the advice and consent of the Lords Spiritual and Temporal, and Commons in this present Parliament assembled, and by the authority of the same . . .'

A statute, therefore, was a measure approved in identical terms, after debate, in both Houses of Parliament, and assented to by the King. Until 1911, as will be seen later, there was no formal difference between the powers of the two Houses. If they disagreed, there might be conferences between representatives of the two Houses, to discover whether the disagreement could be resolved, but unless it could, there was nothing to be placed before the King for his assent. After the reign of Anne (1702–14), if the two Houses were in agreement, the royal veto was never exercised. It only survives today as a shadowy relic of the past. That is to say, that the direct participation of the King, or Queen, in legislation has not existed for over two and a half centuries. Even when George III was struggling to reassert royal influence in government, it was never considered possible by him to extend that influence directly to legislation. Any influence which he may have wished to assert in the legislative sphere could only be asserted indirectly through persons who were members of either House of Parliament.

Parliamentary sovereignty is therefore, at best, a formal, legal concept, which comes close to being a legal fiction, and which is not free from ambiguity. If by Parliament is meant 'King in Parliament,' it is at least remarkable that one element of that composite body takes no part at all in the only function – i.e. legislation – in respect of which, even in the legal sense, Parliament can be said to be sovereign. If we pass from the world of legal forms to that of government, we find that it abounds with anomalies. The government of England, it is said, is a constitutional monarchy. The government is made up of persons who are the King's Ministers, appointed by him, and (in theory at least) capable of being dismissed by him. Government is conducted in the King's name, yet he only acts in a public capacity on the advice of his Ministers, which advice he is constitutionally bound to accept, or else be prepared to accept their collective resignations. At the same time, the

government (i.e. the Ministers collectively) depend for their continuance in office upon the continued dominance of their party in
the House of Commons. They are, in fact, the leading members of
that party. Such an extremely curious state of affairs is incomprehensible without an understanding of the way in which it came
about.

One important aspect of English constitutional history since
1688 has been the progressive elimination of the King (often con-
fusingly termed 'the sovereign') from all direct participation in
government. One has only to think of the parts played in the
national story by George III, Queen Victoria, King Edward VII,
and King George VI, to realise how continuous this process has
been. To the Whig of 1688, the King was still in fact, as well as in
theory, the head of the executive, and his Ministers were in reality,
as well as in theory, selected by him. The Revolution had made it
impossible for a King to persist in a policy which directly conflicted
with the wishes of Parliament, but its formulation was still a royal
responsibility, conditioned by the necessity of obtaining Parliamentary approval and support. The primary lesson of the Revolution was therefore that the King could not rule without Parliament
(as Charles I had done from 1629 until the assembly of the Long
Parliament), and that in a situation in which Parliament and the
King were in conflict, it was the will of Parliament which prevailed, but so far as the conduct of government was concerned, the
monarch still selected the executive, appointing them and dismissing them as policy necessitated. The foreign policy of William III,
for example, was shaped in response to the King's initiative, and
was directed towards curbing Louis XIV's aggrandisement in
Europe – a policy to which the Tories were largely indifferent, and
in the shaping of which the Whigs were reluctant allies. Further,
since William had been called to the throne by both parties, he
attempted initially to form governments selected from members
of both parties. It was only gradually, and primarily on account of
his European policy, that he was compelled to rely increasingly upon
the Whigs, whose opposition to Louis XIV was strengthened by
that monarch's support of the exiled Stuarts.

The decisive change came after 1714, when the House of Hanover was called to the throne. William, Mary II, and Anne, were
all Stuarts, and William's connections with English party leaders
were always close. The Hanoverians, though descended from So-
phia, granddaughter of James I, were German princes, with little

understanding of the complexity of English political life. For this reason they were far less successful in interesting the English parties in the affairs of Hanover than William had been in linking the fortunes of Holland with those of England. Further, the protection of Hanover was not seen to be as vital for England's security as the protection of Holland was, and as it continued to be, so long as France sought to dominate the affairs of Europe. The accession of George I, and the Jacobite insurrection in 1715, brought the Tories into complete discredit, and caused the first two Hanoverians to link their fortunes closely with those of the Whig party, which, until the reign of George III, monopolised government. Partly for this reason, and partly because of his unfamiliarity either with English political life or with the English language, George I ceased to preside over meetings of the inner council of Ministers which increasingly came to be known as the 'Cabinet'. Since those Ministers were the leaders of various sections of the overwhelmingly dominant party in the two Houses of Parliament, they were able to ensure that their policies enjoyed the support of Parliament. At this period, party politics was little more than the reshuffling of rival Whig groups as the result of internal intrigues and periodic gusts of public opinion. Even at this period, however, it would be incorrect to assume that the monarch had no influence on government. When George I died in 1727, it was assumed that the Prime Minister, Walpole, would be dismissed or compelled to resign, because George I, in true Hanoverian fashion, had been on the worst possible terms with his son and heir. Walpole nevertheless remained in office until 1742 because he had taken the precaution of establishing close relations with George II's wife, Queen Caroline, a woman of considerable perspicacity. At a later period in George II's reign, the Elder Pitt was excluded from office, because of George II's deep-rooted aversion to him, until the ineffectiveness of the government during the Seven Years' War made his appointment a necessity.

In some ways, the appointment of the Elder Pitt in 1754 to share the direction of national affairs with the Duke of Newcastle was a turning-point in constitutional development. Newcastle's main importance was that he controlled enormous patronage, and was thereby able to manipulate a large body of members of the House of Commons, and also public officials generally. Pitt, on the other hand, had denounced, both in and out of Parliament, the prevailing jobbery which corrupted every branch of public life. This, coupled with the public recognition of his ability and courage, was largely responsible for the public clamour which swept him to power after the incompetence of the administration had produced a succession of disasters in the early stages of the Seven Years' War. When Pitt arrogantly declared: 'I know that I can save the country, and I know that no one else can' he was right in a double sense. Only his ability, and his talent for selecting able young men (of whom General Wolfe was an outstanding example), could turn defeat into victory. In addition, only he could kindle the national enthusiasm and unity, recalling the great days of Elizabeth I's reign, without which victory could not be won. What was most significant of all, however, was that the voice of the nation had made itself heard through the fog of political intrigue. Pitt owed his support to the nation as a whole, and it was to the nation that he appealed. Its voice was to be heard with increasing frequency, and as effectively, in the years which stretched between Pitt's appointment as Minister and the Great Reform Bill in 1832.

The full significance of this development was not immediately apparent. Kings, and Whig magnates, still exercised backstairs influence in the appointment and fall of ministries. There was as yet no theory of the collective responsibility of the Cabinet, and Ministers relied as much upon influence as upon oratory in their management of the House of Commons, and when George III attempted unsuccessfully to break the power of the Whig oligarchy, he adopted similar methods. Except in times of crisis, national opinion had little opportunity to affect the course of government – and this in an age when continental writers saw in the English constitution the perfection of political wisdom! Moreover, in times of crisis, popular opinion did not always express itself so wisely as it did in forcing the Elder Pitt upon a reluctant monarch. The long drawn-out and discreditable story of 'Wilkes and liberty' reflects little credit either on public opinion or on Parliament, and in the still less creditable hysteria of the Gordon Riots, the steadiness of George III showed to greater advantage than the futilities of Ministers and magistrates, the irresolution of Parliament, or the prejudices of the populace of London. Outbursts of public opinion were most likely to be effective when they were rooted in patriotism, and directed towards national safety.

Eighteenth-century Parliaments unfortunately were only vaguely representative of the nation. There had been many changes in the composition of the House of Commons since the Plantagenets had summoned citizens from each city, burgesses from a number of boroughs, and knights of the shire in the fourteenth century. Originally, the Knights of the Shire had been elected in the county court. This was now obsolete, and they were accordingly elected by vociferous support at the hustings. County elections were often shamelessly manipulated by the great local landowners. For example, at the general election for the only Parliament of James II's reign, his Ministers approached every considerable landowner, urging them to use all their interest with their tenants and friends to secure the election of Tory candidates, and in Buckinghamshire Lord Chief Justice Jeffreys at the last moment directed the poll to be transferred from Aylesbury to Newport Pagnell, in order that the Whigs should be taken by surprise.[1] Even in the counties, votes were openly bought and sold, and the costs of purchasing a seat, even as a Knight of the Shire, rose steadily during the eighteenth century. In the boroughs, the situation was much worse. To the mediaeval lists of boroughs represented in Parliament, the Kings made additions from time to time, and a number of Cornish boroughs, mostly small, were added by the Tudors, but until the sixteenth century, representation in Parliament was regarded as a burden, rather than a privilege, since the member expected to be maintained. Thereafter, the advantages and importance of membership of the House of Commons placed the elector, rather than the representative, in a financially favourable position. With the growth of commerce and industry in the eighteenth century, new towns grew in importance, and old ones declined, yet this was not reflected in Parliamentary representation. Moreover, the method of election in the boroughs varied from one town to another. Some boroughs had a moderately democratic franchise, qualification by payment of 'scot and lot' (i.e. hearth taxes) existing in some. At the other extreme were closed corporations, containing only a handful of freemen who were qualified to vote and who could therefore expect considerable financial profit on every dissolution of Parliament. At the end of the eighteenth century, each county in England returned two members, whilst the boroughs were represented by 400 members, many boroughs being in the language of the time 'rotten'. The reform of Parliamentary elections and the redistribution of seats to reflect the change in the weight of population had already been seen to be a necessity in the last quarter of the eighteenth century, but the French Revolution, the Napoleonic Wars, and the

[1] Keeton, *Lord Chancellor Jeffreys*, pp. 249–50.

ensuing reaction, delayed them until 1832. The Reform Act passed in that year effected a modest redistribution of seats, abolishing the franchise completely for fifty-six rotten boroughs and removing one member each from thirty-one others, transferring this representation to towns with greater populations. But equally far-reaching were the provisions which enfranchised, over the country as a whole, about half a million substantial middle-class voters. Later Reform Acts of 1867 and 1882 carried the process forward, the latter Act extending the franchise to almost all classes of adult male. Still a further Reform Act of 1918 conferred the vote on practically every adult male, and upon women over thirty, at the same time permitting women, if elected, to become Members of Parliament. An Act of 1928 conferred the vote upon every adult woman in the same way as it was enjoyed by men and by the Family Law Reform Act, 1969, the age of majority was reduced to eighteen.

The cumulative effect of these changes has been to make the House of Commons representative of the national mood, more especially immediately after a general election, than it has ever been before. Further, the acceptance of the principle of payment of members has opened Parliamentary representation to every class within the community. How far this has actually changed the composition of Parliament will be discussed in a later chapter. So also will be the changed relation of the two Houses of Parliament, which necessarily followed the progressive extensions of the franchise in the nineteenth century. Too much emphasis should not be placed upon correspondence between the mood of Parliament and the mood of the country. Even in modern times, when Parliament in normal circumstances lasts for five years, there can be wide divergence. It is not open to doubt, for example, that the policy of appeasement followed by the Chamberlain government before the outbreak of World War II baffled and humiliated the electorate, however desirable it might have seemed to government and Parliament. This is the more remarkable since with varying degrees of emphasis, all three parties represented in Parliament broadly agreed. In spite of the overwhelming power which any government in office can exercise indirectly to influence public opinion, it is still the case that an independent Press can often prevent the regimentation of opinion, and can prove a truer expression of public opinion than Parliamentary debates.

Parliament has sometimes been described as 'The Grand Inquest of the Nation', and it will be necessary to mention briefly what Parliament actually does. Historically, it has been stated, Parliament was assembled to assent to extraordinary taxation, and to advise the King on matters of general policy. Progressively it assumed the function of bringing to the King's notice the principal general grievances of which his subjects complained. When he and they were in agreement that these grievances should be redressed, legislation was prepared and passed. Gradually, Parliament perceived that it possessed a most powerful weapon in its presentation of grievances which, members insisted, must be redressed before supplies were granted. Hence the historic constitutional principle that 'Redress of grievances must precede supply'. Even today, clear traces of these elementary mediaeval principles of constitutional government still survive in Parliamentary practice. Another principle has also proved to be of considerable practical value. Historically the King asks Parliament for extra supplies, wherewith to carry on his government. Accordingly a private Member of Parliament cannot propose legislation which would have the effect of increasing taxation. Only a Minister of the Crown can do this, and today such a proposal would be one item in the general programme of the ministry in power. Most frequently, too, such an item will appear in the 'Budget' prepared by the Chancellor of the Exchequer, and presented to the House of Commons in April. In his speech presenting it, the Chancellor of the Exchequer reviews the country's financial situation during the past year, and also reports how far the actual yield from taxation has corresponded with it. He then sets out his assessment of the situation during the coming financial year, and his proposals for taxation to cover the needs of the departments, and also nowadays to achieve the economic objectives which the government has in mind. Examples of such objects might be the need to control private spending, or the need to foster the export trade. So far as taxation is raised to meet the financial needs of the great departments of state, these are based upon estimates of expenditure drawn up by each department at an earlier stage, and discussed by the Cabinet from the standpoint of general policy. It has also been necessary for the estimates to run the gauntlet of detailed Treasury scrutiny, for the Treasury has a supervisory function in respect of all departmental spending. A good deal of Parliamentary time is occupied between April and August in the discussion of the Chancellor's Budgetary proposals which, when ultimately accepted, are embodied in two Acts – the Finance Act, which sets out in detail how the money is to be raised, and what changes in the incidence of taxation are to be made; and secondly, the Appropriation Act, which sets out the manner in which the money is to be spent. If the forecast of a government department proves inadequate, it is possible for it to bring forward supplementary estimates of expenditure later in the year.

At the present day, the private member can exercise very little control over the spending of public money. There exists, it is true, a Public Accounts Committee of the House of Commons, with powers to compel the production of all necessary information from a department in respect of its expenditure of public money. Since, however, the department is working within the general framework of government policy, it is only when a department involves itself in substantial unforeseen expenditure that the work of such a committee is likely to prove effective. Unfortunately such situations are not as infrequent as might be wished, as the lamentable history of the construction of the Concorde supersonic aircraft has shown. The project, as originally planned, was to cost less than three hundred million pounds. By May 1969, the cost had risen to over seven hundred million pounds, and the announcement of this staggering increase was accompanied by hints that even this might not be the end. It is only too clearly apparent today that Parliament has lost any control over expenditure that it may originally have had. The question now is whether any effective control over it is exercised by the government. This question, above all others, calls for solution today. In a number of comprehensive social services – for example, education or national health – the annual commitment is almost incapable of any reduction, and in the normal course of operation, it must increase, because of the necessity of renewing, extending, or modernising buildings, and because very large classes of persons employed by them are on incremental salaries. Since both parties are in substantial agreement upon the maintenance in virtually unchanged form of these and many other public services, it would seem that expenditure of public money upon them must inescapably continue to increase.

Besides the raising and spending of public money, and legislation upon the innumerable matters of public concern which any government today considers worthy of its attention, Parliament's competence to debate any matter of public interest is unlimited, and where any matter requires urgent attention, there is a prompt call for a Parliamentary debate. Sometimes a debate on such a topic is conducted simultaneously in both Houses of Parliament. Sometimes, too, where the government considers a matter is not yet ripe for legislation, it finds it useful to focus public attention and discussion upon it by a debate in the House of Lords.

More far-ranging than the Parliamentary debate is the practice of putting questions to Ministers, and question time in the House is often the time at which it is possible to obtain the closest look at departments in action. Very great ingenuity is often used by a member in his effort to elicit information – which, if the department feels it inconvenient to disclose, will be evaded with equal skill. The game is frequently continued by the framing of supplementary questions, within certain clearly established limits, and the game of hide-and-seek between member and department may be prolonged. Even if the member is by no means always successful in his quest for knowledge, it is consciousness of this liability to be questioned, and of the publicity which an inadequate or unsatisfactory answer will evoke, which, as much as any other external factor, keeps the swollen staff of the departments of state on the paths of righteousness.

A great deal of Parliamentary work is done, not on the floor of the House, but in committee rooms. There exist a number of standing committees, but in addition, both Houses of Parliament set up *ad hoc* committees with increasing frequency. Such committees have wide powers to compel the production of documents and the appearance of witnesses, although they have not developed all the quasi-judicial attributes of their American counterparts, with the exception of Parliamentary tribunals of inquiry which are convened under the Tribunals of Inquiry Act, 1921.[1]

[1] See Keeton, *Trial by Tribunal*.

IV

Lords and Commons

THE continued existence of the House of Lords, which disguises the omnipotence of the House of Commons, is one of the miracles of the twentieth century. It can be explained only on the grounds that no political party has been clear (1) if it were abolished, what should replace it, or (2) whether it should be replaced at all. The general feeling has been that if it did not get in the way of government, there was no harm in keeping it, and there might sometimes be little jobs which it would be convenient for it to do. Accordingly, in the last three decades of the twentieth century, it survives somewhat in the way that the Privy Council does – as a body with routine functions, which is nevertheless occasionally useful.

All this is very different from the position of the House of Lords in earlier ages, or even in the nineteenth century. When Parliaments were first summoned regularly, in the fourteenth century, and for some time afterwards, the Lords, who were summoned by writ individually, attended to advise and consent to legislation. The Commons were there to consent only. Historically, the Lords' function was a continuation of that discharged by the magnates in the King's feudal council of tenants-in-chief from the Norman Conquest onwards. The magnates were bound to attend and give advice because of their feudal duty, and it was of the first importance that they should, because, within the lands which they held of the King in chief, they in turn exercised similar functions with the assistance of their tenants. Further, neither the customary feudal law, nor the equally customary feudal taxation, could be changed without their consent. This feudal conception of the structure of society was obsolete when Parliament took shape, but the magnates were still summoned individually to advise, because they held lands of such extent that they were at once the most powerful, and the richest, members of society. Until the Reformation the House of Lords remained a small and compact body, except when the Wars of the Roses divided the lay peers into two hostile factions who alternately sought to destroy their rivals, forfeit their lands, and to exclude them from the House of Lords and from all part in government.

The possession of a peerage gave the holder a right to a personal writ of summons to Parliament, and indeed, ultimately, to assist in clearing up doubts upon who in fact was a peer, it was decided by the Committee of Privileges that a peer was one who had been summoned (1) by name, (2) to a Parliament (as distinct from a session of the King's Council), and who (3) had sat and voted on at least one occasion. It was also established that when this had taken place, every future holder of the title was automatically entitled to be summoned to Parliament. If the peerage existed simply because of a writ of summons, its holder was styled a baron. Sometimes the King conferred an additional dignity. The holder might be invested with an earldom, which was plainly of higher rank. For some time these were the only two ranks. By the reign of Edward III a still higher rank had been introduced – that of duke – at first only for members of the royal family, but later for others of noble birth. Richard II introduced the rank of marquess, and Henry VI that of viscount. Thus, in order of precedence, the peerage are: dukes, marquesses, earls, viscounts, and barons. England has never accepted the rank of prince as part of the peerage, and the only princes known in England are a monarch's sons or grandsons. Similarly, knighthood is a dignity, but it does not constitute a rank in the peerage – not even in that curious and now obsolescent form, the inheritable knighthood possessed by a knight baronet, or more simply a baronet.

In many ways, an inheritable peerage is regarded in the same light as a piece of real property, and a number of the rules of the law of real property apply to it. For example, the rule of primogeniture applies to it, but if it should descend to two or more daughters, it is said to be in abeyance, until one or other line dies out, and the senior male heir of a daughter can claim it. When this situation arises, sometimes after a very considerable interval of time, the claimant makes good his claim to the satisfaction of the Committee of Privileges. As in the Law of Real Property, in the peerage there exist two forms of limitation which look something like a fee simple and a fee tail. If the peerage is an ancient one, a barony created only by writ of summons, it will descend to the heirs general of the grantee, and it is in respect of these peerages that claims proceedings are often complicated and prolonged. From the reign of Richard II onwards, and partly because of the increase in the number of ranks, it became usual to create a peerage by royal letters patent. These set out the dignity, and the manner of its descent, usually in tail male, i.e. to the heirs male of the body of the grantee. There could, however, be a 'special remainder', e.g. to A, and thereafter to the brother of A and the heirs male of the brother of A. This happened, for example, in respect of the earldom conferred upon Lord Kitchener of Khartoum, since he was a bachelor and had no children, and the peerage of the first Viscount Rhondda had a special remainder to his daughter and her heirs male.

A peerage cannot be alienated, either by gift or sale, nor disposed of by will. Until recently, it could not be surrendered, but the Peerage Act, 1963, has permitted a person on whom a peerage descends to disclaim it within a short time of his succession, or of the Act coming into force. Several peers have already done so. The disclaimer extends only to the peer himself, and the succession on his death is unaffected. The Earl of Home became Sir Alec Douglas-Home (since his titles included a knighthood of the Thistle, which was not surrendered); the second Viscount Hailsham became Mr Quintin Hogg; and Lord Stansgate became Mr Wedgwood Benn. The reason was in each case to continue a political career in the House of Commons which would have been destroyed by exile to the House of Lords; but no reason for disclaimer need be specified.

Four classes of peer call for special comment – life peers, women, clerics, Irish and Scottish peers – and something must be said about courtesy titles. In the middle of the nineteenth century, the Liberal government of Lord Palmerston attempted the experiment of creating life peers. At this date the legal element in the House was noticeably weak, and difficulty had sometimes been experienced in finding sufficient well-qualified persons to sit in the House as a final Court of Appeal. In 1856, therefore, the Palmerston government created a High Court judge, Parke, a peer for life only, with the title Baron Wensleydale. This was very generally opposed by the House itself, and was rejected by the Committee of Privileges, on the ground that it would give the government power to ensure that its policy prevailed in the House of Lords by the creation of a sufficient number of peers to carry government legislation. The unhappy Baron Parke was therefore created a hereditary peer, which made no difference, as he had no heir, and the matter rested until, in 1876, three years after the Judicature Act, statutory power was given to create a limited number of life peers to serve in the House of Lords in its judicial capacity, and to receive a salary for doing so. These are life peers, and they are able to participate in the normal political business of the House. Moreover, if they should retire from their political duties, neither their status as peers nor their membership of the House is affected. By the Life Peerages Act, 1958, the Crown was given a statutory power, apparently unlimited in extent, to create life peers on the nomination of the Prime Minister. The Act was passed by a Conservative government primarily with the object of strengthening the representation of the Labour Opposition in the House of Lords. Free use of it was made by the Wilson government, and the number of life peers created under this Act is already large.

Although a peerage may remain in abeyance if two or more daughters inherit, there is nothing to prevent a single daughter from inheriting the dignity, but in such a case, until recent times, it did not confer also membership of the House of Lords, a peeress being disqualified by sex, and the Committee of Privileges decided, in 1922, in Lady Rhondda's Case, that the Sex Disqualification Act of 1918 in no way affected this disability. However, at a later date, the committee reversed its decision, and the House now contains a sprinkling of peeresses, including life peeresses. To add to the confusion, it can happen that life peerages may be conferred separately on husband and wife. Apart from special creation, a wife of a peer has no right to sit in the House of Lords.

Until the Reformation, the ecclesiastical peers usually outnumbered their lay colleagues. The 'Lords Spiritual' were the archbishops, bishops, and abbots, but the abbots disappeared at the Reformation, leaving the archbishops and twenty-four bishops. In modern times the number of bishops has been substantially increased, but the Bishoprics Act, 1878, provided that the number of Lords spiritual should not be increased thereby. The bishops should be limited to the Bishops of London, Durham, and Winchester, and twenty-one other bishops in order of seniority in consecration. The continued membership of the bishops is highly anomalous. If it be suggested that there is room for the representation of religion in a second chamber, then the exclusion of representatives of other churches is remarkable. Apart from the historic association of the bishops with the business of the House of Lords, possibly the only remaining circumstance justifying their membership is the fact that the Anglican Church is a Church established by law.

At the time of the legislative union with Scotland in 1707 and with Ireland in 1800, both those kingdoms had separate peerages. In 1707, the power of the Crown to create further Scottish peerages was ended, but it was provided that sixteen representative peers of Scotland should be elected for each Parliament to sit in the House of Lords. At the time of the union with Ireland, there was a provision that twenty-eight representative peers of Ireland should sit for life. In practice, very few Scottish peers are unable to sit in the House of Lords, for it was decided in 1782 that if a Scottish peer had an English peerage conferred on him, he could sit in the House of Lords in respect of his English peerage. Most Scottish peers today also have English peerages. So far as Ireland is concerned, it was settled at the time of the creation of the Irish Free State in 1922 (and confirmed on the establishment of the Irish Republic) that there would be no further election of Irish peers to the House of Lords. Accordingly, they have progressively disappeared, unless they too have held English peerages. So long as these two types of peer existed, however, as distinct elements, there was a curious distinction between them. If a Scottish peer were not a representative peer, and had no English peerage, he was excluded from Parliament altogether, for he was not eligible for membership of the House of Commons. On the other hand, an Irish peer who was neither an English peer nor an Irish representative peer was so eligible. This explains why Lord Palmerston, an Irish peer, lived the whole of his political life in the House of Commons.

One further point may be mentioned. The eldest sons of dukes, marquesses, and earls, normally bear their father's second title as a courtesy title during their father's lifetime. Thus, the eldest son of the Duke of Bedford is styled the Marquess of Tavistock, and the eldest son of the Marquess of Bath is styled Viscount Weymouth. This does not affect the eldest son's legal status as a commoner, and he is therefore entitled to be elected to sit in the House of Commons during his father's lifetime. Thus, the Marquess of Hartington, the eldest son of the Duke of Devonshire, was one of Gladstone's principal lieutenants, and it has been suggested that he might have been Prime Minister, but for the death of his father and his transfer to the House of Lords. It is circumstances such as these, and also the fact that the younger children of peers were always ranked as commoners which for a very long period gave the two

Houses of Parliament an underlying feeling of unity, which was particularly demonstrated during the Civil War. All the early leaders of the Parliamentary forces were members of the Upper House, which divided over the constitutional issue in something like the same proportions as the Commons.

After the Revolution of 1688, although there was a slow and almost imperceptible change in the political centre of gravity from the Lords to the Commons, the Lords nevertheless exercised a dominating influence in public affairs. Throughout the eighteenth century, although industry and trade were making vast strides, the peers were still the wealthiest order in the community, as the great palaces which they erected in this period sufficiently witness. As yet there was no income tax, and the possibility of estate duty had not even been conceived. Moreover, each peer of any standing jealously guarded his right of individual audience with the King, and upon occasions, expressed himself upon public affairs with a freedom which would be unusual even today. There were, however, other and deeper reasons. The great Whig families were closely connected by an extremely intricate system of intermarriages and they could exert their vast landed interest in favour of their relations and dependants, when these offered themselves for election to the House of Commons, whether as representatives of the towns or of the counties. County elections could be swayed, not only by social influence and economic pressure, but also by the artificial creation of small freeholds for clients, satisfying the 40/- freehold qualification, which were regularly surrendered back to the magnate's steward, once an election had been completed. Their holders were the 'faggot-voters', who assembled in strength in the hustings, and who, if the opposition seemed to merit it, did not disdain upon occasion to use physical force to secure the return of their nominee.

In the boroughs, the system was even worse. Until after the passing of the Great Reform Act of 1832, there was no procedure for the reallocation of Parliamentary representation, which had therefore taken no account at all of social and economic changes over the centuries. In the reign of Edward I, 166 of the most flourishing boroughs and cities were directed to return members, two for each, except London, which returned four. Not every town complied, for members were supported financially in Parliament by their constituents and, in addition, a borough which returned members to Parliament was assessed higher than a borough which was unrepresented. Between the reigns of Henry VIII

E

and Charles I, when representation in the House of Commons came to be regarded for the first time as a valuable right, there were substantial additions to the numbers of boroughs returning members, by charter, by statute, and finally, by way of petition for the revival of rights which the borough had allowed to lapse. Whilst some of the additions made at this time reflected a growth in civic pride and prosperity, a number of additions, particularly in counties such as Cornwall, where royal estates were extensive, were made because it was thought that their members would strengthen the court party in the Commons. Others again desired representation as a valuable perquisite, for which a substantial cash price could be exacted. Where, as was the case in many decayed boroughs, the franchise was confined to members of a small corporation, which in turn exercised a monopoly in respect of its own membership, individual benefits at election time could be substantial. In the eighteenth century, representation of the boroughs was openly put up for sale, and the price rose steadily as the century progressed. At the end of the century, it was alleged that 306 members were returned by the influence of 160 persons, many of whom were members of the House of Lords – or their close connections. In Scotland their influence was almost absolute, for in a country with a population of two and a half millions, only 2,500 possessed the Parliamentary franchise. In Ireland, the situation was even worse.

This extraordinary system had two major characteristics. It ensured that there was a continuing harmony in outlook between the two Houses of Parliament. It also ensured that young men, trained in a highly sophisticated political and social environment, could be certain of entry into political life through the intervention of a patron. To name only three examples, Charles James Fox, the Younger Pitt, and Gladstone not only entered Parliament at the earliest possible age, but also attained high ministerial office in their early twenties. Beside this there should, however, be set the permanent exclusion from political life of men of ability of all classes who were outside the magic circle. It was because the entire country recognised that the passing of the first Reform Bill would put an end to oligarchical domination that its passage was so fiercely contested, for the Reform Bill ended for ever the power of members of the Upper House to control the elections to membership of the House of Commons. Certain other changes were also taking place. During the long premiership of the Younger Pitt, which largely coincided with the struggle against Revolutionary and Napoleonic

France, Pitt had found it politic to bind the wealthy manufacturers and merchants to him by a freer distribution of peerages. This tendency continued, although with varying pace, throughout the nineteenth and twentieth centuries so that, even without the frequent creations of life peerages since 1958 especially during Labour governments, the House of Lords grew to quite unmanageable proportions, totalling nearly a thousand members, of whom a very large number never attend Parliament at all. Of the remainder, less than a hundred and fifty can be said to be in regular attendance. In the nineteenth century, the successive creations of peers fall into clearly defined groups. Some were created for distinction in public service, whether political, administrative, or in the armed forces. One successful commander-in-chief in a prolonged war, with a final and decisive victory – the Duke of Wellington – climbed the entire hierarchy of the peerage, but for most successful commanders, such as French, Haig, Roberts, or Kitchener, the reward has been an earldom, although Montgomery, at the conclusion of World War II, received only a viscountcy. No civilian has emulated Wellington, although Freeman Freeman-Thomas, a successful member of the House of Commons, who ended his career as Viceroy of India, attained the rank of Marquess of Willingdon, and Rufus Isaacs, an outstanding Liberal lawyer who was Lord Chief Justice, and Ambassador to the United States during World War I, was created Marquess of Reading. The usual reward for a retiring Prime Minister has been an earldom, an honour which Attlee, the Prime Minister of the powerful Labour government which came to power in 1945, accepted as a matter of course. Successful Foreign Secretaries have sometimes received earldoms, but for most retiring Cabinet Ministers, the reward has usually been a viscountcy. Sir Winston Churchill is reputed to have declined a dukedom, with the comment that one in the family was enough. The result has been that, quite independently of the Peerage Act, 1963, his grandson, another Winston, has been able to embark upon a political career without the threat of ultimate translation to the House of Lords hanging over him.

As not infrequently occurs in English political life, the extent of the revolution which had occurred in 1832 was a long time in becoming apparent. Education, social contacts, and local influence could still ensure the return of ambitious young members of great families to the House of Commons without recourse to the corruption which disgraced English political life until 1832. Throughout the century the House of Commons was still largely monopolised by persons of gentle birth and by members of the professional classes, although after 1870, businessmen increasingly secured election. If the Cabinets of the nineteenth century are scrutinised, it will be found that the peerage appears almost as prominently in them as it did in the eighteenth century. For example, W. E. Gladstone's Cabinet of sixteen in the government which took office in 1868, was equally divided between members of the two Houses. In the Tory Cabinet of Lord Derby, which preceded it, there were nine peers and seven commoners, and in the Conservative Cabinet of Benjamin Disraeli, which succeeded Gladstone's in 1874, there were six peers and nine commoners.

Further, in the last four decades of the nineteenth century, the office of Foreign Secretary was invariably occupied by members of the House of Lords, and two Foreign Secretaries – a Liberal, Lord Rosebery, and a Conservative, Lord Salisbury, combined this office with that of Prime Minister. These two are probably the last two members of the House of Lords to attain the supreme office in government. The change in the relations of the two Houses, and the decline of the House of Lords as an effective political chamber, have made such an appointment today impossible. Lord Rosebery, on resigning in 1895, after an unhappy tenure of power in which differences with his Leader of the House of Commons, Sir William Harcourt, had been a regular feature, said bitterly that he would never consent to head a government from the House of Lords again. Lord Salisbury's passage was a smoother one, largely because the Leader of the House of Commons was his nephew, Arthur John Balfour, in a party which included several other members of the Salisbury clan. The last time when the appointment of a peer as Prime Minister was seriously considered was on the death of the Conservative leader, Andrew Bonar Law, in 1922. On this occasion, the Marquess Curzon, who had been an outstanding Foreign Secretary and Viceroy of India, and a dominating figure in the Conservative Party, confidently expected to receive the royal summons, but King George V sent for Stanley Baldwin instead, correctly interpreting the changed climate of government. It has been suggested that Neville Chamberlain, on his disastrous fall in 1940, suggested the Earl of Halifax (another former Foreign Secretary and Viceroy of India) as his successor, but this suggestion, if pursued, would have found very few supporters, when the country had already decided that Winston Churchill alone was capable of extricating Great Britain from disaster. Still more recently, yet another Foreign Secretary, Lord Home, was designated by Harold Macmillan, the Conservative Prime Minister, as his successor on his retirement in 1963, but on this occasion, it was regarded as axiomatic that this could only be done if the Earl of Home renounced his earldom, taking advantage of the recently-passed Peerage Act. Although the earldom was renounced, Sir Alec Douglas-Home (as he then became) failed to win the general election of 1964, and in spite of his great qualities, the Conservative Party subsequently replaced him as leader with Edward Heath. After the Conservative victory in the general election of 1970, Sir Alec could claim to have the distinction of having served as Foreign Secretary both in the House of Lords and in the House of Commons, reversing the progress of Lord Salisbury as Foreign Secretary from the Commons (where he sat under the courtesy title of Lord Cranborne during his father's lifetime) to the Lords.

In spite of the substantial participation of the peerage in nineteenth-century Cabinets, there was a progressive and decisive change in the relationship of the two Houses. Members of the House of Commons no longer looked to powerful patrons, but to electorates, and beyond them to the nation at large for support, and general elections were increasingly fought on agreed programmes on the lines of a national campaign, in which the principal party leaders conducted tours of the electorate, rallying support by appeals which could now directly reach national audiences through the spread of literacy and the creation of cheap popular newspapers with mass circulations. Because of its limited size the United Kingdom has been almost the ideal country in which the struggle for power can be conducted. Even before the intervention of the aeroplane, almost any part of it could be reached in a few hours from London, where also the most influential element in public opinion was concentrated. By a strong constitutional convention, the members of the House of Lords were debarred from playing a direct part in election campaigns, and little by little their influence upon them dwindled. Gladstone may have been generous in his inclusion of Liberal peers in his Cabinet, but he permitted none of them to enjoy the limelight in public speaking. In the period between Gladstone's resignation in 1890 and the outbreak of World War I in 1914, Lord Rosebery and his son-in-law, the Marquess of Crewe, were among the most influential leaders of the Liberal Party, but in the popular estimation, they could not compare with Sir Henry Campbell-Bannerman and H. H. Asquith, primarily because their voices were never heard at election time, when controversy was fiercest.

These were outward and visible signs of an impending decline in power, the real causes of which were more deep-rooted. Most peers of the older creations were still great landed magnates, and as yet the great estates, some of them extending to several hundreds of thousands of acres, were unbroken, but they were already under threat. From 1880 onwards, both parties increasingly turned to social reform as a method of securing the support of the newly enfranchised masses. Social reform necessarily involved expenditure on a scale far greater than that which earlier generations had contemplated. Side by side with such expenditure went the necessity for extensive rearmament, as the country faced a succession of external threats – from France, from Russia, and finally and most serious of all, from a united and self-confident Germany. The international situation might dictate which of these objectives enjoyed temporary priority in the mind of the government of the day, but neither political party could fail to regard them as permanent features of their policies. Both objectives required considerable increases in taxation, which were strongly resisted by the propertied classes, which in turn found their principal spokesmen in the House of Lords. In the three decades before World War I, there was an unanswered question in the constitution. The House of Lords had abandoned its right to amend money bills before the end of the seventeenth century, but it was assumed that it still possessed the right to reject them. Would that right ever be used? If so, in what circumstances? Further, was there a distinction between a simple money bill, e.g. to impose a new tax, and a measure of social reform which involved the expenditure of large sums of public money which again must be met by additional taxation? The situation was potentially explosive because it could be represented that in rejecting such a bill, the House of Lords was not only impeding progress, but was also placing its own interests before those of the people as a whole. Already by 1880, the Liberal Party was raising the cry of Lords versus People, and was stating, in forcible terms, that the 'backwoodsmen' of the House of Lords should not be permitted to make fleeting and silent visits to the House of Lords to obstruct the march of progress and the achievement of social justice.

A conflict between the two Houses could not, in any case, have been averted indefinitely, even though the House of Lords exercised restraint upon numerous occasions, and thereby averted a head-on conflict. For example, although they offered persistent obstruction to Gladstone's weak Liberal government of 1894, compelling him to abandon a number of proposed measures, they nevertheless did not reject the Finance Act of 1894, which imposed a revolutionary new system of levying death duties, which was a major factor in the break-up of great estates and which therefore has contributed as much as any single measure to the destruction of the wealth of the peerage, as an estate of the realm. Even so, Gladstone, in the same year, in his last speech in Parliament as Prime Minister, squarely raised the issue of the position of the House of Lords. 'I think honourable gentlemen opposite must feel, as I feel,' he said, 'that in some way or other a solution will have to be found for this tremendous contrariety and incessant conflict upon matters of high principle between the representatives of the people and those who fill a nominated Chamber. It is the authority of the nation that must in the last resort decide.'

There were other factors directly leading to an explosion. The Irish question had plagued the nation and had seriously impeded the transaction of public business for nearly half a century when, in 1880, Gladstone announced that the Liberal Party accepted the principle of Home Rule for Ireland. This decision posed many very difficult problems. It involved ultimately the destruction of the Protestant establishment in a predominantly Roman Catholic country, for as yet the possibility of partition had not been seen. In the long run, too, the numerous English peers who had inherited considerable Irish estates could not overlook the threat of expropriation either directly or by punitive taxation from an Irish Parliament. To the alliance between the Liberal Party and the Irish Nationalists, the majority in the House of Lords offered unrelenting opposition, with the support of the Conservatives, who now became Unionists, i.e. pledged to maintain the Union. With them were associated an influential body of Liberal Unionists which included most of the former Liberal peers with extensive Irish estates. In spite of the fervour of Gladstone's oratory, and inflammatory speeches from his Irish auxiliaries, a Home Rule Bill, passed by the House of Commons, was rejected by the Lords in 1893, but the struggle could not be indefinitely prolonged. Liberal propaganda increasingly denounced the Lords as the enemies of the people. It remained only until the tide swept a strong Liberal government to power to choose a battleground upon which it was impossible for the Lords to win.

From the moment when a Liberal government, with a large Parliamentary majority, came to power in 1905, led first by Camp-bell-Bannerman, and then, on his death, by H. H. Asquith, conflict between the two Houses was always imminent. Many Liberal leaders had particularly mentioned the need to curtail the powers of the House of Lords during their election campaigns, but on the assembly of the new Parliament, with its decisive Liberal majority, the Lords sought to postpone the conflict as long as possible, and they therefore permitted the bulk of the legislation promoted in the early years of Liberal rule to pass without serious opposition. This was a wise course to choose, for the Liberal leaders had not hesi-tated to point out the one-sided nature of the participation in government by the Lords. When a Conservative government was in power, they said, the Lords were co-operative. They only be-came obstructive, and at the same time conscious of the rights of the people, when the Liberals were in power. It was in vain that Conservatives pointed out that at times the Lords had rejected Conservative measures also. Until the secession to the other side of the Liberal Unionist peers over Irish Home Rule, the two parties were by no means unevenly balanced in a House in which, in an earlier age, the Whig peers had been all powerful. Further, it was difficult to compare in importance the Liberal and Conservative measures rejected, or seriously modified, by the Lords. The Con-servative measures were, on the whole, neither seriously con-troversial nor of major importance. The Liberal measures which had been rejected or mutilated by the House of Lords included Irish Home Rule, the disestablishment of the Anglican Church in Wales, and many measures of major social policy, such as Employ-ers' Liability and national education.

In the event, the Lords accepted the challenge of the Liberal Party over Lloyd George's controversial Budget of 1909. This in-cluded major proposals for a national system of unemployment and sickness insurance, together with other measures. These measures necessarily involved additional taxation, and particularly a new Land Tax, which bore heavily upon the propertied classes, and a graduated income tax. The Lords therefore rejected the Budget as a whole, and thereby raised the greatest constitutional issue since the first Reform Bill. Ever since the Restoration in 1660, the Lords had abandoned all claim to amend money bills, and ever since the practice had arisen in the nineteenth century of putting the government's financial proposals for the year into a Budget, to be ultimately embodied into the annual Finance Act, the Lords had never rejected a Budget. Even in 1909, their legal right to do so was not questioned. The matter was simply one of constitutional propriety; and for the Lords it was argued that the valuation clauses in the Land Tax introduced in the Budget of 1909 had no proper place in a money bill. They were proposals on social policy which the Lords were entitled to pronounce upon as freely as upon any other legislative proposal, and, in rejecting these clauses, the Lords were referring them to the electorate for further consideration. Nevertheless, it was easy for the Liberal government to raise the cry of 'Lords versus People'. They therefore recommended a dissolution of Parliament, announcing as they did so that they were resolved to secure the passage of two measures – the rejected Budget, and also the passage of a bill in which the legislative powers of the Lords would be drastically curtailed.

In 1910, there were two general elections, in January and December, and at each of these Liberals and Conservatives were almost equally divided. Nevertheless, the close alliance between Liberals and Irish Nationalists, who would be among the first to profit from a Parliament Bill, ensured the continuance in office of the Liberal government. During the interval between the two elections, King Edward VII had died, and the country thereby lost an experienced and influential mediator at a critical moment. It is not surprising, therefore, that repeated meetings between the leaders of the two parties, and more formal conferences between the two Houses of Parliament, failed to produce an agreed solution of the constitutional problem. Further, the Liberal Prime Minister had secured from King George V the final political weapon available to a Prime Minister when facing a conflict between the two Houses – a promise to create sufficient Liberal peers to force the passage of the Parliament Bill through the House of Lords. It was the knowledge of this undertaking on the part of the monarch which prevailed upon a sufficient number of Conservative peers to abstain from the critical division – as their Tory predecessors had previously abstained from a similarly critical vote upon the Reform Bill of 1832. Only once in English constitutional history has this ultimate political weapon been actually used – when, in Queen Anne's reign, the Tory ministry induced her to create twelve Tory peers to carry the Treaty of Utrecht, to end the war of the Spanish Succession, in 1712, against bitter Whig opposition. On this occasion, the Marquess of Wharton, a Whig magnate, asked, as the twelve Tory peers entered the chamber: 'Gentlemen, do you propose to vote singly, or by your foreman?'

Exactly two hundred years later, something between two and three hundred creations would have been necessary to secure a safe majority, and whilst it was the intention to mobilise, as a first line, the eldest sons of a number of Liberal peers, the list included, among other Liberal stalwarts, many prominent in local affairs, whose disappointment must have been considerable.

The Parliament Act, 1911, provided that until such times as the second chamber itself should be reformed, the powers of the Lords should be curtailed in the following way: so far as money bills were concerned, the power of the Lords to amend them was abolished, together with their power to reject them. They retained only power to delay them for no more than one month. The result has been that since 1911, the Lords have ceased to be concerned with money bills at all, and they are passed by the Lords after a formal presentation, substantially without comment. So far as other bills are concerned, the Lords retained the power to delay the passage of a bill for two years, during which time it must be passed by the Commons three times. It is not without interest that the Parliament Act, 1911, was only invoked for two bills by the Liberal government which secured its passage – for the Irish Home Rule Act and the Welsh Church Disestablishment Act. Both were introduced in 1912 and became law by virtue of its provisions in 1914.

Like many fundamental constitutional changes, the full effects of this one only became apparent with the passing of time. During the inter-war years, with only temporary and weak Labour governments, the House of Lords rarely found itself at odds with the government which, although Conservative, found no reason to modify so convenient an arrangement. Accordingly, in spite of the findings of numerous committees, the composition of the House of Lords remained unaltered. Gradually, there emerged the hypothesis that such change was best achieved by agreement between the major political parties, and these differed widely in their views of the proper functions of a reformed second chamber. Since the debates in the Lords could no longer affect the existence of governments, there was an increasing tendency for all important ministerial posts to be held by members of the House of Commons, with an under-secretary of state in the House of Lords. Attendance in the Lords declined, in spite of the size of the chamber, and business tended to be confined to a collection of peers, varying from one hundred to 150, who had enjoyed public office, either in Britain or abroad, and who included a number of former members of the House of Commons, who had gone into semi-retirement by accepting a peerage, at the same time retaining their party allegiance. It is interesting to note that of 566 hereditary peers created between 1901 and 1957, 317 were former members of the House of Commons. From time to time governments found it convenient to stage a debate in the House of Lords on some topic of public interest, on which it was desirable to focus public attention, even though the time had not yet arrived for government action. But the Act of 1911 had made it essential that every important legislative proposal must first be considered by the House of Commons. Only occasional bills with non-political content have been first introduced in the Lords since 1911. Orthodox constitutional doctrine in the inter-war years stated that the most important remaining function of the Lords was to act as a revising chamber, since some clauses of some bills were inadequately discussed in the House of Commons. Whilst it is true that the House of Lords has often performed valuable services of this kind, it would seem more appropriate, and certainly not less convenient, for a drafting committee of the House of Commons to undertake them.

In 1948, the Attlee Labour government reduced the delaying power of the House of Lords from two years to one, and the Wilson government of 1966 suggested reducing even this short period. Obviously at this point any suggestion that the House of Lords has any appreciable influence upon the conduct of public affairs becomes unreal. Not unnaturally, attendance has diminished still further, although this has been partly disguised by the creation of nearly 200 life peers, on the ground that such creations would enable it to discharge its functions (whatever they may be) more efficiently. But this curious exercise of patronage by the Prime Minister has scarcely achieved this result. The great majority of these life peers attend only occasionally, and outside their particular fields of interest they contribute little to the conduct of the general business of the House. Even today, the discussion upon the reform and future role of the House of Lords continues spasmodically between the parties, but so far without a conclusion having been reached, either by agreement or by the parties separately. One is forced to the conclusion that both parties have found what is, in reality, single-chamber government highly convenient.

The almost total disappearance of the power of the Lords to influence governmental legislation is now an accepted fact. Since 1948, the power to reject a bill for one year has never been used, and its power to amend legislation is normally used to remove defects in bills, and only rarely upon questions of substance. In 1968, the Lords did in fact reject a government order dealing with the Rhodesian dispute, but beyond drawing down upon them the wrathful condemnation of the Labour government, it aroused little, if any, public interest. Indeed, one of the conditions affecting the work of the House of Lords today is that it receives very little attention in the Press, and practically none on the radio or on television.

Two major questions therefore remain: how should the House of Lords be reformed or replaced, and second, what should such a chamber do? Before answering them, it may be valuable to consider briefly whether a second chamber is really necessary. This is not an idle question, since both political parties have found it convenient to operate what is virtually a one-chamber system for over forty years. In doing so, the United Kingdom has joined a very small group of states – New Zealand, Norway, and Denmark – who alone find single-chamber government attractive. All three of them are relatively small and homogeneous, but even so, all three operate single-chamber government within a written constitution, which defines and limits the function of the legislature. The United Kingdom is large, with diverse elements within it, and its constitution remains unwritten. So long as the tradition of compromise and consent continues to dominate English public life, the dangers of this situation remain latent. Yet it should not be forgotten that in the thirties, Sir Stafford Cripps, Harold Laski, and other left-wing publicists openly advocated the employment of this highly vulnerable system for the establishment of a left-wing dictatorship. To this a single-chamber legislature could have offered no opposition at all – not even the possibility of delay or a reference to the electorate – provided that those who wished to bring about these changes possessed a majority – even a temporary one – in the House of Commons.

As Professor Max Beloff pointed out in the *Sunday Telegraph*, in September 1968, there has always been within the Labour Party a strong Jacobinical and even totalitarian trend, which views Parliament merely as a vehicle by which the wishes of the ruling party are transformed into legislation with the minimum of delay. He further pointed out that the single-assembly constitution was imposed on the 'People's Democracies' of Eastern Europe as a prelude to their communisation after the war. The United Kingdom is particularly vulnerable to such a transformation, since the absence of any formal constitution or of limits to the legislative omnicompetence of Parliament (in reality, already the House of Commons) would make such a development one of little difficulty for a party with a firmly disciplined majority in the House of Commons. It is, therefore, significant that when the latest proposals for reform of the House of Lords were presented to the House of Commons in the autumn of 1968, no less than 132 members voted for the abolition of the House of Lords altogether.

If it be accepted that a two-chamber legislature has been found to be the normal mode of government in Western democracies, then the problems of composition and function must be solved.

Nearly a hundred years ago, Walter Bagehot, in writing a lengthy introduction to the second edition of his *English Constitution*, assessed the change in status of the House of Lords which two extensions of the franchise had caused, and then added: 'If the House of Peers ever goes, it will go in a storm, and the storm will not leave all else as it is.' The prediction was only partially true. The storm, long expected in the last two decades of the nineteenth century, burst in 1910, threatened the destruction of the House of Lords, but died away without further upheavals. Discussions of reform in the inter-war period produced only hesitations, divisions, and ultimately boredom. Any attempt today to rouse the electorate with the battle-cry of 1910, 'The Peers versus the People', would produce perplexity and perhaps amusement. In terms of political action, who *are* the Lords and what do they do?

The problem of the House of Lords is really a complex of problems. There is, first, the relation of the peerage to the legislature; second, assuming a second chamber is necessary, how it should be selected or elected; and finally, what it should do, and in particular how far, if at all, it should have power to delay legislation. Perhaps the difficulties which have been encountered in the past arise from the fact that attempts have sometimes been made to solve all these questions together.

Difficulties in connection with the first question have arisen from the fact that until recently peers were members of the House of Lords, and were therefore ineligible for election in the Commons. Accordingly, most schemes for reform provided for the election of a number from this body for membership of a reformed House. If, however, the hereditary principle is rejected as a criterion for membership, it is difficult to see how selection by hereditary peers from hereditary peers can be justified. The situation is now further modified by the increasing use made of the power to create life peers, in virtue of a recent Act. Life peers now number over 150 in a House nominally of over one thousand members, of whom 200 or so have obtained formal leave of absence.[1] The problem of reconstruction would be greatly simplified if the possession of an hereditary peerage did not involve inability to be a candidate for the House of Commons, but at the same time conferred no right to sit in the second chamber. Membership of that body would then be conferred upon persons who might be styled Lords of Parliament, and who would hold office, either for life, or for some lesser period.

The preamble to the Parliament Act, 1911 (which substituted two years' delay for the absolute veto of the Lords), stated that the Act was a temporary solution until a new second chamber could be devised. World War I postponed consideration for a time, but in April 1918, side by side with proposals for the extension of the franchise, to include women, there appeared the report of the Bryce Committee. The report dealt with the two questions of function and composition. The essential functions of a second chamber, it said, were: (1) the revising function; (2) the initiation of bills dealing with subjects of a comparatively non-controversial character; (3) 'the interposition of so much delay (and no more) in the passing of a Bill as may be needed to enable the opinion of the nation to be adequately expressed on it'; this, it was thought, would be particularly important where the bill introduced an important change in the constitution; (4) discussion of broad topics and important questions for which there was insufficient time in the House of Commons. In 1918, foreign policy was still seen as one of the most important of these. Today it would probably be the protection of individual rights against arbitrary interference.

[1] In November 1968, the composition of the House of Lords was stated to be: hereditary peers by succession, 736; hereditary peers of the first creation, 122; life peers created under the Life Peerage Act, 155; Law Lords (including retired Law Lords), 23; bishops, 26; total 1,062.

The committee therefore proposed the creation of an Upper House of 300 members, each holding his seat for twelve years, one-third retiring every four years. Of the total number, one hundred were to be elected by the peers, from their own number; one hundred were to be elected by the House of Commons, members being grouped into regional areas for that purpose; and one hundred were to be nominated by the government, from persons eminent in public life – for example, ex-ambassadors, ex-colonial governors, and today presumably trade union leaders, leading academics, and similar persons. The report failed to receive either extended discussion or support. The Commons by this date, it was apparent, were not prepared to relinquish, even to this extent, the dominating position they had secured in 1918, or to concede to the Upper House an independent function within the constitution.

The Bryce Committee's conception of function, it will be seen, accepted in full the lessons of the great constitutional struggle of 1911, but it should be added that it also reflected a long political tradition, which first found expression in the speeches and conduct of the Duke of Wellington after the Reform Bill of 1832, which is echoed in a speech of Lord Lyndhurst in 1858, and which, until the crisis of 1910–11, had implied that where the opinion of the nation had been plainly expressed through the action of the Commons, the Lords should give way with such grace as they could muster. It must be added, nevertheless, that even the conclusions of the Bryce Committee bristle with difficulties. For example, what is meant by revision? When does revision become interference with the will of the Commons? Revision is exactly what the House of Lords has in 1968–69 done in respect of two bills. Again, what are bills of comparatively non-controversial character? What is meant by reasonable delay? Two years was agreed upon in 1911. It was reduced to one year in 1949. If the Lords are not to amend bills passed by the Commons, as is now suggested, it is difficult to see what connection with legislation, apart from an occasional right of initiation, remains to them. Further, if the power to delay legislation by one year is too long, is there any point in providing for any lesser period?

It will be seen that even the definition of function is not easy. Moreover, too much may perhaps be claimed for the importance of discussions of broad questions of public policy by the Lords, unconnected with any specific legislative proposal. Broadcasting, television, and the popular Press have created far more competitors for the attention of the nation than existed in 1918. Nevertheless, with the few exceptions already mentioned, all democratic countries have found a two-chamber system desirable, mainly for the reason which is often given for the abolition, or further curtailment, of the functions of the House of Lords – the provision of an opportunity to think again. Both the United States and Australia have strong second chambers and neither is noticeably undemocratic. In both cases, the second chambers reflect the federal principle, which has no place in Britain, but their functions are general, and are not confined to the defence of states' rights. There is, moreover, a further factor of the greatest importance to be considered in relation to American and Australian practice. Both second chambers function under written constitutions. In Britain there is nothing resembling a constitutional document, which can be changed only by some special process, which in Australia includes a referendum. Abolition of the House of Lords, or of its very limited power to delay legislation, would mean that the entire political structure could be changed to any extent, simply by the passage of a bill through the House of Commons, followed by the Royal Assent. If such comprehensive changes were introduced by a government with a small majority, or towards the end of its five-year term, the anomaly would be even more striking, and it is not difficult to imagine the terms in which its conduct would be described, or the degree of resentment which it might provoke.

The sole remaining function of the House of Lords today was very concisely stated by T. E. Utley in an article in the *Sunday Telegraph* in November 1968. 'Let us recognise,' he wrote, 'that the sole legitimate function of the Upper House is to offer respectful, competent and detailed advice to government; that, in fact, the Lords can be only an extension of the Civil Service.' If this is the position, why should those who offer such advice, however distinguished, masquerade as a second chamber of the legislature?

In comparison with a problem of function, the questions of the size and the composition of the House of Lords, the term of office of members, and modes of election, are of lesser importance. The Bryce Committee would have retained a minority hereditary element, in a House of approximately 300, and one-third of the members would have been selected by panels of members of the House of Commons. Since 1918, the problem of composition has been repeatedly debated. Nomination by the Crown, which in reality means by the Prime Minister, has found favour with some, occasionally on the basis of the representation of interests, e.g. trade unions, or religious bodies. Regionalism has its advocates, replacing an older suggestion that county councils should elect. The real difficulty in connection with this aspect of the problem is always the same. If the House of Lords has no effective voice in government, and if also it is dissociated from the peerage, who will be prepared to serve in it? The reservoir of former Empire and colonial statesmen is now almost exhausted. There may still be former public servants of distinction, who are prepared to serve, but even if there are, they will most frequently be elderly. Perhaps if the period of service were limited, and at its expiration there was freedom to stand for the House of Commons, it might be possible to regard service in the House of Lords as a form of political apprenticeship for younger men; but it would be an unusual development, and its constitutional value is not immediately apparent.

The important constitutional innovation whereby the Prime Minister exercises an additional mode of patronage by way of substantial creations of life peerages has evoked little in the way of comment or criticism – possibly because it is recognised that the House of Lords is now so powerless that the presence of a hundred – or even two hundred – life peers who owe their elevation to the Prime Minister makes little difference to the proceedings. When this innovation was first made, it was explained that it was partly to strengthen the Labour ranks in the Lords, and partly to strengthen the debates in that House. In the early days of his ministry Harold Wilson showed considerable enthusiasm for this device, if the number and nature of his creations are examined. Whilst the majority of those so ennobled were either Labour supporters or well-known left-wing publicists, there were some others who belonged to the other two parties, and others again whose creation was due to eminence in public life. For a time, Harold Wilson was evidently attracted by the idea of finding life peers in the common rooms and administrations of universities, but this early characteristic has waned, as the volume of criticism of the administration's achievements has grown. Moreover, the participation of some of the life peers in the proceedings of the House has been too intermittent to be of any general value. Experts, including academics, have tended to intervene only when their own fields of interest have been under discussion, and they have taken little part in the work of committees. Many of them claim that the time they can give,

F

having regard to the posts which they hold, is extremely limited. Few retain, or acquire, any real interest in the workings of party government. All in all, the value of their contribution to general debates, as distinct from debates on specialist topics, has been disappointing.

The attempt of the Labour Party in the session 1968–69 to reshape the House of Lords was remarkable for the confusion which it produced in both the major parties, which had unsuccessfully attempted to produce an agreed scheme. The scheme which ultimately emerged evoked general condemnation from the Press, and from many different groups of members in the House of Commons, and it emphasised the extent to which both major parties were out of touch with public opinion. Its principal characteristic was that the second chamber should be wholly nominated, thus yet again extending the power of the party leaders. Upon this, *The Times* (2 November 1968) commented acidly:

> 'A House nominated by a succession of Prime Ministers is likely to be a badly composed House. The power to nominate the whole of the House of Lords, even when subject to restrictions on the party balance inside the House, is not one which party leaders should be given. There is already in this country too much patronage and too much seeking of patronage. It is an odious thing to see able men who ought to value their own independence adapting their minds towards a new government or a new Prime Minister like flowers turning their faces towards the sun. A wholly nominated House of Lords would enshrine the principle of patronage and would increase this toadyism.'

Since the bill was abandoned by the government after passing a second reading in February 1969, there is no need to consider its proposals in detail. They provided for the abolition of the hereditary element from the second chamber, a wholly nominated House of 230 members, chosen by successive Prime Ministers, but providing that at each change of ministry, new life peers should be appointed so as to give the government a ten per cent majority over the combined strength of the other parties.

To the extraordinary proposal that Prime Ministers should nominate all members of this curious body, there was added a further item of patronage – the payment of a salary of £2,000 a year, or some similar figure to be decided. This was rightly condemned in a leading article in *The Times* as a prospective reward

by way of dignified retirement which the Whips could dangle before party members. In the event, few proposals for change have
been accompanied by such a chorus of disapproval, more especially
from the government's supporters, than this ill-considered piece
of political sleight-of-hand, and after the debate in both Houses on
19 November 1968, it was always apparent that legislation upon
the proposals could not be proceeded with. One of the most effective contributions to the debate in the Commons was made by
Maurice Edelman, Labour M.P. for Coventry West, who said the
proposal for an élite and privileged hierarchy with a number of
political vestal virgins sitting on the cross-benches had a Byzantine
quality which had little relevance to what the people wanted for
their constitution. What was wanted was a second chamber with
useful functions, limited powers, and which was indirectly elected.
The proposals before them implied the takeover by the executive
of a branch of the legislature, one of whose functions was the
scrutiny of the actions of the executive. As the power of Parliament
had been whittled away, it had become increasingly important to
check the power of the Prime Minister. These proposals would
substantially add to them. Little part in the debate was taken by
leaders of the Conservative Opposition, which once again lost an
important opportunity to set out the principles upon which the
English constitutional system should be based. Possibly the last
word upon this tragi-comedy was uttered by a senior Conservative
backbencher who said that in thirty years, he had never known the
two front benches to be so completely isolated in a storm of criticism from all parties. The episode has at least demonstrated what is
not wanted by way of 'reform' of the House of Lords.

V

The Monarchy

THERE IS NO aspect of the English constitution which is so bewildering to the outside observer as the position of the monarchy in
English public life. For one thing, far too many English writers
have described the monarchy in sentimental terms, or worse. For
another, it is extremely difficult to say what the monarchy in Britain
really is, or what it is meant to do. For example, several different
words are used to describe it, and some of them are extremely misleading. The King or Queen today is quite certainly not a ruler,
still less is he a 'sovereign'. In a number of items of public business,
we habitually speak of 'the Crown'. For example, all major criminal proceedings in England take the form of 'the Crown' or 'Rex'
or 'Regina' against the defendant. In this case 'Crown' is simply a
personification of the state, although it perhaps retains an echo of
the mediaeval conception that the King had an active interest in the
preservation of public order, one element of which was the suppression of crime. Many other executive acts, and especially foreign
policy, are conducted on behalf of the Crown, and of course foreign
diplomats are accredited to the King or Queen. This, again, is a
survival from the time when government was not only carried on
in the King's name, but by the King in fact, acting through Ministers chosen by him and responsible to him. A century ago Bagehot,
in writing of the monarchy, gave a long list of acts of major policy
which the King, or Queen, could still carry out without any formal
intervention. These things are still frequently done without direct
Parliamentary control, although usually not without Parliamentary
discussion; but everyone knows that the use of the Queen's name
is formal only, and that the acts and decisions are those of the
Ministers of State. One obvious illustration of this is the 'Queen's
Speech' at the opening of Parliament. This, in reality, is the statement by the government of the policy which it proposes to follow,
both in legislation and in government, during the ensuing session.

The history of the monarchy in England has been the history
of the progressive atrophy of its governmental powers. At no period

has the power of the monarchy been absolute. From the Norman Conquest onwards, the King's policy on major matters was the product of advice tendered by his Council, which, in course of time, and after prolonged constitutional struggles, gave birth to Parliament. Even after the evolution of the mediaeval Parliament, the King was for some time still the dominant party in legislation. He could reject proposals from the two Houses, he could amend them, or he could initiate legislation himself. The power to initiate was certainly lost after Henry VIII's reign, by which time the power to amend was already obsolescent, for in the reign of Henry VI it had become customary to put forward proposals for new legislation in the form of 'Bills', which the King could accept or reject. By this date, it was accepted doctrine that an Act of Parliament was necessary for all legislation of major significance, but for lesser matters, or matters of temporary importance, the King still possessed an independent power to legislate by ordinance or, as it was more usually termed, by proclamation. Already in Tudor times, this independent legislative power was being challenged in Parliament, and Henry VIII was careful to legitimate his powers to legislate by Parliamentary sanction, which lapsed at his death. One of the matters of contention between the Stuarts and Parliament was the claim of the King to independent legislative powers, with which was joined the claim to dispense with, or suspend, the operation of laws which the King found unpalatable – for example, in the reign of James II, the laws disqualifying Roman Catholics from all public office. All these claims were declared to be unconstitutional, and the exercise of them unlawful, at the Revolution in 1688, and thereafter, until the astonishing delegation of law-making authority to the departments of state in the present century, the omnipotence of Parliament in the legislative sphere has been unchallenged. So much has this been the case that the disappearance of the Royal Veto on legislation since the reign of Queen Anne has passed almost unnoticed.

The loss by the Crown, first of control, and, later, of effective influence, upon the process of government, has been more gradual. Throughout the eighteenth century Ministers were appointed by the King in fact, as well as in theory, and a King might resist popular pressure to appoint a person successfully. George II's dislike of the Elder Pitt, and George III's dislike of Charles James Fox are examples which readily occur to the mind. Similarly, the King could dismiss Ministers, and governments, in spite of the fact that they appeared to command majorities in Parliament. Such majorities could be undermined by influence and corruption, and the hostility of groups within a party could be exploited to bring about the disruption of an apparently firmly established government. Such a system was always possible so long as the unreformed House of Commons could only be relied upon to promote the public interest in times of national emergency. Since 1832, the fact that representation in the House of Commons has been firmly based upon popular support has had the consequence that the King's power of appointment has been exercised only subject to the desires of the most powerful political party, and his power to dismiss has been completely replaced by an adverse vote of the House of Commons. Constitutionally, the King could only dismiss a Prime Minister and his government if he could find an alternative Prime Minister and government who would assume responsibility for such an act. Such an alternative choice would only be possible if the alternative Prime Minister and government could be relied upon to obtain the support, either of the existing House of Commons, or of a new House of Commons assembled after a dissolution of Parliament. If such a situation existed, the intervention of the Crown would be unnecessary, for the inability of the government to make its wishes prevail in Parliament would ensure its resignation – at any rate, so long as it was acting within the limits of a constitution which, it has been pointed out, is unwritten, and which rests as much upon convention as upon law.

Bagehot, in discussing the changed position of the monarchy, ensuing from the rise to a dominant position of the House of Commons on the one hand, and of the Prime Minister and Cabinet on the other, explained that it still performed an important constitutional function by way of advice, based upon long experience. In other words, Ministers change with the swing of the party pendulum; the monarchy is the permanent factor, and since the monarch has access to all important documents of state, he or she accumulates a wealth of experience which can be placed at the disposal of an incoming Prime Minister and Cabinet. This view was quite plainly influenced by the long reign and high qualities of Queen Victoria (although when Bagehot wrote, the reign had not yet approached its climax), and it is more than doubtful if he could have written in similar terms had the sovereign been any of her three predecessors. Moreover, even the history of her reign and the memoirs of those who played leading parts in it, show that her Ministers were by no means always willing auditors. Much is made of the part which she played in seeking to curb the activities of Palmerston as Foreign Secretary, but it may be suggested that her intervention would have been of little effect, but for the notorious antagonism of Palmerston and his Prime Minister, Russell. In any event, the nature and degree of the sovereign's influence are directly dependent upon the personalities of the sovereign and his Prime Minister; whilst the first characteristic of royal discretion must quite plainly be the avoidance of party bias. Finally, the ever-increasing volume and complexity of modern government makes it at least doubtful whether a modern monarch is as well qualified to express opinions upon it as Queen Victoria apparently was.

More recent writers than Bagehot tend to suggest that with steady development of national self-consciousness in the Dominions, with the evident possibility that they might develop centrifugal policies, the monarchy remains a unifying symbol within a world-wide Commonwealth. This indeed was a factor of considerable importance on the eve of two World Wars, and the strength of the tie with the monarchy was again plainly evident at the time of the Abdication crisis in 1936. On the other hand, events have moved fast since 1945, and the Commonwealth nations which have emerged since 1945 have not experienced the same sentimental attachment (nor could they have been expected to do) as the older Dominions, predominantly settled by persons of United Kingdom stock, have done. Today, the Commonwealth tie is slender in the extreme, and the awkward term 'Head of the Commonwealth', which has been devised to describe the changed position of the monarch, is almost meaningless. For example, it has had no influence whatever upon the course of the unhappy civil war in Nigeria, nor upon the expulsion of non-African British subjects from Kenya. If the Commonwealth has any effective function at all, it is not because the monarchy unites it.

A recent writer[1] concluded his chapter upon the British monarchy, after remarking that the Queen was called upon to do many dull things, and that the monarchy today counts for much less than it did, with the observation that 'free government lasts much better with a King than a President'. This conclusion was founded upon the often-noticed fact that, in Europe, monarchy has survived only in the north-west corner – in the United Kingdom, in Holland, Belgium, and Scandinavia – Greece being a recent casualty. The

[1] Ian Gilmour, *The Body Politic*, p. 324.

statement is, nevertheless, highly questionable. It ignores the United States and France. It also ignores the fact that many nations have failed to preserve freedom whilst possessing Kings, France before 1789 being a very notable instance, as Italy was more recently.

One of the few surviving prerogatives of the Crown which, in exceptional circumstances, the monarch might be called upon to exercise upon his own initiative, is the prerogative to dissolve Parliament before the statutory limit of its existence has been reached. In all ordinary circumstances, it is for the Prime Minister to advise upon a dissolution of Parliament, and it is accepted constitutional doctrine that the Crown must then accept such advice. Are there any circumstances in which a dissolution could be refused? It has been suggested that a Prime Minister of a minority government could not expect automatic compliance, if there existed a viable alternative government, and Parliament had still some appreciable time to run. In fact, a dissolution has never been refused, even to the Prime Minister of a minority Labour government in the inter-war period, and it seems reasonable to suppose that the possible leader of an alternative government would desire a dissolution at least as much as a minority Prime Minister. For one thing, it is a reasonable supposition that a minority Prime Minister who wishes to dissolve is losing ground with the electorate, and a general election will confirm this hypothesis, and strengthen the position of the alternative government. If an alternative party leader accepted office after a dissolution had been refused to his opponent, it would presumably be necessary for him to work with the existing Parliament before he could, with propriety, himself ask for a dissolution. In any event, it would be difficult, both in Parliament and in the eventual general election, to avoid the introduction of discussions of the monarch's conduct into public debate. From the standpoint of practical politics, it looks as though the power to refuse a dissolution, in any foreseeable circumstances, is also obsolete.

Such considerations have led many writers reluctantly to the conclusion that the monarchy today is not only outside the field of political action, but is also devoid of constitutional function. This is not to say that it is without significance. The monarch is the person to whom foreign diplomats are accredited; he entertains the heads of foreign states; on state occasions he, in a sense, personifies the body politic. The monarchy is, in essence, both an ideal of public behaviour and a point of stability in a world which is changing with unprecedented speed. In the early Middle Ages, monarchy possessed a deep mystical significance, and something of this has been retained, when almost all other attributes have dropped away. To transform the United Kingdom into a republic would require only one short Act of Parliament, but English life would be much more drab afterwards. Monarchy survives because the majority of British people still feel an attachment to it, not because it has any political importance. In a country in which, after unending political vicissitudes, the House of Lords has miraculously survived, albeit in a form that would have been unrecognisable two centuries ago, the survival of the monarchy is not, after all, so very anomalous. In Japan, another country which remains attached to monarchy, the Emperor remained for centuries a cypher, all his political functions being exercised in his name by the Shogun. When, a century ago, Japan found it necessary to emerge from a seclusion which had lasted for two and a half centuries, the power of the Shoguns was broken, and the country was rallied in the name of the Emperor. Very much the same process was repeated after the usurpation of the Emperor's functions by the army in the thirties, and the catastrophic defeat which their assumption of power involved. The existence of a monarchy has given a superficial appearance of continuity to the national life both of the United Kingdom and Japan. There, however, the parallel ends, for it is extremely difficult to imagine a national revival in the United Kingdom with as its starting-point a demand for the monarchy to have the exercise of some of its former prerogatives restored to it.

VI

The Party Game

EVERY discussion of the British constitution is based upon the twin assumptions of cabinet government and the party system which produces it, yet the political parties are unknown to constitutional law. No statute or judgment recognises them, or defines their functions or conditions of existence, nor does any legal text contain a declaration of the right of political association. Nevertheless, they exist, and their organisation has continuously developed. Even a century ago, Walter Bagehot, in his classic exposition of the principles underlying the British constitution, did not think it necessary to devote a special chapter to the activities of the political parties. His reflections upon them are mainly to be found in the chapter devoted to the House of Commons. The party system – indeed, the two-party system – is the key to the working of the British constitution. Without the parties, it would be impossible for government to carry on, at any rate in the form in which it now exists, and further, without them, the ordinary citizen would feel even further removed from political life than he does at present. If one asks for what purpose the political parties exist, one answer would be: to perpetuate themselves, and though it would not be the whole truth, it would be an important aspect of it. Indeed, when a movement or politician of sufficient magnitude emerges to threaten the vested interests of the two parties, it, or he, is subjected to what might be described as Ordeal by the three Ds – Derision, Distortion, and finally Denunciation. This has recently been particularly well illustrated by the history of the Irish, Scottish, and Welsh Nationalists; and also by the experience of J. Enoch Powell from 1966 onwards.

In view of their place in modern times in the political and constitutional structure of the United Kingdom, it is interesting to recall that when parties for the first time emerged in recognisable form in the latter part of Charles II's reign, they were frequently termed 'factions' – a description which implied that they were disruptive in tendency. Naturally, each party regarded the other as a 'faction', they themselves being the true instruments of government; but in an age when government was still in fact, as in theory, the royal prerogative, party strife could be regarded as in itself 'factious', and there were many loyal subjects who must frequently have echoed Mercutio's dying words in *Romeo and Juliet*: 'A plague on both your houses.' At this period, the Whig party, which was the first to organise itself under a popular leader, the Earl of Shaftesbury, could certainly be termed factional. Made up of a motley collection of landed magnates, city merchants, nonconformists suffering under repressive laws against Dissenters, republican survivors from Cromwell's day, and finally, the London mob, they could express their dissatisfaction chiefly by public demonstration, since all, except the magnates and the city merchants, were without power to vote or to influence Parliamentary elections. Although differing widely in their ultimate objectives, they were united upon some pressing problems. They sought to prevent the succession of James, Duke of York, to the throne on the death of Charles II; they fiercely resisted the reassertion of personal rule by Charles II, which was primarily provoked by this threat to his brother's rights; and they attempted to win a control of local affairs, when any similar attempt in respect of national government seemed vain. To counter this threat, the King's friends organised themselves into the Tory party, and more gradually established a national organisation. It is not without significance that, in origin, both Whig and Tory were terms of abuse.

After the Revolution of 1688, and still more plainly, after the accession of the House of Hanover in 1714, the position of the parties was reversed. The Whigs were united in preserving the Protestant succession and the Anglican establishment. The Tories were for a time completely divided. Some, either openly or surreptitiously, continued to support the exiled Stuarts, and therefore were, in the true sense, factious. The majority of the Tories, however, who had been reluctantly compelled to join the Whigs in bringing about the Revolution of 1688, accepted the principles underlying that revolution, but disapproved of much of the policy of the Whigs, more especially that which encouraged the expansion of British commerce overseas, with its inevitable interference in the affairs of continental Europe. From the accession of George I in 1714, to the beginning of the premiership of the Younger Pitt in 1783, Great Britain was governed, with only brief interludes, by varying coalitions of Whig families and their dependants. It was only when the impact of the American and French Revolutions had produced deep divisions among the Whigs that Toryism once again became a major political force. It proved to be a rallying point for wide sections of the nation who saw, in the excesses of the French Revolutionaries, and later, in the absolutism of Napoleon, a threat not only to national safety, but also to the political and constitutional settlement of 1688, and to the way of life which it had engendered in Great Britain.

It would be quite wrong to suppose that the Whigs were the party of progress, and the Tories the party of reaction, and much the same judgment can be passed on their nineteenth-century successors, the Liberals and the Conservatives. The Whigs, especially in the eighteenth century, were not infrequently 'reactionary'; the Tories as frequently were progressive. Although the Whigs were the architects of the first, the Great, Reform Bill of 1832, conferring the vote upon their most constant supporters, the prosperous middle classes, the Tories, under Sir Robert Peel, passed the Catholic Emancipation Act in 1829, and repealed the Corn Laws, whilst Disraeli's Reform Act of 1867 went a good deal further than the Whigs had at that time intended to go. Similarly, it was the Tories, under the initiative of Lord Shaftesbury, who passed the first Factory Acts in the teeth of Whig opposition, for the Whigs derived support from the factory owners, and were firm adherents of *laissez-faire*. Finally, Gladstone's conversion to Irish Home Rule in 1886 narrowly anticipated a similar step by the Conservatives, with the consequence that the Liberals were split, and the Conservatives became Unionist, ultimately absorbing the dissident Liberal Unionists. Often, indeed, during the nineteenth century, opportunism rather than principle decided, at a particular moment, which party should claim credit for a major change which both parties had come to regard as inevitable.

If one asks, therefore, for what purposes the two major political parties exist today, it would not be cynical to say: to perpetuate themselves, and to achieve office. It is for this purpose that an elaborate nationwide organisation has been built up, and it is for this reason that both parties turn the full weight of their organisations relentlessly against interlopers. They are, in essence, very large and shifting combinations of men and women, united chiefly in their desire to dominate the political scene, and although their organisations are now regulated by constitutions to which members subscribe, the parties have no place in the formal constitution of the country. Theoretically they could be replaced at any time by other organisations. Their power is derived principally from the fact that only by their assistance and support can a candidate expect to be returned as a Member of the House of Commons. Every time the franchise has been extended, the power of the parties, and their control of Parliamentary elections, has increased. The organisation of constituency branches of party organisations calls for the expenditure of time and money, and each party now retains a considerable full-time, paid staff, which includes not only local organisers, but also a well-qualified headquarters staff and research departments.

The most obvious virtue of the party system is that it ensures stable government, and that it always presents the possibility of an alternative government. It is party coherence which enables the government, as the leaders of the most powerful party in the House of Commons, to secure the passage of their programme of legislation, and it is the same coherence which gives the government the support of a sufficient body of opinion within the country to support the pleasing illusion that it is governing 'democratically', in accordance with the wishes of the majority of citizens. In reality, it is doing no such thing. Many aspects of government policy do not receive attention at general elections, and are not even discussed in the Press until they crystallise into government action. Even when they are, the treatment of these issues by party politicians is so perfunctory as to be of little informative value. For one thing, party leaders, whether in or out of office, do not wish to be tied too specifically before action is necessary. For another, they feel it undesirable to do more than express their views in broad terms, so as to appeal to the broad spectrum of varieties of opinion which exist within their own party, and finally, they have felt it necessary to conduct debates on public issues in terms which are comprehensible with relatively little intellectual effort, and in this respect, the daily Press readily follows their lead. For example, the question whether it is desirable or advantageous for Britain to enter the Common Market is an extremely complicated one. Entry would involve far-reaching changes in the conduct of industry and commerce, but also in Britain's laws and public institutions, and ultimately in her external relations; yet politicians, whatever their political allegiance, have made little attempt at serious exposition of these problems, and their advocacy of entry or opposition to it appears to be based upon assumptions which require full and detailed analysis before the electorate can be expected either to understand or to accept them; but for this, we have waited in vain.

The primary object of every government is to govern and to preserve the unity of the party. In actual fact there are relatively few measures of the government's party that command the support of all of its Parliamentary members, and it is therefore the policy of any government to ensure, if it can, that dissidence is neither prolonged nor numerically important. Once a measure is through Parliament, it is the object of everyone within the party to restore the façade of unity again. The alternative for a dissident member is to cease to receive the party Whip, with the implication that he will forfeit party backing at the next general election. Since without that support he has virtually no chance of securing his re-election, a member who persists in his revolt is virtually signing his political death-warrant. On the other hand, the knowledge that a substantial body of opinion within the party is opposed to a proposed measure will have an important influence upon what a government does. The irreconcilable opposition of the trade union wing of the Labour Party to a Trade Unions Bill, which would have brought unions to a limited degree within the law, by making them legally responsible for certain types of strikes, inflicted a humiliating defeat upon the government by compelling it in 1969 to drop the measure altogether. Significantly, as soon as the measure had been dropped, harmony between the unions and the government appeared to be restored, and the whole question was discussed in a minor key at the Trade Union annual Congress in September 1969. The importance of the overall association of the trade unions with the Labour Party for electoral purposes was recognised by both.

The test of a party leader is to be found in his plausibility with the electorate, and in his capacity to unite his party behind him, not only in office, but in opposition. This is not at all an easy task, for to make a national appeal, and to secure a majority of seats at a general election, it is necessary to embrace men of very different opinions, with widely differing aims. Within the Labour Party, for example, the trade union member may frequently be at odds with the intellectuals of the party, and leaders must walk a tightrope in the effort to reconcile their views. If divisions are less clearly defined in the Conservative Party, it is only because the party is less obviously a coalition of distinct groups; but in the past thirty years, Conservatives have frequently found themselves sharply divided –

over the proper attitude towards the dictators in the thirties, and particularly over 'appeasement'; over the Common Market; over Suez; and, more recently, over immigration. Unless considerable dexterity is exercised by leaders, issues such as these can lead to secessions which would be fatal to the party's chances at the next election. Accordingly, the first rule of party politics is that, whilst everything may be discussed, and whilst there may be considerable latitude in respect of opinions held, in the last resort, the party must be held together, both in the House of Commons and in the country at large. All three parties – Conservative, Labour, and Liberal – therefore make a considerable parade of their adherence to the principle of free debate of issues likely to divide the party, and of the fact that this is simply evidence of their democratic outlook and of their desire to reflect public opinion, so far as it is discoverable. Obviously, too, debate at annual party conferences is of considerable importance in shaping party policies, and in determining priorities within programmes. Above all, it is an aid to the clarification of party doctrine, but underneath it all is the well-founded assumption that the party's representatives in Parliament will give support to the activities of its leaders, for if they did not, the party system could not continue to dominate the political scene as it does today.

It would be quite wrong to suppose that there is anything immutable in the policies to which parties may at any time adhere. In the first half of the nineteenth century, the Tories fiercely opposed Catholic Emancipation, Parliamentary reform, and repeal of the Corn Laws – and eventually passed all three. In our own day, the Labour Party has fiercely attacked restrictions on immigration, especially upon coloured immigration, and devaluation; and in office has initiated both. In opposition, it was as directly opposed to any attack upon the privileged position of the trade unions. It has only been prevented from passing restrictive legislation by the opposition of the unions, upon whom it depends for electoral support. Such variations are neither surprising nor blameworthy, for situations change, and measures must be varied accordingly. Winston Churchill as a young man, defending his change of party, once remarked that only a fool never changed his opinions – and he might have added that the parties themselves were certainly not composed of fools. The programmes of all three political parties have changed continuously with the passage of time. If they did not, they would produce political stagnation. What is less praiseworthy is that they are not infrequently couched in terms designed to catch the current mood of the electorate. The most striking illustration of this in modern times is the emphasis placed by the National Government's programme in the general election of 1935 upon collective security and support for the League of Nations in a policy of sanctions against Italy. Once the election was over, this was completely sidetracked, and eventually the Prime Minister's successor, Neville Chamberlain, was able to describe a policy of sanctions against Italy as 'midsummer madness'. During the same period, Baldwin was eventually to confess that if he had given the true facts about rearmament in Europe, and Britain's weak position in face of it, he would have lost the election.

The corner stone of the English party system is the single-member constituency in which the member is elected by a simple majority vote. It can produce some curious results, for if a number of candidates, some of whom represent minor groups or parties, contest the election, then it can be won, and a government can be appointed, by a minority of voters. At the same time, the system is merciless to groups or parties which intervene in the unending mock-battle of the two major parties. Since 1945, the Liberal Party has made repeated efforts to stage a revival as a major Parliamentary party. On several occasions the number of Liberal candidates at general elections has been between two and three hundred. On a similar number of occasions, the total votes cast for Liberal candidates has exceeded three million. Nevertheless, the number of Liberal Members of Parliament sunk after the election of 1970 to six. Not unnaturally, therefore, virtually the only constant feature of the Liberal Party's programme has been its advocacy of proportional representation. Equally, this electoral change has been ignored by the two major parties, both of whom would lose seats if it were adopted. Possibly the most useful function which the Liberal Party fulfils at the present time is that it is a party of protest, in a double sense. Its active members most frequently express a protest against the ritualistic antics of the two major parties; whilst the majority of those who vote for Liberal candidates know (1) that their candidate has little chance of election and (2) that even if he is elected, there is absolutely no possibility of him being joined by sufficient other Liberals in the House of Commons to exercise a considerable influence upon the conduct of public affairs. Those who vote for Liberal candidates must therefore be regarded as expressing their disapproval of the policies of both the major parties. It is, in fact, almost the only way in which the ordinary citizen can express dissatisfaction with the operation of the two-party system, and with the policies professed by the two parties themselves.

An elector who is placed in this position may legitimately ask whether such a system is a really satisfactory one. Does the undoubted fact that it produces a stable government really compensate for the lack of a wider choice, and is stable government synonymous with good government? What happens today at a general election is not that the elector chooses between rival policies, for the policies themselves today increasingly show only variations of emphasis, and, as will be mentioned below, they are often as noteworthy for what they omit as for what they include; the real purpose of a general election is to select the persons who will govern the country during the next four or five years.

The political parties are notable products of the British talent for voluntary association. Their membership is a cross-section of the country as a whole, and the qualifications are nominal. Indeed, probably an important proportion of those who are ranked as party members are not persuaded of the value of the policies they nominally support, and a number of them probably do not support their party by voting at general elections. At any rate, it is clear that party membership fluctuates with the variations in the party's fortunes in the country. When the tide is running strongly, there is a sudden upswing of membership, and meetings tend to be more representative of the constituency. When the party is out of favour, or in times of apathy, only the faithful few, mainly committee members, can be relied upon to put in an appearance. As with other voluntary associations, the activity of a constituency party branch depends upon an energetic chairman, who can keep a body of unpaid helpers together. At election time, there are never enough of them to canvass the constituency, to organise social gatherings, and to distribute literature. The English parties have never imposed binding obligations upon their members, and there have rarely been any rewards by way of honours, dignities, or public offices, to which loyal party members may aspire. Formerly, the branch chairman of the party in office had some influence in appointments to the office of Justice of the Peace, which carried some local prestige, but today this is greatly diminished, and in any event it is now the policy of the Lord Chancellor's office to dissociate the local magistracy as completely as possible from local political activity –

G

a reform which was long overdue. In every Honours List, it is possible to detect the names of a small number of party workers amongst the recipients of very minor honours – but it is doubtful whether, in many cases, the possibility of obtaining one plays much part in securing, or retaining, the voluntary service of party members.

In nothing is the party system so typically British as in the relation of the constituency organisation to Central Office. Throughout the twentieth century, there has been a tendency for the control of the branches by the Central Office to increase. This is because organisation has steadily become more extensive, and also more expensive, so that a number of branch organisations may need support from central funds, either continuously or at election time. Moreover, the Central Office produces a steadily-increasing volume of information, and it promotes conferences, and week-end schools, where branch members can meet and extend their political education. The Central Office also seeks to guide constituencies in the selection of candidates, the choice of whom is tenaciously retained by the constituency. The constituency again sends delegates to the annual party conference, and it not infrequently proposes or supports motions to be discussed there; but the selection of topics for debate remains in the hands of the Central Committee, and in spite of the democratic façade of these conferences, they are often little more than an opportunity for party leaders to assess the state of opinion within the party. Compared with American Conventions, they are amateurish in the extreme – and they are none the worse on that account. And whilst it is true that there is little chance at annual conferences for the views of the rank and file to prevail against those of the leaders, in the event of a conflict, the leaders will take careful note of the trend of opinion within the party in formulating policy, and also in emphasising particular aspects of it. There can be no doubt, for example, that recognition of the extent to which Enoch Powell has been able to make articulate the views, and even the prejudices, of the rank and file of the Conservative Party, has produced a marked change in emphasis amongst Heath and his colleagues upon such topics as immigration and Britain's application to enter the Common Market.

It will be evident, therefore, that one of the tasks of the party leader is not only to secure the highest measure of agreement within the party upon particular topics, but to ensure, so far as is possible, that headquarters, the Parliamentary party, and the consti-

tuencies remain in step. Further, since general elections turn upon
the ability of parties to attract to their support the important body
of uncommitted voters, it follows that a party leader must have in
mind, not only those who are already his supporters, but also
those who, with a little encouragement, might become supporters.
A leader, therefore, should never be drawn from one extreme wing
of the party or the other. Unfortunately, this has too often meant
that he has been opportunist rather than statesmanlike, and that his
speeches have tended to become increasingly platitudinous, the
longer his tenure as party leader has lasted. Many of the speeches
which a leader is called upon to deliver can be, and possibly are,
written well in advance. He is against war, and will use his best
efforts to reduce international tension, wherever it may exist. He is
anxious about the balance of payments, but (if he is in office) he is
satisfied that we are making progress in extricating ourselves from
our difficulties. If he is in opposition, he wishes the government
well, but thinks their efforts are misconceived and likely to fail. He
is in favour of increased social benefits and also of lightening the
burden of taxation simultaneously – and so on, indefinitely. So
platitudinous has this type of oratory become, that it is very generally disbelieved, and few bother to listen to it. For most people, a
party political broadcast on television is synonymous with a tea
break. For the same reason, debates in Parliament have come to be
regarded as ritualistic exercises, in which the utterances of those
participating are predictable with precision.

In spite of the amateur character of much of the activity of the
British parties, they are nevertheless increasingly expensive to
maintain, and, as has been indicated, even constituencies cannot
always support themselves, although it is one of the main tasks of
constituency committees to seek out persons who may make substantial contributions to local funds. So far as the Labour Party is
concerned, it is highly doubtful whether it could continue to exist
as a nationwide party, were it not for support, both in finance and
manpower, that the trade unions give to it through the political
levy which unions are empowered to exact from their members.
Beyond this, the Labour Party has, since 1945, received extensive
support from entrepreneurs and industrialists who regard such
support as a form of insurance against activities too hostile to their
interests. So far as support of this kind is concerned, the Conservative Party is naturally much more broadly based, but unlike the
Labour Party, it cannot rely upon any equivalent to the trade

union levy on its members, nor can the constituencies today extort large subscriptions from Conservative candidates. In both parties, substantial gifts by individuals are rarer today than they have been, for they cannot be deducted for tax purposes.

In one important respect the British party system compares most favourably with that of the United States. Whilst there exist no checks upon the ordinary running expenses of the parties, there are severe statutory restraints upon what can be spent, and for what purposes, on behalf of candidates at Parliamentary elections. Failure to control election expenses has made the American candidate even more dependent upon the party than he is in Britain – to such an extent, in fact, that a successful candidate for a major office, whether of President, Governor, Mayor, or Senator, may find himself enmeshed in a mass of promises which he has given in exchange for financial support.

As one would expect, the structure of the Conservative Party, even today, is a good deal less formal than that of Labour. The National Union of Conservative and Unionist Associations is now over a century old, having been formed in 1867, and there is a pyramid of representative institutions, but the National Conference members are not delegates, and often attend at their own expense. The result is that they are free to speak and vote as they choose, but this is not of major importance, for although members may, and do, criticise particular items, the conference does not formulate policy, and it does not elect either the party leader or his principal lieutenants. Before the recent changes in party organisation, which resulted in the choice of Edward Heath, it sometimes seemed that the leader was either selected by Divine inspiration or was self-appointed. In fact, he was selected by the leading members of the party in Parliament (including members of the House of Lords), often after a good deal of manœuvring, and not without expressions of opinion from the rank and file, conveyed to the leaders by the party Whips. In 1963, however, when Macmillan was contemplating resignation as a consequence of illness, the views of the Cabinet were ascertained by the Lord Chancellor, the views of Conservative peers were obtained by the Conservative Whip in the House of Lords, and those of the members of the party in the Commons were communicated to the Chief Whip. Local associations, the Young Conservatives, and the Women's National Advisory Committee were also given the opportunity to express their views. At the end of this consultation, Macmillan advised the

Queen that the preponderance of opinion favoured the Earl of Home, now Sir Alec Douglas-Home.

Unhappily, the length of, and lack of secrecy in, these proceedings had produced strong reactions from disappointed contenders and others. Accordingly, the party leaders, now out of office after the general election of 1964, evolved an elaborate procedure of election by secret ballot of the party members in the House of Commons, as a result of which Heath became the first elected leader of the party. Even today, therefore, the ordinary Conservative voter has no share in the selection either of the leader himself or of his colleagues who, if the party is returned to office, will sit with him in the Cabinet. These are selected by himself, with due regard to their standing in the party, and to opinion in the House of Commons, and also more remotely in the country. It is from their collective opinions, influenced by the opinion of party members in Parliament, that party policy is evolved.

As one would expect, the organisation of the Labour Party is, in appearance at least, a good deal more formal than that of the Conservative Party, and there have at various times been solemn expulsions from its ranks – a procedure unknown in Conservative ranks. Formed for the purpose of promoting the interests of working men, and especially trade unionists, in Parliament, it has developed in course of time, and coincidentally with the disintegration of the Liberal Party, to be a truly national party which is a cross-section of the community, although with a different emphasis among differing social groups from that within the Conservative Party. Because of its origins, its attachment to socialism, in the continental sense, has always been somewhat artificial. Indeed, in a recent book,[1] Christopher Mayhew, a Labour Member of Parliament, has pointed out that in recent years the Labour Party has virtually abandoned all its socialist creed, and has become completely disillusioned with those objectives, such as the nationalisation of key industries and planning, which it has virtually achieved. In his view, in Britain today, 'working class power is less an instrument of social justice than a means by which one section of the workers promotes its own interests at the expense of others.' Unhappily, many of the consequences of the Great Illusion may very well prove to be long-lived.

Mayhew also develops a theme which has been expounded by other writers, and more especially by Ian Gilmour in *The Body*

[1] *Party Games*, 1969.

Politic. It is that the parties today are not divided on principles. They tend to approach politics in much the same way, albeit with differences in emphasis. Both they and others therefore conclude that party performances in the House of Commons are largely meaningless, and Ian Gilmour also draws attention to the unspoken understanding between the parties upon some issues upon which meaningful discussion, though possibly embarrassing, is nevertheless vitally necessary. Foremost among these is immigration, which the parties had swept under the carpet, until Powell inconveniently uncovered it. This issue, possibly more than any other, has demonstrated how far official party opinion, whether of Left or Right, is removed from the opinion and feeling of ordinary persons. But it may be added that the great decision to dissolve the British Colonial Empire was never the subject of party debates nor was any attempt made to ascertain the views of the electorate upon it.

The decline of the Liberal Party, and its supersession as the alternative force in British political life, is a classic illustration of the truth that in the conduct of public affairs, gratitude is unknown. Until the end of the nineteenth century the cause of the urban worker had been linked with the fortunes of the Liberal Party through the attachment of that party to the expansion of British industry and commerce. The advocacy of extension of the franchise, of popular education, of Free Trade, and of the privileges of trade unions all stemmed from this alliance, which at an earlier period had ensured the repeal of the Corn Laws. At the same time, the Liberals failed to include the leaders of the newly enfranchised working class among their electoral candidates, with the consequence that the Independent Labour Party was formed in 1893, and the Labour Representation Committee came into existence five years later. By the time of the general election of 1906 the Liberal Party had achieved a working arrangement with the representatives of Labour that the Liberals would refrain from contesting approximately thirty seats, where the electorate was strongly working-class and trade unionist; whilst Labour would refrain from putting up candidates in opposition to Liberals elsewhere. The result was that in 1906, and again in the two general elections at the beginning and end of 1910, the first Labour members entered the House of Commons, and the Trade Disputes Act of 1906 owed its shape to their alliance. But it was not until the general election of 1918 that Labour became independently a substantial element in the Commons. Labour candidates then won fifty-eight seats, the majority of them by the unaided efforts of a party whose following had very greatly increased during the war years. Thereafter, the Labour Party rapidly increased in strength, and profiting from the divisions in the Liberal Party, which arose from the bitter hostility of Asquith and Lloyd George, it found itself in office for the first time, but as a minority government dependent upon Liberal support, in 1924. Nevertheless, in less than a quarter of a century, amid social changes and domestic difficulties which were largely the product of World War I, Labour had established its claim to be regarded as the true alternative to Conservative government. Although in eclipse after its failure to face the twin problems of unemployment and the maintenance of the pound, and suffering a shattering defeat at the general election of 1931, Labour once again gained greatly in strength during the years of World War II, and profited by the ineptitude and irresolution of Baldwin and Chamberlain in face of the obvious belligerence of the dictators, to win a victory as overwhelming as that of the Liberals in 1906, at the general election of 1945. Thereafter there has been a regular alternation between Conservative and Labour, with a marked tendency on the part of the electorate to permit each party in turn to remain in office sufficiently long for its achievements and failures to be assessed in detail. At each election since 1945, too, the steady atrophy of Liberal representation has been apparent, the country as a whole indicating its preference for a clear choice between alternative groups of leaders, and its distaste for third-party intervention.

The modern Labour Party dates from the establishment of a national constitution in 1918, creating local branches of the party. These, however, are organised within municipal wards, and it is significant that in the years following the adoption of this constitution, Labour made a determined and largely successful onslaught on municipal government, culminating in Herbert Morrison's capture of the L.C.C. in 1930, followed by the retention of control for over thirty years. This attack found their rivals largely unprepared, since before 1914, party politics had not penetrated deeply into local government. The ward Labour parties send a delegate to the Constituency Management Committee, which consists exclusively of such delegates, and which selects the Labour candidate for the constituency. Considerable independence is shown by many constituencies, although in a number of predominantly working-class areas, the voice of the dominant trade union is all-powerful, since it is the union which will be largely providing the expenses of the campaign, and which may also supplement the Parliamentary salary of the candidate if he is successful. When such an arrangement exists, the constituencies have sometimes been compared with the rotten boroughs of the unreformed House of Commons. Such support was of national importance so long as great disparities in the wealth of candidates existed, and so long as the salaries of members were inadequate. It is harder to justify today.

Again as one would expect, the constitution of the Labour Party in its higher echelons is nominally more democratic than that of the Conservative Party. When in opposition, the party leader, the Shadow Cabinet, and the National Executive are all elected annually, and the Parliamentary party votes weekly on questions of policy. In reality, however, the authority of the party leader approximates closely to that of the Conservative leader, and the control of the Labour Cabinet or Shadow Cabinet differs little from that of the opposing leader and Cabinet. Both from time to time are called upon to face upsurges of opinion within the party, and there seems to be little to differentiate their reactions to them. What is apparent is that Labour national conferences produce a greater body of resolutions, critical and otherwise, and that conference debates are frequently more vigorous and more critical of the leadership than those of the Conservatives. But once elected, the position of the Labour leader seems today as secure as that of his opposite number. His principal problem is not the national party, but, as events in 1969 clearly underlined, his relations with the trade unions, which, in view of their position and resources, often play a major part in shaping policy, especially in the economic sphere. Their power is emphasised by the fact that at annual conferences of the party, the unions are able to cast block votes which, although they have often been used to support the policy of party leaders, and to curb occasional extravagant outbreaks from the constituencies, are a limiting factor which no leader can afford to treat lightly. He does, in actual fact, pay more continuous attention to it than he does to resolutions either of the annual conference or of constituency organisations. From the constitutional point of view, the freedom to decide, exercised by both sets of party leaders, is sound practice, emphasising that the parties are no more than voluntary organisations, whose decisions may not coincide either with the national interest or even with the weight of public opinion.

Although both in the Press and other media of mass communication the Liberals are still accorded the status of a major party, this is rather a salute to the party's past than a true evaluation of its present status. Its representation in the House of Commons is trifling, its leadership problems are recurrent, and its shifts of policy incessant. In addition, in recent years, the difficulties both of maintaining a national organisation and of financing its activities have steadily increased. Its shifts of policy are, in a sense, the least of its difficulties. Situated between the two major parties, whose own policies are by no means constant, it must keep shifting its own position, in order to maintain an attacking posture in respect of both of them. The party still has members who look back nostalgically to the days when Liberal reform had not yet been ousted by Labour's social reorganisation. It also includes younger members who would see in the Liberal Party an instrument of radical advance, unfettered by the paternal control which the trade unions exercise over the Labour Party. Many Liberal difficulties stem from the fact that, of necessity, they make a virtue of being free, both of the unions and 'big business'. For that very reason, their policy lacks predictability and their national difficulties in remaining alive are intensified. As each general election approaches, there is a resumption of discussions within the party, whether to concentrate effort upon winning a limited number of seats, or whether to spread the attack broadly. If the latter policy is pursued, the party runs the risk of speaking with many voices, although it may be hoped that it will serve to disguise the obvious fact that in no circumstances will the Liberal Party be in a position to form a government. Liberals remain, therefore, a party of protest; at times they are not guiltless of political extravagance. At others, they are able to express independent views – for example, upon entry into the Common Market, or defence – with greater clarity and coherence than the other parties, either of whom might find itself hampered, when in office, by over-specific statements. Yet it must be regretfully conceded that such expressions of opinion by the Liberal Party have little or no influence upon the conduct of public affairs.

In its latest efforts to set its house in order, in preparation for the general election, the party conference in September 1969 rejected a proposal that the party assembly should elect the leader, and retained the practice whereby he is elected by the small group of party members who are Members of Parliament, but at the same time it attempted to tighten party discipline by the adoption of a new constitution in place of that adopted in 1936. Under the new constitution there will be a central finance and administrative board, which will operate as the central command of the party, and there will also be, for the first time, a code of conduct for members, with provision for the expulsion of a party member who expresses views contrary to the party's accepted doctrine. In view of the frequent changes in doctrine during the last two decades, these provisions may be difficult to apply, except in the very clearest cases.

The ultimate test of party organisation is not in the performance of the party in Parliament, but in the general election, and the selection of a party manager to plan and execute the campaign is now of major importance. Party managers today resemble the managers of football clubs, in that they are judged by results, and their jobs are at risk if they fail. Timing and publicity are of overwhelming importance in the process of vote-catching, and it is therefore not surprising that very little real effort is made to conduct a reasoned debate upon the issues with which the country is faced. In recent years, these have been predominantly economic, but neither party has made a serious attempt to educate the public, and the appeals to the voter have been oversimplified to the point of absurdity, and have been expressed in controversial terms which hide the real issues. There is no major difference between the parties in the mode of presentation, since each party wishes to preserve the greatest possible freedom of action, should it be successful. Accordingly, the main lines of election campaigns are readily predictable. The Opposition will show that the government has failed dismally to fulfil its promises, and that it has also deviated from the policy on which it was elected. The government will attempt to show that when in office, the performance of the Opposition was worse, and that, in any event, they have given the voter more direct benefits than he enjoyed previously. Topics inconvenient to both parties are largely ignored. Each party recognises that the other is engaged in a ritual war-dance. Happily, the electorate is now sufficiently alert to perceive it also, and the innocent fervour of the pre-1914 party warfare is now obsolete. Even at election time, a large number of viewers automatically turn off the television set whenever a leader of *any* political party puts in an appearance. The number of those who turn off the television set when leaders of parties other than that to which they give their vote appear, is very much larger. Ultimately, the elector will vote for men, and not for measures. That is what general elections are for; and once elected, the leaders of the dominant party will govern the country for the next four to five years, unless some quite unforeseen calamity supervenes. It has the appearance of a democratic process, but very little democratic substance.

VII

The Prime Minister

TWO DIRECTLY conflicting views of the Prime Minister's position are tenable. One is that, so long as he is in office, his powers are almost unlimited, and that he possesses many of the attributes of a dictator. The other is that his powers are extremely circumscribed, and that he habitually follows, but cannot lead, public opinion. The first theory may be described as a formalist, the second as a realist, view of the situation. Since there is no written constitution, no appeal to the letter of the law is possible. The solution of the problem is only to be found in a consideration of the mystery of power in national affairs.

The office of Prime Minister, and the whole institution of cabinet government, has grown up over the past three centuries, entirely outside the purview of any statute or constitutional provision. It rests entirely upon convention, and even the existence of the Prime Minister remained unrecognised by the law until the beginning of the present century, when he was given precedence on formal occasions immediately after the Archbishop of Canterbury. The fact that the Prime Minister's functions, and those of the Cabinet, rest not upon law, but on convention, is sometimes offered as an explanation why the British constitution is unwritten, but the constitutions of the Dominions, where cabinet government has taken root as firmly as in Britain, have found no difficulty in including provisions relating to cabinet government.

The discrepancy between the law and the practice of the constitution most clearly appears in Blackstone's account of the position of the King in the constitution. Writing in the reign of George III, he says:

'We are next to consider those branches of the royal prerogative, which invest thus our sovereign lord, thus all-perfect and immortal in his kingly capacity, with a number of authorities and powers; in the execution whereof consists the executive part of government. This is wisely placed in a single hand by the

British constitution, for the sake of unanimity, strength, and dispatch. Were it placed in many hands, it would be subject to many wills: many wills, if disunited and drawing different ways, create weakness in a government; and to unite those several wills, and reduce them to one, is a work of more time and delay than the exigencies of state will afford. The King of England is, therefore, not only the chief, but properly the sole magistrate of the nation; all others acting by commission from, and in due subordination to, him; in like manner as, upon the great revolution of the Roman state, all the powers of the ancient magistracy of the commonwealth were concentrated in the new Emperor.'

This nonsense was quite untrue when Blackstone wrote it, but since his *Commentaries* were the best-read work among American lawyers at the time of the Revolution, it is not altogether surprising that they were deceived by it, and that they inverted the accepted constitutional convention, and made George III personally responsible for the errors of his Ministers, instead of making the Ministers responsible for the errors of the sovereign. For all that, the pressure which George III exercised upon his Ministers, and his freedom in selecting and dismissing them, emphasises the fact that, until the accession to power of the Younger Pitt, the position both of the Prime Minister and the Cabinet differed fundamentally from their position today.

The office of Prime Minister, it has already been noticed, evolved only gradually, and the continuity of the office dates only from Walpole's long tenure of power in the reigns of George I and George II. His continuance in office was due, not only to his capacity to manage (and to corrupt) sufficient members of the House of Commons to give general support to his policy, but to his retention of the confidence of the King. It would not have occurred to Walpole that he had any direct relationship with the world outside Parliament, and he could not rely upon the collective support of his colleagues in the ministry. He owed his pre-eminence in part to his natural abilities, in part to his access to the secret list and to his patronage, and in part to the fact that, in the absence of the King, he presided at cabinet councils. At this period, the first Minister was no more than *primus inter pares*, and the office of Prime Minister was regarded as possessing undesirable continental overtones. It was indeed one of the charges brought against him on his fall from power, that he had acted, and had described himself, as 'Prime Minister'. At the other end of the century, the Younger Pitt owed his appointment to royal selection, and for some months after taking office, the measures which he brought forward were regularly defeated in the House of Commons. Even at this period, therefore, the opposition of the House of Commons could be outweighed by royal support. On the other hand, Pitt, in bringing about the union with Ireland in 1800, had intended that it should be accompanied by measures removing the disabilities of Roman Catholics, but the unrelenting opposition of the King to such a measure, which he regarded as violating his coronation oath, prevented anything being done until after his death – by which time Irish opposition to the Union had already taken shape.

The real starting-point for the development of the office of Prime Minister is to be found in the first Reform Act, and the emergence of the House of Commons as a body of representatives of the nation. The abolition of rotten boroughs meant that Parliament could no longer be managed, and that the ministry was dependent for its continuation in office upon the support of a majority in the Commons, and not upon royal favour. Party organisation grew in response to the necessity of keeping such a majority together, and of providing an alternative government, but for a period of approximately forty years from 1832, whilst the number of voters was still small, so that the ordinary candidate was generally able to finance his electoral campaign, party organisation remained loose, and the individual member asserted an independence which is quite unknown today. Whilst the dominating theme of party conflict was first between Whig and Tory, and later between Liberal and Conservative, it would be quite wrong to regard them as stable combinations. At various times, there were groups of Canningites and Peelites, and at a later date, Liberal Unionists who eventually merged with the Conservatives, who all changed their nominal allegiance, and the bulk of the members of the House of Commons during this period would have asserted the right to vote in defiance of party affiliations for good cause. On a number of occasions, the fate of a ministry was settled, after debate, by a vote of the House, in which considerable freedom was exercised by members. The classic illustration is the fall of the Aberdeen ministry in 1855, following a debate in the Commons in which an attack by Palmerston on the halting conduct of the Crimean War by the ministry had a decisive influence on the result. The force of Palmerston's attack was increased by the fact that on this occasion, as on many others, Palmerston was correctly interpreting the mood of the country as a whole.

As the century progressed, and coincidentally with successive extensions of the franchise, fundamental changes took place in the relations of government, party, the House of Commons, and the electorate. Members became dependent upon the party for support in election campaigns. Parties became more comprehensive in their national organisations, and party leaders exercised increased control over parties. They were helped in this by the increase in the circulations and influence of daily newspapers. By progressive steps the leader of a party became a national leader, appealing directly to the electorate.

The first party leader to recognise the change in the political centre of gravity was Sir Robert Peel, shortly after the passing of the Reform Bill. As the Tories had consistently opposed it, it was necessary, if they wished to return to office, to define their position in the light of the constitutional changes. In 1834, on the dissolution of the ineffective Whig ministry headed by Lord Melbourne, Peel issued an address to his constituents at Tamworth, which was subsequently known as the Tamworth Manifesto, in which he defined the policy which the Conservative party which he led would follow, if they were returned to office. It was their policy, he said, to correct all proved abuses and real grievances; to preserve peace at home and abroad; to resist the secularisation of church property in any part of the United Kingdom; to fulfil existing engagements with foreign powers; to observe strict economy in the public expenditure; to consider impartially the agricultural, manufacturing, and commercial interests; and finally, 'with regard to the Reform Bill itself, I accept it as a final and irrevocable settlement of a great constitutional question; a settlement which no friend to the peace and welfare of the country would attempt to disturb either by direct or insidious means.'

The manifesto was intended to have, and did have, national currency, and its influence was very considerable, since the Conservatives were returned as the largest single party. A cynic might perhaps observe that in this, the first modern national party manifesto, the ingredients were very much what they are today. A further notable feature of the manifesto is the doctrine of the 'final settlement.' Certain fundamental changes, once accomplished, were to remain unchallenged. Peel himself had already undertaken one – Catholic emancipation – and he was to be the author of another – the Repeal of the Corn Laws.

A further stage in the party leader's direct appeal to the electorate was reached in Gladstone's various Midlothian campaigns. In
the first, at the end of 1879, he set out from Liverpool on 24
November, on the eve of a general election, and in the course of a
fortnight, spoke to great and enthusiastic audiences at Carlisle,
Newcastle, Galashiels, Edinburgh, Dalkeith, Motherwell, and a
score of lesser places. Wherever his train stopped, or his carriage
travelled, he was attended by cheering crowds and eager reporters,
remarkably reproducing the whistle-stop campaigns of American
Presidential candidates from the time of Lincoln onwards. As Lord
Rosebery put it, in presiding over a meeting at Waverley Market,
'there has been no Scottish village too small to afford a crowd to
greet him; there has been no cottager so humble that could not find
a light to put in his window; as he passed, mothers have brought
their babies to lisp a hurrah, old men have crept forth from their
homes to see him before they died. These have been no prepared
ebullitions of sympathy; these have been no calculated demonstrations. The heart of the nation has been touched.'

And, it may be added, for its entire duration, the reports of it
dwarfed all other news in the Press. It was recognised that a new
electoral technique had come into existence, and that the leader of
the party now enjoyed a new prestige and a new place in the national
life. So striking was Gladstone's success that he followed the
campaign with a second, which proved equally successful. In the
ensuing general election the results were plain, for the Liberals
swept to a decisive victory.

Gladstone's campaigns have often been imitated, but none of his
successors have achieved the same stunning impact which Gladstone's did in 1879, and there were some who saw in them a
threat to the constitution itself in the direct appeal to the emotions
of a vast audience. Nevertheless, even today, with access to radio,
television, as well as the Press, no national leader since Gladstone
has equalled his mastery of popular feeling except Winston
Churchill, and then only in the extremity of a war for survival.
Nevertheless, the popular appeal of the Prime Minister and of the
Leader of the Opposition remains as important a factor in the winning of general elections in Britain as in the election of American
Presidents.

The nineteenth century rather unexpectedly reproduced one of
the characteristics of the eighteenth – the frequency with which
peers, or their close relatives, became Prime Ministers. The list is a

long one, and in some measure misleading, for Melbourne and Palmerston were both Irish peers who sat in the House of Commons and Lord John Russell and Disraeli only went to the House of Lords at the end of their political careers. On the other hand, the Earl of Liverpool, Earl Grey, the Duke of Wellington, the Earl of Derby, and (at the end of the century) the Earl of Rosebery and the Marquess of Salisbury, all presided over governments from the House of Lords as a normal incident in their political careers, and in addition, Rosebery and Salisbury held the Foreign Secretaryship whilst they were Prime Ministers. So long as the two Houses were on a nominal equality, this was always a possibility, but since the government in the Commons must, in these circumstances, be led by another member, harmony could only be preserved where the association between Prime Minister and leader in the Commons was close. The arrangement was probably seen at its best during Salisbury's last premiership, when the Commons were led by his nephew, A. J. Balfour, who succeeded him as Prime Minister. It was at its worst when Harcourt led the Commons during Rosebery's premiership. Their lack of sympathy was notorious, and on his resignation Rosebery made plain his determination never to serve again. The concentration of power in the House of Commons after the Parliament Act, 1911, has made it practically impossible for a peer now to be selected as Prime Minister, although Lord Curzon erroneously assumed that he would be asked to form a government on the resignation of Bonar Law in 1922. The fact that a group of Conservatives in 1940 considered the possibility of Lord Halifax succeeding Chamberlain, in preference to Winston Churchill, merely emphasises the extent to which they were out of touch with public opinion, and how much they underestimated the peril in which inept policy had placed the country. Today, the heir to a peerage who cherishes political ambitions may disclaim his peerage, thereby becoming eligible for election to the House of Commons, but it is not entirely irrelevant to notice that Sir Alec Douglas-Home, formerly the Earl of Home, who succeeded Harold Macmillan as leader of the Conservative Party, in spite of his generally recognised abilities, only held that position briefly, one criticism of him being that he lacked the necessary degree of popular appeal.

On the morning after winning a general election, the Prime Minister stands at the apex of the political system, and with the prospect of five years in office, his powers appear almost unlimited.

H

Necessarily, a great deal will depend upon his own personality. The impact of some Prime Ministers upon history has been enduring; that of others is scarcely remembered, or if it is, with condemnation. Omitting Bonar Law and Campbell-Bannerman, both of whom resigned and died after a brief tenure of the premiership, it is possible to trace the widest variations in approach between the other premiers of the present century. Possibly the most unexpected premier of recent times was Clement Attlee. Acute and modest, and a loyal lieutenant in a great wartime government, he had achieved leadership of the Labour Party only by a series of unforeseen events and there were few who would have confidently predicted the landslide to Labour in 1945. Many members of his team were already tired men when they took office in 1945, and to many members of the public Attlee himself was still virtually unknown. Nevertheless the achievements of his first government merit direct comparison with those of the Liberal government of 1906, albeit they greatly exceeded those of that government in comprehensiveness. Attlee, by common consent, was not an assertive leader. In cabinet discussions, he was inclined to let each member make his case at length, and then himself tersely sum up. Since dissensions were frequent, it is reasonable to assume that only Attlee's adroitness, and his capacity for lowering the temperature of discussion, could have kept the team together so long.

The Prime Minister's personal influence upon policy may be exerted in more direct, and more decisive, fashion than this, however. Putting aside the immense power wielded by David Lloyd George and by Winston Churchill under abnormal wartime conditions, there exists the decisive change in national policy which followed the replacement of Stanley Baldwin by Neville Chamberlain in 1937, and which, although it was achieved with the general support of the Cabinet, owed its force and direction to the Prime Minister himself. During his brief tenure of office before the outbreak of war, the 'midsummer madness' of sanctions, into which his predecessor had reluctantly stumbled, was wound up; very great efforts were made by him unsuccessfully to detach Mussolini from the Axis, and Chamberlain led the country into the diplomatic disaster of Munich. His policy, which was based upon the erroneous assumption that the demands of the dictators were limited, and could be accommodated, had involved the resignation of Anthony Eden, and the replacement of the advice of Lord Vansittart by that of Chamberlain's chief personal adviser, Sir

Horace Wilson, whose qualifications to proffer advice upon international problems were obscure. Whatever conclusions may be reached upon these events, they at least showed the capacity of the Prime Minister to intervene in all spheres of governmental activity, and to select his own advisers for the purpose. They also showed the power of the Prime Minister, backed by influential opinion and by important sections of the Press, to mould public opinion sufficiently to give the appearance of public support to a policy of appeasement, upon which the country as a whole was very sharply divided.

The Prime Minister, unlike his cabinet colleagues, has no department to administer, for it is unlikely that any future occupant of that office will again combine it with the office of Secretary of State for Foreign, and now also Commonwealth, Affairs. On the other hand, he retains his power to lay down guide lines for the conduct of any branch of public affairs, especially in times of emergency. This was most plainly evident during Winston Churchill's wartime government, but it is always there, even though some Prime Ministers have chosen to leave their colleagues to run their departments in their own way. Asquith, for example, was addicted to this, and it has been frequently asserted that in the Liberal administration of 1906–14, foreign affairs were rarely upon the Cabinet's agenda, and when they were, surprisingly little interest in them was shown. Very much the same state of affairs existed with regard to colonial affairs, both then and at an earlier period, and all the efforts of Joseph Chamberlain to create a lively consciousness of the problems of empire failed to produce a significant change. Such attitudes will not be likely to recur today, when defence, foreign policy, the Common Market, and the economic problems of the United Kingdom are all inextricably intermingled.

In considering the position of the Prime Minister, it is essential to distinguish between the power which he commands and the factors which limit his exercise of it. The powers which he exercises, especially at the outset of his administration, are almost unlimited. Every government now puts forward a programme of legislation which occupies virtually the whole of the time available for legislation during the session, and it is the Prime Minister who takes the lead in deciding what goes into that programme, for there are always many more things which the government considers it desirable to be done than can possibly be achieved. But once decided upon, there is no constitutional check upon the achievement of that programme, for the Prime Minister commands an obedient majority in the House of Commons. For the recalcitrance of one or a small group of dissidents, there waits in the background the threat of withdrawal of the party Whip, or, for the Labour member, expulsion from the party, and perhaps severe damage to a career. If the party itself, or an important section of it, is restive, there is the threat of a dissolution. There are no legal limits to the legislative competence of Parliament, and no court may pronounce an Act of Parliament unconstitutional or void, as is the case elsewhere, and more particularly in the United States. Moreover, although a second chamber still exists, it cannot reject, and can only very temporarily delay, legislation, whilst even its power to amend on points of substance is today exercised only on threat of abolition of the House of Lords altogether. Nor is this all. Acts of Parliament, it has been shown, today frequently only trace the broad outlines of the rules which control people. Details are filled in by departmental orders and regulations which annually grow more voluminous. In the vast majority of cases, this power to make rules with statutory force is not abused, but there is no legal limit to the extent to which it could be employed; and it must not be forgotten that in the inter-war period a 'ginger group' of the Labour Party, which included Sir Stafford Cripps and Professor Harold Laski, wrote that in order to achieve a socialist state, a Labour government should pass a general enabling Act, permitting the government to legislate by decree – exactly as was being done on the continent in countries ruled by dictators at this period. Nothing of the kind has occurred, but the possibility is there. So long as both parties remain convinced of the value of freedom, it will certainly not become a reality; but the constitutional danger is obvious.

Ian Gilmour, in his analysis of *The Body Politic*, assumed this was a basic condition of political life in the United Kingdom, and, whilst admitting the fact of such a concentration of power in the Cabinet, under the leadership of the Prime Minister, suggested that they have tended rather to lag behind public opinion than to lead it. It can be accepted that, on many issues, there is evidence to support this view. It may be assumed as axiomatic, for example, that the United Kingdom today can only be involved in a war which public opinion as a whole accepts as an inescapable necessity. This, in fact, is the strongest argument for the policy of the Baldwin–Chamberlain governments in refusing to face the dictators until the position had already altered greatly to British disadvantage. It was only at that point that all sections of public opinion were united. It may also explain the collapse of the Eden government's intervention at Suez – a classic illustration of the fact that you cannot engage in war with a peacetime mentality – and also the non-involvement of Great Britain in the war in Vietnam. In a country in which the media of communication are free from official control, the ascertainment of public opinion on any major question is often extremely difficult, particularly if it is also desired to discover the point at which the highest measure of general agreement may be obtained. The recent variations in the climate of opinion upon entry into the Common Market are another illustration of this difficulty.

These are examples of the temperate way in which government is conducted in the United Kingdom at present. Perhaps, too, they are examples of the remarkable tolerance of the British people for their leaders. There is no guarantee that either will continue indefinitely. Even in the United Kingdom there are today signs of a drift to violence, which affects the temper of public life increasingly. No constitution, and no definition of the powers of government, can protect a community against the failure to protect its basic freedoms. But there is no reason why failure to face constitutional inadequacies should facilitate the loss of them.

It is for this reason – and not from any doubt of the democratic outlook of either major party or their leaders – that suggestions of similarity between the office of Prime Minister and that of the American President are so misleading. Superficially, they have come closer together, because in the United Kingdom, with a disciplined party supporting the government, it can be regarded as being in office for a fixed term, i.e. the life of a Parliament. Presidential government, however, depends upon one man – the President – and his Cabinet are not colleagues, as in the United Kingdom. They are subordinates, with neither place nor following in Congress. On the other hand, the powers, and more importantly the limits of the powers, of the President are defined in the constitution, which President and Congress alike are unable to alter, and which can be asserted in the Federal Courts. In the United Kingdom, the powers of the Prime Minister and the Cabinet depend upon convention only, and, except in the extremely unlikely event that their exercise involved a breach of law, they cannot be challenged in any court. In any event, if they did, an Indemnity

Act would quickly follow. For example, in 1912, the Bank of England, on behalf of the government, deducted income tax from the dividends of Thomas Gibson Bowles before the Finance Act of the year was passed, involving changes in the rate of taxation. In *Bowles* v. *The Bank of England*,[1] Bowles was able to secure a pronouncement from the court that this was illegal, but an Indemnity Act was passed immediately afterwards.[2] An even more striking example occurred in 1923. In that year, it emerged that Mr Art O'Brien had been illegally arrested and handed over to the Irish Free State on the orders of the government.[3] For this, he and others were granted compensation, and the Home Secretary was absolved, in the Restoration of Order in Ireland (Indemnity) Act, 1923.

The limits of the powers of the President of the United States are most clearly visible in relation both to general legislation and to taxation. Even if the President and the majority in Congress are members of the same party, there is no certainty that the President's proposals will be accepted as they stand. Where they are on opposite sides, there can be major conflict. Accordingly, it is necessary for all Presidents to negotiate with Congress on their proposals, and the check which this imposes is very real. Even if the legislation is passed, the Supreme Court may declare it unconstitutional and void, as happened to important parts of President Roosevelt's New Deal legislation. The effect of this may be either good or bad, but the checks which exist are sufficient to prevent the emergence of a disguised dictatorship. The American constitution, that is to say, has operated throughout the history of the United States to prevent an over-concentration of power in a single, or in few, hands. It is true that, with the ever-increasing pressures of modern life, the office of President is quite different from what it was in President Lincoln's time, and that his powers are much greater; but they operate within the limits prescribed by the constitution, and they may be checked both by Congress and the courts as those of the Prime Minister cannot.

[1] [1913] 1 Ch. 57.
[2] The Provisional Collection of Taxes Act, 1913.
[3] *Secretary of State for Home Affairs v O'Brien* [1923] A.C. 603.

VIII

The Cabinet

BAGEHOT DESCRIBED the Cabinet as 'a combining committee – a *hyphen* which joins, a *buckle* which fastens, the legislative part of the state to the executive part of the state'. This is still true today, albeit with a considerable difference in emphasis. Members of the Cabinet are still leading members of the major party in the House of Commons or (rarely) of the House of Lords, but they dominate its proceedings to a much greater degree than they did in Bagehot's day. Almost one-third of the members of that party in Parliament have ministerial office, and therefore look expectantly towards the Cabinet for the advancement of their political careers. The remainder are subject to the supervision of the party Whips.

Like the term 'Prime Minister', the term 'Cabinet' was first used in politics with a derogatory significance, being linked in some minds with 'Cabal'. Its emergence as a closely knit body of leading members of a single party, pledged to a particular policy, was gradual, and the evolution of cabinet government to its present proportions has also been a gradual one. It has already been mentioned that the decisive step forward occurred after the accession of George I, when sovereigns absented themselves from cabinet meetings, and the Prime Minister occupied the vacant seat. Largely because of the nature of the business transacted, and partly because cabinet Ministers were in origin the King's confidential advisers, cabinet meetings have remained quite secret. Secrecy was also closely linked with informality. Until modern times, there was no formal record of cabinet proceedings, and members were expected to destroy papers on which they may have recorded cabinet business. It is for this reason that former cabinet members have sometimes differed widely in their recollections of what occurred at such meetings. All this is now changed. It would in any case have been quite impossible to conduct two World Wars on this basis, and in 1917 Lloyd George instituted a cabinet secretariat. With the development of its functions, order has been introduced into cabinet business, and the secretariat now collects and distributes

material relevant to its meetings; it keeps a record of cabinet discussions and of the conclusions reached, and it communicates these
to the departmental Ministers, thus emphasising and increasing
the Cabinet's control over them.

The development of cabinet government in the United Kingdom has depended throughout on convention, and not upon the
law of the constitution. It has therefore remained fluid, and this
has been a main reason for its strength and flexibility. Conventions
regulate its formation, its relation to Crown and Parliament, and
the business which it transacts. The Crown, by convention, must
accept the advice which it tenders, or else it must find other
Ministers who will accept responsibility for the Crown's action,
and also carry on the business of government. The last sovereign
who attempted to control the actions of the Cabinet in this way was
George III, and this explains many of the political and constitutional conflicts of his troubled reign. Ultimately, even George III
learned the political lessons that the King reigns but does not govern
and that whilst the King could at that period influence cabinet
policy, he could neither initiate nor vary it.

So far as Parliament is concerned, the Cabinet now enjoys a
virtual monopoly of the initiative in legislation. Where progress is
made with the rare private member's bill, it is because the Cabinet
permits it, and even these bills are not infrequently modified during
their passage through Parliament at the prompting of the government. So far as taxation is concerned, a major constitutional
convention, based on the old historical rule that Parliament voted
supplies only when the Crown asked for them, makes the initiation
of all financial proposals a government monopoly. Conventions
themselves are fluid, and the nature and extent of a constitutional
convention may itself become the subject of political controversy,
or it may be abandoned in an emergency, temporarily or permanently. The constitutional conflict which was solved by the passage
of the Parliament Act, 1911, arose upon a fundamental disagreement between Liberals and Conservatives upon the convention
governing the power of the House of Lords to reject the government's financial proposals. During the controversy, the existence
of other conventions was asserted and denied – notably, an alleged
convention that if the Lords considered a government measure,
other than a financial one, was not approved by the electorate,
the Lords had a right to reject, and so force a general election.
With this convention there was the corollary that if the election

clearly showed that the electorate supported the government, the Lords would not press their opposition to the measure. Such a convention, if accepted as binding, would have made the House of Lords the arbiter between government and electorate, and was energetically refuted by the Liberals, and any assertion of it died with the Parliament Act of 1911 – although even in recent years it has been suggested that the shadowy suspensory powers of the Lords might be used in a similar situation. Two points may be noticed about this alleged convention. The first is that at the second election in 1910, fought primarily upon the Lords' veto, the Liberals were returned with a substantially reduced majority, and indeed, thereafter they depended to an undesirable extent upon the support of their Irish Nationalist allies, for whom this election brought Home Rule measurably nearer. But did the election endorse the Liberal attitude on the Lords' veto or not? Those Conservative 'diehard' peers who asserted, even after the 1910 elections, that the Parliament Act should be rejected, continued to assert that the electorate had not given a clear decision on this controversy. In fact, the whole controversy raised the fundamental difficulty over such an alleged convention. Who is to decide when an occasion to invoke it has arisen, and what happens when (as in this case) the electorate is almost equally divided, and gives no unambiguous decision?

The economic crisis in 1931, which was responsible for the formation of the first inter-war 'National' Government, illustrated how a convention could be jettisoned in a time of national emergency. The National Government contained members drawn from all three parties, and when, shortly after its formation, it was necessary to decide upon economic measures essential to bring about a national recovery, it became necessary to consider in detail the imposition of protective tariffs. When the search for agreement proved fruitless, the Cabinet was compelled to consider its position with regard to the major convention that it should preserve unanimity in the presentation of its measures to Parliament. Ultimately it published the following statement:

'The Cabinet has had before it the Report of its Committee on the Balance of Trade, and after prolonged discussion it has been found impossible to reach a unanimous conclusion on the Committee's recommendations.

The Cabinet, however, is deeply impressed with the paramount importance of maintaining national unity in the presence of the grave problems now confronting this country and the whole world.

It has accordingly determined that some modification of usual Ministerial practice is required, and has decided that Ministers who find themselves unable to support the conclusions arrived at by the majority of their colleagues on the subject of import duties and cognate matters are to be at liberty to express their views by speech and vote.

The Cabinet being essentially united in all other matters of policy believes that by this special provision it is best interpreting the will of the nation and the needs of the time.'

Several things may be noticed about this most interesting pronouncement. The first is that a major constitutional convention, previously regarded as one of the foundations of cabinet government, has been down-graded to 'the usual Ministerial practice'. The second is that the Cabinet has adopted it as 'best interpreting the will of the nation and the needs of the time'. This is a flexible concept, and, as was seen in the constitutional controversy of 1911, one on which sharply conflicting opinions may exist. The circumstances of 1931 being quite different from those of 1911, the abandonment of a major convention provoked little opposition.

Possibly the most remarkable feature of the British constitution is the convention that the Cabinet is responsible to Parliament for what it does. The whole conception of responsibility, as applied to the Cabinet, is a shadowy one. At various times, it has been alleged that the Cabinet is responsible to the Crown, to the law, and to Parliament. Responsibility to the Crown derives from the fact that Ministers are appointed by the sovereign and proffer their resignation to him. In the eighteenth century the sovereign held them accountable for what they did, and he might dismiss them if he was dissatisfied with their acts. In the nineteenth century, Queen Victoria frequently expressed criticisms of the conduct of Ministers, and the celebrated dismissal of Palmerston from the Foreign Office by Lord John Russell in December 1851 for his independent action in recognising Louis Napoleon's *coup d'état* without informing either his colleagues or the Queen followed upon the Queen's protests to the Prime Minister. It is impossible to imagine a repetition of the incident today. All that remains of the responsibility of the Cabinet to the Crown, beyond the formal acts of appointment and resignation, is the communication of public business, including cabinet business, to the sovereign.

Responsibility of the Cabinet in law is a formal consequence of the responsibility of every subject for his acts before the ordinary courts. No special law protects cabinet Ministers, and, as was shown above, if they break the law, they can be made legally responsible – subject to the qualification that an Act of Indemnity will be quickly put through Parliament.

Finally, there is responsibility to Parliament, or rather to the House of Commons. When Bagehot wrote, just over a century ago, he explained that it was the special virtue of the constitution that the House of Commons controlled the actions of the Cabinet. Already in 1915, in the last (the eighth) edition of *The Law of the Constitution* for the editing of which he was responsible, Dicey had stated in the Introduction: 'It may be maintained with much plausibility that under the quinquennial Parliament created by the Parliament Act the British electorate will, each five years, do little else than elect the party or the Premier by whom the country shall be governed for five years,' and he concluded: 'The plain truth is that the power which has fallen into the hands of the Cabinet may be all but necessary for the conduct of popular government in England under our existing constitution.'

Over the half-century and more which has elapsed, and after two World Wars, that power has continually increased. Today, if it is necessary to talk of responsibility, one should rather speak of the responsibility of Parliament, or rather the responsibility of the major party in Parliament, to the Cabinet, and not *vice versa*. Theoretically, an adverse vote in Parliament can still defeat a ministry. In practice, such adverse votes, in a full debate, will not be given, and unless such a vote were the result of a loss of control by the government, even if such a vote were to be given, it would almost certainly be followed by a dissolution of Parliament.

It is the existence of this power of dissolution at the Prime Minister's request, and the resulting certainty that he will be supported by a vote of the members of the party in the House, which has robbed debates there of major significance, and has made speeches, during debates, formal exercises which the Opposition inevitably opposes, without expecting their opposition to change what is proposed, and government supporters automatically support. Recently, it has been suggested that reality would be restored to Parliamentary proceedings if the power to request a dissolution were removed from the Prime Minister, so that Parliaments lasted for a fixed term of years. Coincidentally, it should cease to be regarded as a constitutional convention that a government should resign after an adverse vote in the House. Only votes of confidence should be treated as requiring its resignation, and other matters could then be debated on their merits. If a Prime Minister were defeated, it is suggested, he would resign, and the Leader of the Opposition, or some other person, would be asked to form a ministry. Only if a government could not be formed would the sovereign order a dissolution. It is axiomatic that any such proposal would be opposed by party leaders, for it would remove the most powerful weapon which a Prime Minister possesses, the existence of which is sufficient to bring a turbulent party to order. It would, moreover, weaken party discipline within the House, and ultimately lead to the formation of groups whose moves and countermoves could determine the fate of government. Possibly the most serious objection is that it would seriously curtail the government's powers to carry out a consistent policy, since the fate of any particular measure in the House would be uncertain until it had passed its third reading. This would delay action on measures which are deemed to be urgent, and it would seriously delay the process of decision-making by the government. One response to such a measure to stabilise the life of Parliament would be to tighten party discipline still further by making it clear that a member who failed to support the government's proposals would certainly fail to receive party support at the next election. At the end of the day, therefore, Prime Minister, government, and party would emerge even stronger than before. Those who advocate fixed Parliaments often cite the example of Congress; but under the American constitution, President and Congress lead separate lives. So long as members of the government in England are also leading members of the House of Commons, it is hard to see how their control over its proceedings can be relaxed, or that any British Prime Minister and Cabinet could accept the hard and prolonged bargaining with the House of Commons over finance which a President undertakes each year with Congress.

This last objection also points to another. Independent voting in the House would not only make the issue of debates uncertain, but would also make the progress of public business slower. It would run completely counter to the present practice of governments to increase the pressure upon their supporters in the

Commons to dispatch the government's programme of legislation. In the spring of 1968, when the government was attempting to push through the House simultaneously four major measures – the Finance Bill, the Prices and Incomes Bill, the Race Relations Bill, and the Transport Bill – sittings of the House were prolonged, and the resentment of the House increased to such a degree that for a period it was almost unmanageable. One difficulty is the way in which a government presents its measures to Parliament. Generally, the pace of Parliamentary proceedings is a leisurely one from the opening of the session until February. Thereafter, pressure builds up rapidly as the government strains every nerve to complete its programme of legislation by August.

The Prime Minister selects his cabinet colleagues (as well as the members of the ministry who are not in the Cabinet), and when he resigns, they also relinquish their offices. This is also the position when a Prime Minister resigns during the lifetime of Parliament, and it is expected that the government will remain in office – for example, when Eden resigned and was succeeded by Harold Macmillan. On such occasions, the resignation of the Prime Minister's colleagues is largely a formality, but it allows the new Prime Minister the opportunity to make any changes which he considers necessary.

The Prime Minister's range of choice is limited by a number of factors. Whilst the party has been in opposition, they will have been led in the House of Commons by a 'Shadow Cabinet', in which each member, other than the Leader of the Opposition (who is also the party leader) will have assumed responsibility for the affairs of a particular department, and will have taken the initiative in debates upon it. He will naturally expect to be appointed to that department, and to sit in the Cabinet as the head of it, when the party comes to power. Today, therefore, there tend to be fewer surprise choices of cabinet members than there were before 1914, and the progressive disappearance of peers (other than the Lord Chancellor) from the Cabinet has emphasised this tendency. Another factor which limits the Prime Minister's choice is the preference of the colleague whom he approaches. Office has frequently been refused because the man approached has felt it to be all-important that he be offered the post to which he considered himself entitled or (less frequently) because he felt he had not the qualifications to fill that which he is offered. Now that the activities of the great departments of state have become so specialised, a Prime Minister will rarely deviate from the positions established in the Shadow Cabinet whilst the party was in opposition, at any rate at the outset of his administration. After it has been in office for a period, there may be a reshuffle, particularly if the performance of some cabinet members has failed to justify expectations. A reshuffle may also provide the opportunity to promote ambitious and able younger members of the government.

Cabinets vary in number from time to time. Last century, they frequently numbered as few as fourteen or fifteen members. In recent years they have had as many as twenty-three or even more members. The majority of Prime Ministers are understood to prefer smaller Cabinets, but they have not always found it possible to achieve them. Certain offices always carry cabinet rank – for example the Chancellor of the Exchequer, the Home Secretary, the Foreign Secretary, and now the Minister of Defence (who has replaced the Parliamentary heads of the three service departments), as well as the Lord Chancellor. The Lord Chancellor is a curious survival from an earlier age. Until the Revolution in 1688, he was most frequently the head of the King's administration as well as the head of the judiciary. After the emergence of the Prime Minister, the Lord Chancellor's political functions have atrophied. Today his cabinet membership presumably depends upon the fact that he is the leader of the government party in the House of Lords – a curiously anomalous position for the head of the judiciary. Today, he is increasingly concerned with law reform, with the administration of justice, and the activities of lay magistrates, and in some of these duties it is manifest that there may be an overlap with the Home Office. It is sometimes said that it is valuable for the government to have the Lord Chancellor in the Cabinet, since there are occasions when his colleagues need his advice as a lawyer. Here again, however, there is an overlap with the functions of the Law Officers[1] – neither of whom sits in the Cabinet. Today, the continued presence of the Lord Chancellor in the Cabinet has a slightly archaic appearance, recalling that in the eighteenth century, before the ministry of the Younger Pitt, the Cabinet had at times contained the Archbishop of Canterbury, the Lord Chamberlain, and even the Lord Chief Justice of the King's Bench. It was to Pitt that we owe the decisive change, by the exclusion of these dignitaries, and the inclusion of those members of either House who were the heads of the great administrative departments.

It was not until the same period that the principle was estab-

---

[1] The Attorney-General and Solicitor-General.

lished (subject to the important deviation in 1932, which has been mentioned) that all members of the Cabinet must support all government measures, or if they do not, then they must resign. During the reign of George III, Lord Camden whilst Lord Chancellor had publicly expressed his opposition to the policy of the Cabinet of which he was a member, and at a later date, Lord Ellenborough who, although Lord Chief Justice, was a member of Fox's Cabinet, sought with the Prime Minister's approval to establish that he would not be responsible for cabinet decisions on legal proceedings, in respect of which he might subsequently be required to sit in judgment. Such attitudes became impossible to maintain with the development of party discipline in the nineteenth century, and the doctrine of collective responsibility emphasises at once the fact that cabinet policy is not, either formally or in fact, the policy of the Prime Minister alone (as an American President's is) and that the members of the Cabinet have a position distinct from that of the Prime Minister, both in Parliament and in the party. This is a circumstance which a Prime Minister must always take into account, for the resignation of one or more leading members of his Cabinet must necessarily have far-reaching repercussions in both places, which he will wish to avoid so far as this is possible.

Conversely, a cabinet member himself will normally hesitate before he offers his resignation, for apart from possible suggestions inside the party that he is 'rocking the boat', there is the very real danger that the reasons for his resignation may be quickly forgotten, and that his standing in the party will suffer an eclipse. One of the most recent illustrations of this is the resignation of George Brown, who had been both Foreign Secretary and Deputy Prime Minister, from the Wilson government in 1968.

The fact that Ministers have a collective responsibility for the formation and advocacy of cabinet policy, has one important qualification, and one important by-product. The qualification is that so long as a question remains an open one, in the sense that the Cabinet does not yet have a settled policy on it, convention permits considerable latitude in the expression of views until a policy is formulated. Thus Joseph Chamberlain, whilst Colonial Secretary (1895–1903), had been a strong advocate of a protective tariff, before either the Cabinet, or even Balfour, the Prime Minister, had expressed a settled view upon it; and at an earlier date, such questions as the repeal of the Corn Laws and Irish Home Rule had been similarly treated, before cabinet policy was decided. Kite-flying by Ministers is a well-known political gambit, and has value in testing the reactions of the public.

The important by-product is that cabinet Ministers, whilst in office, are not free to write, either in the Press or in books, upon political questions when their views may not coincide with those of their colleagues. This rule of cabinet procedure was established by Baldwin, as Prime Minister, when Lord Birkenhead was seeking to supplement his income by applying his very considerable talents to political journalism. In 1969 Harold Wilson reaffirmed the same rule at the expense of a junior Minister (not a cabinet colleague), Jeremy Bray, who had written a book, criticising the political structure of the country, and the Labour Party's reaction to it. The rule is a wise one, and in both these instances, its application plainly deflected much political criticism away from the government of the day. For a Minister to use outside opinion to reinforce his dissent from the policy adopted by colleagues would clearly go some way towards undermining the authority of the Cabinet.

One unusual part which the House of Lords plays in the political life of the country is that it sometimes permits a Prime Minister to select as a colleague a person who is not prominent in political life. An outstanding example of such a selection was that of Lord Woolton as Minister of Food during Winston Churchill's war-time government. Conferment of a peerage satisfies the convention that cabinet members should also be Members of Parliament, and it also helps the Prime Minister to satisfy the requirements of the Ministers of the Crown Act, 1937 (as amended by the Acts creating new Ministries), regulating the distribution of offices of state between the two Houses. Very exceptionally, no such solution is possible, and other expedients are sought. In 1931, for example, J. Ramsay MacDonald appointed Sir William Jowitt as Attorney-General, but it proved impossible to find a seat in the House of Commons. Jowitt, who had no desire to prejudice his political prospects by accepting a peerage, accordingly resigned. Fourteen years later, in the Labour government which took office in 1945, Jowitt accepted a peerage, and sat in the Cabinet as Lord Chancellor. The Scottish law officers have also, upon occasion, provided difficulties for the Prime Minister. In the Labour governments of 1924 and 1929, and in the Conservative government of 1923, the Lord Advocate was not in Parliament at all.

The Machinery of Government Committee, which reported in 1918,[1] defined the primary functions of the Cabinet as: (1) the final determination of the policy to be presented to Parliament and, it may be added, to the electorate at a general election; (2) the control of the national executive in accordance with the policy so presented to Parliament, and approved by it; and (3) the continuous co-ordination and delimitation of the authorities of the various departments of state.

The first of these functions is today of overwhelming importance. Any party programme which is expected to win the approval of the electorate must convey the impression that there is a great deal which needs changing, and that, if elected, the party will initiate a spate of legislation on a great variety of topics. Similarly, a government which appeals to the electorate for a fresh term of office will proudly enumerate the long list of measures it has passed, changing things from what they were before. Inevitably in enumerating the things they are going to change, the parties compete against each other, and accordingly, modern elections have increasingly assumed the character of public auctions, in which the country is knocked down to the highest bidder. One result of this is that every government must at all times give the impression of furious activity, coupled with a readiness to change things, which has added not a little to the confusion which is today characteristic of the transaction of public business, and especially the business of Parliament. Regularly the public is informed that time can only be found for some measure at the expense of deferring another, and one is left with the impression that the government is like the White Queen in *Alice Through the Looking Glass* – always running, and never getting anywhere. In the sphere of public finance, this is unfortunately only too apparent.

The collective responsibility which members of the Cabinet share for the conduct of public business implies (1) that members know what is being done; and (2) that they share a similar outlook, sufficiently to be able to compromise when their views of the manner in which a particular problem should be approached do not coincide. So far as the first point is concerned, there exist a few exceptions, the most notable of which is the preparation of the Budget by the Chancellor of the Exchequer. The proposals are communicated orally to the Cabinet very shortly before the Chancellor introduces them into the House of Commons, but prior to

[1] Cmd. 9230.

I

that, cabinet members will have been as ignorant as anyone else. On the other hand, in these days, when Great Britain's financial difficulties are a constant preoccupation, any perceptive cabinet member, like any perceptive member of the public, will be able to conclude, without undue difficulty, the Chancellor's probable line of approach.

Apart from such exceptions, which are few in number, cabinet members are kept informed of the work and the views of their colleagues, by the circulation of papers, and in this way the work of members has grown, and with it, the cabinet secretariat, which prepares and distributes this material, and which keeps a record of points made in discussion and of cabinet decisions. This has removed the possibility, which always existed down to 1914, that there should be no clear opinion upon what actually was decided. It was the experience of World War I, and the very great expansion of the cabinet secretariat which it necessitated, that has controlled the future development of cabinet procedure. In particular, it demonstrated the necessity for an increasing amount of cabinet work to be delegated to cabinet committees and sub-committees. Of these, the largest and most important is the Defence Committee, which became a permanent cabinet committee as early as 1904, and was known until 1939 as the Committee on Imperial Defence. Its composition has varied from time to time, and especially during the two World Wars which have occurred during its existence, but it has always included the Prime Minister, the heads of the armed services (replaced now by the Minister of Defence), the Chancellor of the Exchequer, and the Home and Foreign Secretaries. Subordinate to this committee is the Chiefs of Staff Committee, which investigates the problems of defence as a whole, and the co-ordination of the armed forces. One important function of the Chiefs of Staff Committee is the presentation of an annual report to the Defence Committee, in which defence is linked with the varying climate of foreign policy, and in which proposals arising out of them are made. During World War II the Committee of Imperial Defence was merged into the War Cabinet, and its sub-committees were very greatly extended. With the appointment of a Minister of Defence in 1946, the Defence Committee emerged again as a separate cabinet committee, with its Chiefs of Staff Committee, and other sub-committees. The Prime Minister is still the Chairman of the Defence Committee, with the Minister of Defence as Deputy Chairman.

Besides this major committee, other cabinet committees have progressively emerged, notably the Home Affairs Committee, which considers the bills which the Cabinet is proposing to initiate in the House of Commons, not only from the standpoint of general government policy, but also in their more technical aspects. In the discharge of this latter function, the Home Affairs Committee will have the assistance of the Law Officers, and of Parliamentary counsel to the Treasury, and also of officials of the departments which are concerned with the proposed legislation. From time to time other committees are established, not necessarily on a permanent basis, and recently, problems of economic planning have engaged the attention of a special committee, to which experts outside Parliament have been summoned.

It scarcely needs to be stated that the business of a modern Cabinet is far more taxing, both in time and energy, than it was in the time of Gladstone and Disraeli, or even in the era which closed in 1939. The Cabinet today is constantly concerned with every aspect of national life, and indeed, through the departments, it is attempting to regulate the daily life of all citizens. New problems of the greatest magnitude are constantly emerging, crises are recurrent, and over all, there looms the constant menace of economic insecurity. Whatever view may be taken of the assumption of such an immense load of responsibility, the question which immediately presents itself is whether the Cabinet is organised to deal with this task efficiently. In 1949, Clement Attlee remarked acutely: 'The Cabinet as now constituted sins against the first principle of good administration, in that it does not distinguish between the function of planning broad strategy and making decisions as to the detailed execution of plans.'[1] In spite of some minor changes in organisation, largely brought about by changes in the structure of individual Ministries, the disappearance of some, and the emergence of others, Lord Attlee's criticism remains substantially true, although the functions have much increased since 1949. It would be interesting to know how much cabinet time is spent upon the functioning of the nationalised industries, or upon the changing structure of British industry, and how well informed cabinet members are upon the extremely complex process of entering the Common Market. To press the inquiry a stage further, how many cabinet members have the time, or the will, to read and to form views upon the mountain of reports which issue from the

[1] *The Labour Party in Perspective*, p. 128.

government printers from committees set up at the initiative of the government itself. The layman may be forgiven if he concludes that by the time some of these reports appear, the Cabinet has forgotten why the committee was set up in the first place, or if he concludes that the process of government today is largely one of rush and muddle, in which an apparent answer to a problem must be found somehow. No other conclusion would, indeed, appear to be possible, having regard to the volume and scope of the Cabinet's activities, or to the way in which solutions to the intricate problems are announced in the form of new legislation. To take only one example – at what point, if at all, did the Cabinet consider the effect of the legislation which created the Land Commission, whose ill-conceived activities produced such a widespread crop of individual injustices that its activities had to be hastily curbed? No one will question that in times of rapid social change, and of rising social tension, Cabinets must be responsive to the public mood. This makes it the more important that their activities should be the response to circumstances, rather than to pre-determined views or prejudices. They can only have this character if the members of the Cabinet have the time for reflection which they at present lack, and for lack of which government tends to be conducted at a progressively lower level. In a special article in *The Times* of 18 December 1968 Louis Heren wrote:

> 'I was told, and can believe, that Cabinet discussions can be painfully trite and shallow. A synoptic view of what is required for the national good is rarely if ever achieved. Certainly it seems to explain the series of bad decisions which has brought the country to the precipice of financial disaster.'

Earlier in the same discussion, Louis Heren was properly ironic over the secrecy and foolish mumbo-jumbo which accompanies much cabinet activity – for example, 'the traditional news photographs of the Chancellor standing at the door of No. 11 on Budget Day holding up the battered dispatch box to the respectful populace as if it contained tablets handed down from some private Mount Sinai.' This, alas, is only one side of the coin. On the other is the portentous apparatus of official and semi-official government handouts, inspired leaks, and 'well-informed spokesmen', who comment on the action (or inaction), rather in the manner of the Chorus in a Greek play, but who are rapidly reducing it to the level of farce. The whole of this machine was brought into operation in May 1968, to explain how James Callaghan, the Home Secretary, had been the subject of Mr Wilson's displeasure for his independent views on the Trade Unions Bill, and accordingly for a time he would not be summoned to cabinet meetings when that thorny piece of intended legislation was being discussed. What Harold Wilson and Callaghan thought when the government ignominiously dropped the bill a few months later was not made the subject of similar handouts – but ludicrous episodes such as this have much to do with the general indifference to the activities of politicians, which is now the prevalent public mood.

Faced with the persistence of this mood, political writers have sought to find an alibi for the politicians. Ian Gilmour, in *The Body Politic*, Crossman, in public speeches, and numerous others, have put forward the thesis that, although nominally the Cabinet and the Prime Minister are all-powerful, in reality this is quite misleading, because a party majority, television, the Press, the public, or some other mysterious agency may at any time remove them – so that, in order to stay in office, they achieve, and seek to achieve, very little. One is irresistibly reminded of the wife of a Crusader, who proudly greeted her husband, after an absence of fourteen years in the Holy Land, at the head of a row of twelve small children, with the words: 'I, too, have not been idle.' Cabinets are perpetually busy, and if it is not upon projects dear to the hearts of members, they have only themselves to blame. In any event, it is difficult to think of any government, however absolute, which has habitually acted in defiance of public opinion.

One of the longest-standing and remarkable features of cabinet government is its secrecy. As Privy Councillors, cabinet Ministers are bound by oath not to disclose information of their proceedings, and this is reinforced by the Official Secrets Act, which prevents the publication of cabinet papers, except after a long interval. The justification for this secrecy is the necessity for protecting free discussion on major questions of policy. The same veil of secrecy is thrown over the activities of cabinet committees and their agencies, for example the Secret Service, which are responsible to them. Bagehot regarded this secrecy as wholly admirable, protecting the High Priests of politics from the gaze of the vulgar, but this, more than any other single factor, has progressively separated government from electorate, whilst at the same time totally concealing the process of policy-making from outside criticism. It also totally conceals from view the extent to which the Cabinet or its committees invoke, or rely upon, the advice of specialists, or the way in which such specialists are appointed. In this respect, it is not unreasonable to suggest that we have a good deal to learn from American experience, although it should be emphasised that the Cabinet of an American President is not at all comparable with an English Cabinet. The President's Cabinet is composed of men appointed by him, they are only loosely associated in their policy, they are dismissable at the President's pleasure, and they are not members of Congress, or even, necessarily, leading party men at all. All these things stress that the ultimate responsibility in America rests with the President, and not, as in Great Britain, with the Cabinet. On the other hand, a glance at recent political developments in Australia and Canada would show that the Prime Ministers and Cabinets of these Commonwealth nations have apparently been readier to avail themselves of outside advice than English Cabinets have been.

There are few who would question that the increasing pressure of public business, as the state assumes more and more functions, has brought about a sharp decline in the quality and value of cabinet discussions, if they are to be judged by their results. Some time ago, the late Lord Samuel, with his wide experience of cabinet procedure, wrote shortly after World War II:

'Recent events show that the governing machine is not working well. The pressure of business – international, imperial and domestic, legislative and administrative – is too heavy for it in normal times, and leaves no reserve of energy and power for times of crisis. Even if the present programme of legislation were lightened, the rapid expansion of the functions of the State during this century makes an adaptation of the old mechanism essential.'

The position is far worse today, and one is tempted to suggest – in direct opposition to the prevailing trend – that one major reform would be to have a lengthy close season for new legislation, during which Britain would have an opportunity to digest that which had been passed recently, for the conclusion is irresistible that one of the most persistent diseases which afflicts modern Western democracy is legislative dyspepsia.

One example, the Land Commission Act, 1967, produced such a devastating crop of injustices, to which the Press, led by the *Daily Express*, gave full publicity, that the policy of the Land Commission was abruptly modified, after only a few months of operation.

An equally ill-considered Act is the Trade Descriptions Act, 1968, which has produced something like chaos in the catering trade. Armed with wide new powers, local authorities and inspectors have interpreted their duties under this Act very differently in differing parts of the country, so that grocers are quite unable to comply with the provisions of the Act, even though they may have used their best endeavours to do so. In October 1969, the Chief Inspector of Weights and Measures for Westminster, Chelsea, and Hammersmith admitted: 'The Act is far from satisfactory in operation . . . . . . We must assume that the law will, at some future date, be examined and redrawn.' Possibly it would have been better to think a little further before rushing such ill-drawn legislation on to the statute-book, more especially as wide powers to make orders under the Act are scattered liberally through its sections, and very wide powers of entry upon premises and to seize goods and documents are conferred upon the enforcing authorities.

A third example is the Road Safety Act, 1967, which introduced the notorious 'breathalyser' test for motorists. In quashing a conviction of a motorist under this Act, Mr Justice Hinchcliffe said on 20 November 1969: 'They will have to scrap this Act and Parliament will have to have another try,' to which Mr Justice Sachs added: 'It is time for a breath of commonsense.' Although a working compromise upon the breath-test has now been reached, it might possibly have been better if more time and thought had been given to its preparation in the first instance.

Lord Samuel pointed out that, in spite of the strong recommendation of the Haldane Committee on the Machinery of Government, which reported in 1918, that there should be a small Cabinet largely freed from departmental preoccupations, little had been done to implement this recommendation. It is understandable that cabinet Ministers should be reluctant to hand over the direction of large and important departments to others, but the inescapable consequence of failure to do so is that cabinet Ministers attend cabinet meetings with a departmental attitude which may be productive of a good deal of conflict when the policy of one department impinges upon that of another. Lord Samuel's suggested solution was that the departments of state should be organised into five groups, each group being presided over by a Minister of cabinet rank who himself had no departmental duties. These, with the Prime Minister, the Chancellor of the Exchequer, the Foreign Secretary, the Home Secretary, and the Lord Chancellor, might form a new Cabinet of ten. Ultimately the group departments might evolve their own Cabinets, under the presidency of the cabinet Minister, dispatching a good deal of general departmental business, but reserving matters of general concern and those likely to provoke considerable controversy for the major Cabinet. The details of departmental grouping in Lord Samuel's scheme need not now be considered, as the departments themselves have changed considerably since he wrote, but it is at least a scheme which boldly attempts to dissociate national policy-making by the Cabinet from the running of the departments. Lord Samuel's final conclusion was:

'The proposal springs of necessity from the urgent needs of the actual situation. It is in fact long overdue. The present functions of the executive have come to it from two opposite directions, from above and from below. Some have been delegated by the Crown: the King, in early days, inviting to his assistance various Ministers to handle the affairs concentrated in his own hands – law and order, finance, foreign relations, national defence. To these have been added, with rapidly growing volume and speed in modern times, a great variety of services coming up from the body of the nation itself, services that began with voluntary organisations and private enterprise, education, health, social agencies of many kinds, the conduct of industries, housing and the like. The old duties, handed down, have been overwhelmed by the new ones pressing up. The result is confusion and inefficiency. The time is ripe, and more than ripe, for a fundamental change.'

The proposals of Lord Samuel, it will be seen, represented an attempt to meet the shrewd criticism of Clement Attlee, which has been mentioned earlier, but which has remained unanswered until the advent of the Wilson administration. From an earlier predilection for the creation of new Ministries, such as the Ministry of Technology and the Department of Economic Affairs, which added further complications to an already intricate pattern, in which inter-departmental committees attempt to iron out inter-departmental clashes, Harold Wilson turned to simplification and with it a reduction in the number of cabinet members. One important simplification came when the Foreign Office was united with the Dominions and Colonial Offices under Michael Stewart, and a further step was taken by merging the Ministry of Health with the Department of Social Security in 1968; but a more far-reaching change occurred when in October 1969 the Ministry of Technology absorbed the Ministry of Power, under Wedgwood Benn, and when at the same time a new department under Anthony Crosland, the Department of Local Government and Regional Planning, became responsible for housing, local government, transport, and regional planning, absorbing at the same time the Department of Economic Affairs, so far as its activities relate to regional problems. The remaining functions of the Department of Economic Affairs pass mainly to the Treasury or (in relation to industrial organisation) to the enlarged Ministry of Technology. The changes made possible a reduction in the Cabinet from 23 to 21 Ministers. Perhaps they drew their original inspiration from Lord Samuel's suggestion, but they do not do what he suggested should be done, and what Lord Attlee advocated – namely, free cabinet Ministers from immediate departmental responsibilities. On the other hand, they do permit these super-Ministers to make decisions within their spheres, and in so doing, they make it possible to avoid lengthy inter-departmental wrangles.

The principal criticism of these changes was that they had a transitional appearance. The Cabinet is still too large, and under the reconstruction of 1969, some members were plainly retained for personal, rather than functional, reasons. Nevertheless, they point the way along which further changes may be made at a future date, and they are a recognition that there is need for increased effectiveness in the formulation of cabinet policy. This, however, is not the only change of structure which has been achieved by Wilson's government. One evident source of weakness in the past has been the gap between the Cabinet and the rank-and-file of the party in the House of Commons. It has depressed the status of the ordinary party member, and curtailed his usefulness. This has often been one of the major disappointments faced by young, enthusiastic, and ambitious members on their first entry into the House of Commons, and, so far as the Labour Party was concerned, it stood in sharp contrast with the position which existed when the party was in opposition. Then the party elected at the beginning of each session, not only the Leader and Deputy Leader, but also the Chief Whip and a Shadow Cabinet of twelve members. Policy decisions of the Shadow Cabinet were reported to weekly meetings of the Parliamentary party for discussion and approval. During the session also there existed specialist groups, which included both

Shadow Cabinet members and backbenchers, undertaking investigations and discussions on many important topics, and as a result of them, reporting back to the Shadow Cabinet. Out of such reports and discussions policy decisions eventually emerged.

When the Labour Party came to office, there was a sharp change. The intimate contact between Cabinet and backbenchers was lost, and the new role of the party in the House was to support government policy. Liaison was maintained through the Chief Whip and a small, elected liaison committee. This, however, was a poor substitute for the intimacy which had existed in opposition, and accordingly during the 1968–69 session, the Labour government initiated regular weekly talks with the chairman of the backbenchers, at which impending government bills, governmental policy, and many allied matters were discussed. Whether this had the desired effect of narrowing the gap between government and 'other ranks' in the party is not yet apparent. It will depend upon the extent to which backbench views are seen to influence the formation of government policy. So far as the Labour Party is concerned, it is part of a complex of activities with this object in view, which included too the frequent holding of party meetings, where Ministers attended and answered questions, and of which a full account was given at the conclusion to lobby correspondents. In addition, the studies and discussions undertaken by groups of specialists whilst the party was in opposition were continued during the existence of the Labour government, and the chairmen of these groups had regular monthly meetings with the Prime Minister, and more frequent meetings with the Minister whose department was within the special area of interest of a group. If the contact between Minister and specialist group was close, much friction could be avoided, and in addition the backbenchers could, in this way, exercise some real influence upon the formation of policy. Conversely, failure by a Minister to maintain sufficiently close contact may impair his usefulness, or, on a controversial matter, even put his proposals at risk.

The real significance of this development is that it offers the backbencher some prospect, however slender, of taking some share in the process of decision-making, not only on the broadest questions of national policy, but in the work of the departments, which has become all the more important since investigation by Select Committee has fallen progressively out of favour. There is also another aspect. In 1968, Crossman, then leader of the government in the House of Commons, introduced a number of changes in its procedure, which were intended to expedite its business, and at the same time to extend the control of the business of the House by the government. One important feature of these changes was the institution of new specialist committees to scrutinise the activities of particular departments or particular branches of government activity. Already there existed the prototypes of such committees in the Estimates and Public Accounts Committees. To these there have more recently been added committees on science and technology and on agriculture, the Nationalised Industries Committee, the Education and Science Committee, and the Committee for the Parliamentary Commissioner. It is contemplated that these specialised committees should do a good deal of work, and progressively acquire a considerable body of specialised knowledge. Gradually, no doubt, special committees with adequate professional staffs will cover the entire field of governmental activity. These proposed developments will be an important step towards enabling the backbenchers of both parties to take a close look at government in action, and to make informed criticism, but their creation has paradoxically raised from members protests that they are being pressed too hard. Members, however, cannot have it both ways. Either they must take the necessary steps to equip themselves to make informed criticism of the activities of government, or they must remain, as they have tended to be recently, largely in ignorance of what is being done, unless some particular matter is brought to their attention, not infrequently by a constituent.

The record of members of the House of Commons in dealing with the reports of its committees is not an impressive one. The Public Accounts Committee was formed as long ago as 1851, and its investigations into the expenditure of public money are extensive. In the session 1968–69, the committee took evidence on thirty days between 27 November and 23 June, and interviewed the heads of seventeen departments or government agencies.[1] Its report, extending to 615 pages, sharply criticised the lavish spending of money on Concorde without the knowledge and sanction of Parliament; the excessive recruitment of staff by the Land Commission; and numerous other matters. The debate on the committee's report lasted only two and a half hours, and was conducted almost entirely by members of the committee themselves – a situation which also exists in respect of reports of other committees.

[1] David Wood in *The Times*, 23 November 1969.

One response, though a very limited one, to the restiveness of backbenchers of both parties, has been to encourage them to participate in outside activities, especially in their constituencies. Another cause of dissatisfaction is the perpetuation of conditions, such as inadequacy of accommodation in Westminster, and an absence of secretarial facilities, which an American Congressman would find quite intolerable. At long last their needs as legislators are beginning to receive recognition, but improvements in this area will miss their point unless they are accompanied by an improvement in communication and knowledge between members on the one hand and Cabinet and department of state on the other. In a series of articles in *The Times* in 1968, Louis Heren wrote that the oligarchs of the Cabinet see the backbencher as an ombudsman for constituents, possibly as a ministerial trainee, and above all, as a supporter of the oligarchy, and he concluded that this was a principal factor in bringing Parliament into disrepute. A member who is constantly acting as a general welfare officer for his constituency may be pleasing his party leaders, but he may not be, and frequently is not, fully discharging his responsibilities as a member of a sovereign legislature, and he is leaving the Cabinet even freer than it was before of that scrutiny, criticism, and ultimate control which is essential if democratic government is to be a reality.

IX

Government by the Departments

DURING THE last century and a half, a major revolution has occurred in the structure of politics in the United Kingdom, mainly unperceived by citizens at large. It is the progressive transfer of governmental functions from Parliament and, in some measure, from the Courts of Law, to government departments, which operate independently of public control, and even to a considerable extent beyond the range of public scrutiny. It is almost as if the increasing participation of the ordinary citizen in the largely formal process of electing members of the House of Commons must necessarily be accompanied by a shift of power to organisations less responsive to public pressure. From time to time, when expressions of anxiety have been heard upon this continuing process, the public have been soothed by the irrelevant, and not entirely accurate, remark that the British civil service, like the police force, is the best in the world. In so far as the governmental structure depends upon any general theory, it is that general lines of policy are established by the Cabinet, and it is then for the departments to give them detailed application. As the late Sir Carleton Kemp-Allen put it:

> 'There are really two entirely different kinds of executive bodies within our system. The Cabinet is what may be called the high executive, subject to the vital principles of Cabinet solidarity, Parliamentary responsibility and ultimately the will of the people. But the actual machinery of execution is carried on by a large body of persons one of whose principal characteristics is that they are wholly detached from politics, or even (in theory) from policy, and who are responsible not to the electorate but only to the Crown. It is they who, apart from abstract doctrines, are the real executive in the constitutional system.'[1]

This fundamental change in structure has taken place, as Lord

[1] *Law and Orders* (2nd ed.), p. 15.

Samuel explained in the observations quoted at the end of the last chapter, by the assumption of more and more functions by the state, as a result of a general acceptance of theories upon the functions of government, sharply differing from those assumed by the political philosophers of earlier ages. Even so late as the middle of the nineteenth century, departments were still small, and permanent appointments were filled largely by patronage. The growth in volume, and the changes in the nature, of their work, not only involved a continuing and very great expansion of their staffs, but also the selection and organisation of a civil service, competent to deal with this business, and accordingly appointments to all but the minor posts were filled by competitive examination. One of the most valuable reforms affecting the entire edifice of government, achieved in the nineteenth century, was the substitution of open competition for patronage and favour in this field, and the establishment of permanent and progressive careers for those who were selected. This major change was not brought about without heart-searching among politicians, whose patronage would disappear, and the Order-in-Council of 1870 which made entry into every government department, except the Foreign Office, depend upon a competitive examination had one built-in safeguard. The civil service itself was divided into two main classes, an upper and a lower. So far as the upper division was concerned, the examination was so arranged that it was almost impossible for anyone other than a graduate of Oxford or Cambridge to obtain entry. Although there was some liberalisation after World War I, it remained true until after 1945 that the monopoly of the older universities was not gravely challenged. The result was a close-knit community, with a common social background, common interests, close links with the Common Rooms of Oxford and Cambridge and with the professions, and a remarkable degree of detachment from the outside world. In the seventy years during which this system operated, with only surface changes, an entire society passed away, the position of the United Kingdom was profoundly modified, and the older universities ceased to dominate every sphere of public and commercial life. Nevertheless, the values cherished by the older universities still dominated the thinking, and conditioned the lives, of those who spent their lives in the departments of state. They were accepted without criticism, not only by those who were themselves products of those two institutions, but also by those less favoured mortals languishing in the lower ranks of the service, who, under favourable conditions, might hope to achieve some minor honour – a junior grade in one of the various orders of knighthood – before they retired.

In more stable times than the present, the system of selection has been defended because it produced men and women of some culture, who could be relied upon to give loyal service and sound advice, no matter what party was in power. Indeed, the service has frequently expressed pride in its detachment from the storms of party political life. But the fact that the civil service has no party political affiliations has not meant that strongly held departmental attitudes have not been developed, or that strong departmental pressure, masquerading as advice or appreciations of situations, had not been exercised upon a Minister. A great deal has therefore depended upon the personality of the Minister himself, and it has sometimes been the case that the Minister most valued by a department has also been the weakest from the standpoint of initiating policy.

In recent years the civil service has frequently been the subject of public discussion, principally because it has been thought that methods of selection and modes of training have become increasingly out of touch with present-day problems, and with the increasing emphasis upon technology. It was this which prompted the setting-up of a committee under Lord Fulton, charged with the duty of reporting upon changes which might be regarded as desirable. The report of this committee appeared in June 1968. Its basic assumptions were that there was today a greater need for management, rather than for administration, for the assumption of personal in place of collective responsibility, and for research and expert knowledge in place of the carefully meditated decisions of the cultivated amateur. One consequence of this latter proposal will be that there will be a good deal less movement from department to department, and that the staff of a department will in course of time acquire expert knowledge of high quality. In the long run, this may well mean that bureaucracy, since it will be more efficient and more professionally alert, may also become more oppressive. If this is not to occur, then not only must Ministers exercise greater control than they have sometimes done, but also specialist committees of the House of Commons should be constantly watchful, more especially since the management conception implies that departmental policy should be derived from expert knowledge, and that it should take less account than is taken at present of political considerations. Amongst these are the reactions of members of the House of Commons, of reports of Parliamentary committees, and of pressure exercised by groups which send deputations to the Ministry, or which take space in the Press to explain their reaction to impending departmental action.

If the approach of the Fulton Committee is to be accepted, it follows that the professionalism of the civil servants must operate within the department. This, in turn, will operate within the framework of a national policy, which it will be the responsibility of the Cabinet to formulate. In fact, this is the motivation behind the changes in the structure and functioning of the Cabinet and of the departments in October 1969, and it emphasises yet again the increasingly managerial outlook on government which its leading practitioners affect; which led Barbara Castle, in a television interview following her speech upon equal pay for women at the Labour Party Conference at Brighton in 1969, to speak of the national dividend and its distribution. The analogy, though at first sight attractive, is a dangerous one. Unlike commercial corporations, governments do not earn dividends, although today they stimulate the earning of profit by others. There is, however, a more fundamental difference in function. The business of the government is to govern, and this involves the consideration of many factors of which a commercial enterprise may remain in ignorance. The main argument which can be advanced in support of the managerial concept is that it will enable departments to delegate some of their activities to other agencies – either the autonomous administrative agencies which occupy so prominent a position in the United States and in Sweden, or to regional authorities, the creation of which is now under consideration.

It is in conformity with this managerial concept of government (which led Wilson to reorganise the Cabinet, and which underlies the proposals for change in the Fulton Report) that the changes of October 1969 were followed by strong hints from Whitehall that the Prime Minister was about to undertake a major rationalisation of all state agencies concerned with corporate activities. These would include the National Board for Prices and Incomes, the Monopolies Commission, the Consumer Council, the British Productivity Council, the Commission on Industrial Relations, the National Economic Development Office, and the Registry of Restrictive Trade Agreements. What is contemplated is the creation of a National Trade Practices Commission, which will include the scrutiny of company behaviour, including possibly the registration of important policy decisions of major corporations, and the enforcement of consumer protection. Another contemplated change is the extension of the powers of the Monopolies Commission on the model of the American Federal Trade Commission. The multiplication of autonomous agencies with wide powers of supervision and control is one of the favoured expedients of modern governments, and it has much to commend it as a method of implementing policy. The rights of the individual will, however, need special protection in face of this major advance by government into the industrial and commercial spheres.

The evolution of a permanent civil service which is politically neutral, has been based upon two major principles. The first is yet another manifestation of ministerial responsibility, and the second is secrecy of inter-departmental activity. So far as responsibility is concerned, in theory it is the Minister who acts, and the civil servant who informs and advises. Under modern conditions, with a civil service numbering approximately half a million, this is a self-evident fiction. A great deal must necessarily be done, of which the Minister is either totally unaware, or else of which he is aware only in the very barest outline. When the departments are engaged, as they are today, in the day-to-day control of very wide, and constantly extending, fields of human activity, it is plain that the Minister can at most lay down general principles, and that, even in the best-regulated departments, accidents will occur. Nevertheless, the civil service is completely faceless, and a Minister may be called upon to assume responsibility for actions of which he was totally ignorant until the Press, possibly, brought them to light. Responsibility, in this context, means that the Minister must explain, and justify if he can, what has occurred, to the House of Commons. If the error is a gross one, the Minister may have to resign, as Sir Thomas Dugdale, then Minister of Agriculture, did over the Crichel Down Scandal in 1954. Even in this case, however, the Minister's resignation was due rather to his own sense of propriety than to Parliamentary pressure, and it is certainly true that resignations on this ground are rare, and tend to become rarer. There are good reasons for this. The Minister's own party will naturally not wish the episode to be magnified, whilst all members of the House are well aware that with departments operating on the present scale, the Minister's personal involvement may be minimal. Such

K

episodes, therefore, usually terminate with a caution from the Opposition, and a promise by the Minister that the matter will be looked at again. From first to last, constitutional convention will have completely protected the actual persons within the Ministry who are responsible from both publicity or criticism, and the matter will then be relinquished to whatever departmental procedures may be appropriate. It is, from the constitutional point of view, quite extraordinary that the doctrine of ministerial responsibility permits government departments to operate with a degree of secrecy which is not paralleled either in government abroad or in other spheres of activity (other than Freemasonry) in the United Kingdom. One has only to think of the searching, and at times ruthless, inquiries conducted by Congressional committees in the United States for the contrast to become apparent.

Ministerial responsibility has as its necessary corollary the doctrine of secrecy within the department. This not only prohibits any civil servant from revealing, or commenting on, the affairs of the department, but it also legally protects departmental activities from the scrutiny of the Courts of Law. Having regard to the extent to which the internal affairs of companies, corporations, universities, and many other organisations are now exposed to public view, and to legal control, the legal immunity of government departments becomes year by year more anomalous. The problem whether the activities of the state should enjoy a privilege which no other organisation or individual enjoys is not a new one, and few would wish to dissent from the proposition that the stages by which important branches of public policy are formulated should not be exposed to public view. This conclusion has particular force in its application to foreign affairs; but there are also many aspects of domestic policy which enjoy, and deserve, similar immunity. No government, for example, could guarantee the preservation of public order, if confidential policy reports were to be made available to the public. Even in the past, when the activities of government were small, in comparison with those of the present day, the exercise of this privilege was not only resented, but it sometimes produced injustice. Nevertheless, the courts were powerless – or they considered themselves to be – to intervene, and this is the more serious when many branches of governmental activity are not distinguishable in nature from those of an ordinary company, and where they can adversely affect the individual in a similar way. For example, a report of an accident, made by a railway company to the Ministry of Transport, was privileged, even before the railways were nationalised,[1] and in *Duncan* v. *Cammell, Laird & Co.*[2] the House of Lords conceded official privilege in the widest terms, even though it might prejudice the interests of a private litigant, as in this case it did. The case arose out of the loss of the submarine *Thetis* in 1939, and a strong House of Lords of seven members held that documents vital to the claims of relatives of the victims could not be produced, when the Admiralty objected. More recently, however, the courts have shown a less liberal attitude towards claims of official privilege, and have required Ministers to state their reasons for refusing to produce documents.

The problem of departmental secrecy was not considered by the Fulton Committee, since it was regarded as outside its terms of reference, but it would seem logical that if administration gives way to management, and if this is also accompanied by delegation to administrative agencies and to regional authorities, wide areas of official secrecy must be abandoned, since it will be difficult even for a member of a specialist committee to pursue the ramifications of action through such delegations, and even if that is done, there will be difficult questions of responsibility to solve. The abiding danger is that in this vast extension of governmental activity, the rights of the individual will once again be ignored or submerged. Long before these extensions were part of the fabric of Western civilisation, several continental nations had developed systems of administrative law, precisely for defining and regulating the respective rights of official and private citizens. This has necessarily involved making civil servants accountable for faults of administration before administrative courts, and the time is overdue for the consideration of the introduction of such a system in the United Kingdom, coupled with the abandonment of the comfortable blanket of ministerial responsibility for the failings of subordinates.

Such a system implies the existence of a hierarchy of administrative courts, applying clearly understood rules independently of the departments. In his *Law of the Constitution* Dicey proudly explained that no such system (the purpose of which he completely misunderstood) was necessary in Britain because of the supremacy of Common Law. In face of the increasing control exercised by the departments, however, both the supremacy of the Common

---

[1] *Ankin* v. *L.N.E.R.* [1930] 1 K.B. 527.
[2] [1942] A.C. 624.

Law and the sovereignty of Parliament have proved ineffective shields for the ordinary citizen. During the past century there has developed in the United Kingdom a system of very great complexity, which is termed, for want of a better general designation, administrative law, but which differs fundamentally from the *droit administratif* of continental systems, which exists for the purpose of protecting the citizen against illegal activities by officials and organs of the state. The British system is the creation of government departments. It impelled Lord Hewart, then Lord Chief Justice, to write, forty years ago, of this system: 'The conclusion is irresistible that it is manifestly the offspring of a well-thought out plan, the object and the effect of which are to clothe the departments with despotic powers.'

Lord Hewart's attack in *The New Despotism* created, as it was intended to create, a deep impression; and it was followed by a number of others, some of which condemned the system which he had described so clearly, and others which explained and justified it. Underlying Lord Hewart's argument was the conviction that the departments had usurped functions which properly belonged to the courts and to Parliament, and that these powers should be restored to the bodies to which, in his opinion, they properly belonged. In the forty years which have elapsed, the activities, and also the powers, of the departments have increased to a greater extent than even Lord Hewart foresaw, and today the argument is not whether these powers can be removed, but whether they can be controlled, for no Parliamentary session passes without substantial additions being made to them. In fact, it is only too apparent that modern government would be impossible without them, and that, in this respect, the United Kingdom is no different from any other developed society, whether east or west of the Iron Curtain. There is, however, one major difference. In every other modern state these great and all-embracing powers of control are exercised within the framework of a constitution which cannot be altered by ordinary legislative processes.

The reasons for this apparently unlimited transfer of power to the departments are not difficult to discover. Progressive extensions of the franchise, coupled with the rapid development of industry, have produced a total change in the philosophy of government. It is no longer sufficient for the state – or the government – to hold the ring, by the preservation of order, the maintenance of national security, and the administration of justice. It has been called upon increasingly to intervene in every sphere of national life. Today, taxation is openly declared to be a principal method of reducing inequalities, and of redressing social injustices. Industry and commerce are regulated in accordance with a national plan, the object of which is declared to be increased prosperity. No party today can hope to secure public support sufficient to return members to Parliament unless it reiterates its determination to secure or invent increased benefits for all; very great benefits have been secured, but the price is not always appreciated.

In a number of respects, the price is a heavy one, and taxation is only one part of it. It includes a vast extension of bureaucracy, and with it, a progressive removal of choices formerly open to every citizen. Policies originally limited in their application become extended almost to the point of absurdity. To take only two examples: planning in relation to the use of land was first introduced to check unsightly and undesirable developments in areas particularly exposed to them. It now envelops every aspect of land usage to such a degree that the use of a single room cannot be altered without planning permission, whilst the planning authority has power to decide what type of bricks shall be used for the construction of a dwelling-house, and even what colour shall be used for the painting of windows. Again, a national system of education was introduced in the heyday of Liberal rule, to make provision for the education of the children of persons who were unable to provide it themselves. Today, the discussion centres upon the question whether a single, uniform system of comprehensive schools should be imposed upon all secondary education, whether parents, or their elected local representatives, want such a system or not.

These despotic powers (in Lord Hewart's phrase) are exercised in a rarefied atmosphere, remote from the cut-and-thrust of debate in Parliament or from popular control. They are shielded by the fiction of ministerial responsibility to Parliament, and they are, to a large extent, protected from the supervision of the courts. They depend upon statutory concession, but once that concession has been made, control of them is remote and intermittent. Their principal pillars are the power to make rules and regulations; and the existence of administrative tribunals of very many kinds.

The power to make rules and regulations is derived from

delegation by Parliament, and in theory, it is limited by that fact. A great constitutional struggle was fought in the seventeenth century to establish (1) that the Crown had no independent legislative power; and (2) that the legislative power of Parliament was unlimited. This struggle engendered in the Parliaments which followed the Revolution of 1688 a deep suspicion of the practice of delegating legislative powers, so that it was not until the middle of the nineteenth century and the progressive abandonment of a *laissez-faire* philosophy that the practice developed to any marked degree, and when it did, it needed a modernised and efficient civil service both to frame rules and regulations under the powers conceded in Acts of Parliament, and to carry out the policies contained in those rules. As a natural consequence, a more centralised administration, based on Whitehall, replaced a host of localised and semi-autonomous boards, commissions, and similar authorities.

In this sphere, the appetite has grown steadily with what it fed upon. In the last decade of the nineteenth century, the average annual number of rules and orders was approximately a thousand. In the next fourteen years the number increased steadily, the annual average being 1,349. Shortly after World War I, the number exceeded 2,000 for a time, and then dropped to approximately 1,500 a year until 1939. Since 1945, the annual output has increased greatly, not only in the number of rules and orders, but in their content, and also in their range and impact upon the individual citizen. They now exceed 6,000 annually, and in fact, they form the submerged nine-tenths of the legislative iceberg. Nor is this by any means all. Many subordinate bodies, statutory monopolies, and other branches of governmental activity are given powers to make sub-delegated legislation, and upon occasion, no less than six tiers of subordinate legislation have been detected. Still more recently, another and even more objectionable practice has developed – viz. the issue of constant streams of ministerial circulars, containing advice, warnings, and declarations of ministerial policy, which from the formal point of view have no legal force at all, but which those to whom they are addressed ignore at their peril. Year by year it becomes more difficult to determine what is legally binding, and what is not. In this respect, if in no others, the United Kingdom already has some of the characteristics of an authoritarian state.

It is not open to question that delegation, as now practised, is steadily bringing the law into greater disrepute, or that Ministers increasingly tend to regard it as simply one variety of governmental activity. In November 1969 another Lord Chief Justice, Lord Parker, in a case in which bookmakers claimed the benefit of a direction by the Chancellor of the Exchequer, purporting to vary the terms of the Finance Act, 1969, said:

> 'This is about as flagrant as one can imagine. Here is a statute saying exactly what must be done and almost the next day they are doing an utterly different thing.
> This is legislation by Ministerial word. I do not know where we are getting to in this country.'

Manifestly, Parliament cannot control this avalanche of legislation. Much of it is completely unknown to members. Many types of it must be formally presented to Parliament. It is presented, but not read and, as was pointed out in the first chapter, the Committee of the House which is charged with the duty of scrutinising delegated legislation finds it difficult to find sufficient time to discharge its duties efficiently, even with the considerable help of Counsel to the Speaker. It would still be a difficult and time-consuming task if the committee were assisted by a permanent staff of experts. Finally, the purpose of the committee is to establish whether the rules and orders exacted by the departments are within the powers delegated to them. They are in no way concerned with the scope of policies embodied within them.

When the practice of conferring legislative powers upon the departments was in process of development in the two decades before World War I, it was regarded with some complacency, on the assumption (which has proved quite false) that Parliament and the courts could control it. A rude shock was administered to those who had accepted such assumptions so passively, when some early decisions brought to light the extent to which it had already developed. For example, a litigant in *Ex parte Ringer*[1] who sought redress against the Board of Agriculture and Fisheries found that he had been completely deprived of it by an order of that Board, made under Section 39(3) of the Small Holdings and Allotments Act, 1908, which provided that once an order had been confirmed by the Board, it 'shall become final and have effect as if enacted in this Act, and the confirmation by the Board shall be conclusive evidence that the requirements of this Act have been complied

[1] (1909) 25 T.L.R. 718.

with, and that the order has been duly made and is within the powers of this Act'. Such a clause emphasises the helplessness of the courts in such a situation, when there is no written constitution. There were similar miscarriages or denials of justice under other Acts, but in spite of frequent expressions of anxiety by judges both in court and elsewhere, the practice of including such clauses in Acts conferring the power to make regulations upon departments continued. One example, contained in Section 10(6) of the London Traffic Act, 1924, was mentioned by Lord Hewart in *The New Despotism*, but the practice had become common in the years following World War I, and Lord Hewart's condemnation of this authoritarian practice was a general one. It was considered in detail by the Committee on Ministers' Powers which was set up in response to the widely expressed anxiety which followed Lord Hewart's exposure, and they reported that 'finality clauses' of this type were never justified, and also that in any case in which a department declared that such a clause was essential, there should be a period of at least three months, and preferably of six, during which such orders should be before Parliament so that their validity could be questioned. Even at this point the departments did not give way without stubborn resistance, and in 1933, the National Government introduced an Agricultural Marketing Bill containing exactly such a clause. After attacks upon it in both Houses of Parliament, the government eventually agreed that there should be a period of a month during which regulations under the Act could be challenged in the courts. Thereafter, however, this most objectionable clause has been for practical purposes abandoned. It is significant, nevertheless, that the departments devised it; that they were quite plainly attached to it; and that the government of this date at first supported it. Whilst it may also be said that this was an example of public opinion both inside and outside Parliament compelling the Cabinet to modify its attitude, one may question whether public opinion would have been even aware of the danger, but for the publication of Lord Hewart's book, and the Report of the Committee on Ministers' Powers. At the time when the earlier Acts containing such a clause were passed, it certainly was not.

Almost as soon as one device placing the activities of departments beyond the control of Parliament is abandoned, another is conceived. During two World Wars, the executive has rightly and necessarily taken powers to exercise control over the national life and the national economy which would give rise to bitter opposition in time of peace. Such powers have not necessarily been wholly relinquished when the emergency has passed. There was a prolonged struggle after World War I to terminate the powers conferred by Defence of the Realm Acts, and the extremely comprehensive regulations made thereunder. After World War II, the issues were less clearly defined, and the result of the struggle has been less satisfactory. Its implications have been less clearly understood, and the impact upon the citizen less obvious. In 1945 there were in force 342 Defence (General) Regulations and 345 other emergency regulations, and a much greater volume of sub-delegated legislation. Approximately one-third of these ceased to operate at the end of the war. The remainder would have expired in February 1946. They were continued in operation for five years by the Supplies and Services (Transitional Powers) Act, 1945, which also included a power to vary them. Two years later the Supplies and Services (Extended Purposes) Act extended the scope of the earlier Act by conferring on the executive powers:

'(a) for promoting the productivity of industry, commerce and agriculture;

(b) for fostering and directing exports and reducing imports, or imports of any classes, from all or any countries, and for redressing the balance of trade; and

(c) generally for ensuring that the whole resources of the community are available for use, and are used, in a manner best calculated to serve the interests of the community.'

In 1951, at the time of the Korean War, these powers were extended yet again by the Supplies and Services (Defence Purposes) Act, 1951. Of these three Acts, Sir Carleton Kemp-Allen wrote:

'The provisions of these three Acts, taken together, probably represent the high water mark of governmental powers in the whole history of English legislation – at all events, the present writer does not know of any parallel to them. In their economic aspect, it is clear that the phrase "in a manner best calculated to serve the interests of the community" gives *carte blanche* to executive discretion. The words, so far as I know, have never been the subject of judicial interpretation, but it is difficult to see how a Court could attach any meaning to them except that the competent authority was the sole and unassailable judge of the interests of the community. No charter so unrestricted has ever before been conferred by legislation, not even in time of war.'[1]

The correctness of this assessment is illustrated by the fact that in the debate on the 1947 bill in the House of Commons, the Attorney-General, Sir Hartley Shawcross, said:

'The purpose of this Bill . . . . is to ensure that our existing powers – not new powers but powers arising under the existing regulations – are exercisable without the fear that they will constantly be the subject of challenge, and sometimes of frivolous challenge, in the courts.'

And Crossman in the same debate explained that the bill was a necessary step in the march forward to full socialist planning. The connection between this legislation, and much that has been enacted between 1964 and 1969, together with the reorganisation of the Cabinet in October 1969, is plainly apparent. Unfortunately during the thirteen years of Conservative rule which intervened between Attlee's administration and Harold Wilson's, the problem of departmental rules and regulations, though frequently discussed and investigated, remained largely unresolved, for the report of the Committee upon Administrative Tribunals and Inquiries (more commonly known as the Franks Committee), which appeared in 1957, did not deal with this aspect of departmental activity. Its terms of reference were 'to consider and make recommendations on: (a) The constitution and working of tribunals other than the ordinary courts of law, constituted under any Act of Parliament by a Minister of the Crown, or for the purposes of a Minister's functions; (b) The working of such administrative procedures as include the holding of an inquiry or hearing by, or on behalf of, a Minister on an appeal, or as the result of objections or representations, and in particular the procedures for the compulsory purchase of land.'

The effect of this report, which was an important landmark in the development of administrative jurisdiction in the United Kingdom, will be considered shortly, but it is first necessary to say something of the extent to which the ordinary courts can exercise control over the legislative activities of the departments. Whilst the courts have no power at all to question the validity of

[1] *Law and Orders*, pp. 70–71.

any Act of Parliament, they may and do exercise that right in respect of delegated legislation under the doctrine *ultra vires*. By this it is meant that the courts may inquire whether the delegated legislation is within the terms of the grant from Parliament. Hence the former affection of the departments for the now abandoned finality clause. Even without this clause, however, grants are frequently made in such wide terms that the extent of judicial control is minimal. Since in fact regulations and orders will rarely be drafted in direct excess of powers granted, in most cases the utmost that can be done is to investigate whether any forms which may be prescribed by the Act have been complied with. The *Law Reports* contain reports of a number of cases in which regulations have failed to incorporate all the preliminaries which the statute has required, but since grants tend to be made in increasingly wide terms, this type of challenge is not frequent.

A further ground for judicial intervention may be that powers granted for one purpose are being extended and used for a quite different purpose. Many battles have been fought in the courts upon the Housing Acts, under which local authorities were given powers of compulsory acquisition, often at site value only, for certain specific purposes – usually slum clearance and improvement. Gradually, some local authorities discovered that if land were compulsorily acquired under the powers granted by these Acts, it would be used for quite other purposes, or even disposed of at a handsome profit. One such scheme, relating to property in the centre of Derby, came before a Divisional Court of the King's Bench and the Court of Appeal in 1929.[1] It included a provision that the whole of the land could be sold, leased, or otherwise disposed of as the local authority might think fit, and had been confirmed in these terms by the Minister of Health. As Lord Hewart pointed out in the Divisional Court, the Derby Corporation had acquired a valuable piece of land, not for slum clearance, but for the purpose of resale as and when the city thought fit, and when this occurred, the city would make a handsome profit.

On this occasion, the courts were able to hold the scheme *ultra vires*, since its purpose did not fulfil the purposes set out in the Housing Act, 1925. Such victories are often short-lived, however. Subsequent Acts normally concede powers in wider terms. For example, the Housing Act, 1936, provided in Section 25 (3) that a local authority might declare a clearance area, and might then

[1] *R. v. Minister of Health, Ex parte Davis* [1929] 1 K.B. 619.

secure the clearance of the site either by ordering the owner to demolish the buildings, or by purchasing the land themselves, and then either undertaking or securing the demolition of the buildings on it. In *Robins & Son, Ltd.* v. *Minister of Health*[1], the Court of Appeal were faced with an interesting situation, which Lord Justice MacKinnon described in the following terms:

'The appellants (Robins & Son, Ltd.) some years ago bought this property with the sole object of obtaining a vacant site for buildings they wished to erect in the course of development of their existing premises. For some years they had been prevented from carrying out that desire by reason of the operation of the Rent Restriction Acts. The corporation, having power to acquire the site unhampered by those Acts, could and did declare it a clearance area under Section 25 of the Housing Act, 1936. The corporation could then under Section 25(3) secure the demolition of the buildings either (a) by ordering their demolition or (b) by an order for compulsory purchase. Considering that the ground of demolition would be welcomed with alacrity by the appellants, as to whose power to comply with it there can be no doubt . . . one might have expected that an order under (a) for demolition would be made. But the corporation preferred to make an order under (b) for compulsory purchase. Thus they can pull down the buildings themselves, although, as I have said, there is no suggestion that the appellants could not pull down the buildings themselves with equal diligence. The corporation, if they pull them down and acquire the land, can sell it under Section 30 (1)(a), or, without pulling down the buildings having purchased them, they can sell the site under Section 30 (1)(b), subject to a condition that the purchasers shall pull them down. Obviously, in either case, the appellants here, who want to extend their existing premises, must be the most eager purchasers. The possibility in such circumstances of using the provisions of the Act for the indirect purpose of making money out of the appellants is obvious.'

Nevertheless, the Court of Appeal held that it was powerless to aid the appellants.

Inasmuch as the courts have to a very considerable extent been excluded from scrutiny of delegated legislation, is there any machinery whereby Members of Parliament may supply this

[1] [1939] 1 K.B. 520.

deficiency? The answer to this must be, for practical purposes, No. The Select Committee on Delegated Legislation, which reported in 1953, drew attention to the bewildering variety of procedures which are used to bring delegated legislation before Parliament, and to this must be added the fact that most sub-delegation is never, even in theory, scrutinised by Parliament at all. In spite of the proposals of the Select Committee of 1953, which introduced a number of improvements, the procedure can still be described as complex and ineffective, and it becomes even less effective year by year. One major reason for this is the volume of material which in theory should be scrutinised. Another is the necessity for familiarity with the procedure appropriate to the rules or regulations to be considered. For example, the procedure of the House of Commons makes it virtually impossible for a member to raise for discussion the provisions of an order or Statutory Instrument which is to be 'laid' before the House, without further qualification. If it is provided that an Instrument shall be laid before the House, but shall not come into operation until the expiration of a specified period of time, then the order will take effect automatically, unless a member moves to set it aside. Other orders may come into force at once, but they may be annulled in consequence of a 'prayer' to that effect being made within a specified period; and there are a number of other varieties of procedure. One needs to be something of an expert in Parliamentary procedure to be aware of the possibilities, and it is not surprising that members very rarely avail themselves of them, independently of the recommendations of the Scrutiny Committee. One is regretfully compelled to conclude that the control of Members of Parliament is as limited, and as ineffective, as that of the courts.

To this one should add that the torrent of delegated legislation passes almost completely unremarked by the Press. Here again, unless expert staffs were retained, their labours would be largely in vain, for even if excessive powers of delegation were detected, the effects of them would often require a good deal of explanation. When a major scandal, such as the extortionate levies imposed by the Land Commission, arises, the Press is not wanting, although even here, the legislation which conferred these powers was only criticised after its effects had become apparent.

The governmental activity of the departments extends far beyond the making of rules and orders. It involves making innumerable decisions affecting private rights. Sometimes such decisions can only be made after public inquiries have been held. In such an inquiry, every person whose interests may be adversely affected has the right to put forward his objections. Such statutory inquiries are normally compulsory where land is to be acquired for a public purpose, and the procedure for such inquiries will usually conform with the requirements specified in the Acquisition of Land (Authorisation Procedure) Act, 1946. The proposal to acquire compulsorily must be advertised in the local Press, and the owners and occupiers of the land to be acquired must be notified. The period during which objections may be lodged (often twenty-one days) is specified, and if there are objections, there must be an inquiry, which is usually held in public, and in which objectors are not infrequently legally represented. An inspector appointed by the department conducts the inquiry, and submits his report to the Minister, who may accept, modify, or reject it. There is no appeal from the Minister's decision, but if the Minister confirms the proposal to acquire, a person aggrieved may apply within six weeks of confirmation to the court for an order to set aside the decision on either of two grounds: (a) that it is *ultra vires*, or (b) that the statutory procedure has not been strictly complied with.

Public inquiries are now a normal feature of departmental activity, and the very great preponderance of them not only conform to the general conception of fair dealing, but also attempt to balance the policy embodied in the proposal with the views and interests of those who are affected. They are not legal decisions upon conflicting rights, however. They are determinations upon questions of departmental policy, and for this reason, if for no other, the courts must necessarily stand on the side-lines. One of the many clear illustrations of this is to be found in *Franklin v. Minister of Town and Country Planning*.[1] This case arose out of the designation of Stevenage as the first of the new towns to be constructed under the New Towns Act, 1946. A public local inquiry had been held into deep-rooted local objections, but the Minister, who had visited Stevenage shortly before the Act was passed, had said in a speech on that occasion that the Stevenage scheme was going forward. After the inquiry, he confirmed the inspector's report in favour of proceeding, and an attempt was made to set it aside on the ground of bias. The House of Lords held, however, that in confirming such an order under the New Towns Act, 1946, there was no judicial or quasi-judicial duty imposed upon him,

[1] [1948] A.C. 87.

and accordingly the question of bias was irrelevant. The sole question was whether in fact he had considered the report and the objections. The effect of the decision, it will be seen, is to reduce the public inquiry in such a case to a merely formal exercise.

Under some other statutes, Ministers have power – often without appeal – to make decisions directly affecting the rights of individuals or of public authorities. The enormous bulk of these decisions, and the extent to which they can adversely affect the rights of others, has produced a mass of learning, and a number of legal decisions, often very technical, upon the nature of the decision which the Minister makes. Attempts have been made to classify the decisions as judicial, quasi-judicial, and administrative, and to specify the essentials of each, so far as the protection of the rights of the parties is concerned. The question is one of great obscurity, upon which lawyers disagree sharply. The source of the difficulty is that the departments are combining in themselves functions which the purist would wish to see separated. They make the rules, they hold inquiries, decide private rights, and carry out policies. It is not surprising, therefore, that courts and public alike regard some of these activities, at least, with deep suspicion, or that the public feels itself powerless in front of this ever-advancing juggernaut.

Altogether distinct from the decisions implicit in policy-making are the decisions of the many and varied tribunals which have been created by the departments, in the implementation of these policies. It need occasion no surprise that these conform to no pattern, that their procedures vary widely (some, for example, permitting legal representation, and others not), that until recently, provision for appeals was unsatisfactory, or that a number of these courts were long distrusted by ordinary citizens, who regarded them simply as outposts of departmental activity, and by lawyers, since these tribunals had grown up outside the ordinary judicial system. Much has been improved since effect was given (in the Tribunals and Inquiries Act, 1958) to the report of the Franks Committee, which decisively affirmed that 'tribunals should be regarded as machinery provided by Parliament for adjudication rather than as part of the machinery of administration', and it was in accordance with this principle that important reforms were introduced. One of them was the provision that there should be an appeal from decisions of tribunals to the ordinary courts on points of law. Another was that two advisory Councils on Tribunals, one for England and one for Scotland, should be established, to keep the constitutions and working of these tribunals under continuous review, and to advise whenever it was proposed to create a new type of tribunal. Today, these tribunals are a necessary and valuable part of the administrative process, and in recent years, relatively few criticisms of their operation have been made. Today, the still unresolved problem is the extent to which ministerial decisions affecting private rights can be controlled, or even subjected to scrutiny.

The Franks Committee's terms of reference did not extend to maladministration by the departments, where this did not involve a breach of the law. In this respect the United Kingdom still lags behind many other nations, and in particular France, for it is in this sphere that *droit administratif* affords a protection of which the English legal system has, until recently, been quite innocent. Although the Franks Committee owed its establishment to one notorious act of maladministration, its terms of reference nevertheless excluded this type of official activity from its purview – a circumstance which leads one to reflect that even today, the nature of administrative activity is only very imperfectly understood in the United Kingdom. The echoes of Crichel Down have long since died away, but the episode still has important lessons for the present day. A landowner had made persistent efforts to recover from the Ministry of Agriculture land which the Ministry had requisitioned during the war, which it no longer needed for the purposes for which it was requisitioned, but which it now proposed to put to quite other uses. Once again one detects the besetting sin of some departmental activities – the use of powers conferred for one purpose, for quite other purposes. Due to the persistence of the landowner, and to the vigilance of the Press, this abuse of power attracted great publicity, and was ultimately rectified, and the Minister of Agriculture resigned. But the episode left the uncomfortable suspicion that many other 'Crichel Downs' had remained unredressed, because the persons involved had been less persistent, or because the matter had not caught the eye of the Press. Moreover, the upshot of Crichel Down in 1954 was not altogether clear. Following a debate in the Commons, it was understood that in future a department which had requisitioned land for wartime use should offer it back to its original owner when that use was exhausted. Nevertheless, on 26 January 1969, *The Sunday Telegraph* reported another case arising out of the requisition by the

Air Ministry in 1938 of thirty-six acres of land from a farmer at Compton Bassett. In spite of repeated requests, the Ministry of Defence had failed to offer to sell the land back to the son and heir of the original proprietor, but having no further use for it, was proposing to sell the land by auction for the extraction of sand – a transaction which, if completed, would yield a profit of over 2,000 per cent for the Ministry.

It was the suspicion that there were many such cases as Crichel Down which ultimately led to the establishment of what is popularly termed an 'Ombudsman' (from the Danish term for such an official) by the Parliamentary Commissioner Act, 1967. The primary function of such an official is to receive complaints against executive action, and to investigate them and report. All complaints are made, not directly to the office of the Commissioner, but to a Member of Parliament by a person or some public body (other than a local authority) who claims that he has suffered injustice in consequence of maladministration. The work of sifting such complaints has now become a major task for Members of Parliament, but it has the effect of largely relieving the Commissioner of frivolous complaints. In introducing the Act, Crossman explained that it 'provided the backbench Member, once he knows how to use it right, with a new and powerful weapon – the possibility of impartial investigation into alleged maladministration'. Whilst the Commissioner's functions cover the activities of most departments, they exclude foreign and diplomatic affairs, the hospital service, criminal matters, and commercial transactions, as well as the activities of public corporations. Moreover, the Commissioner may not investigate any action in respect of which the complainant has a remedy by way of an appeal to a tribunal established by statute or royal prerogative, or by way of proceedings in a court of law, unless in the circumstances it is not reasonable to expect the complainant to have taken such proceedings. As Sir Dingle Foot pointed out in an article in *The Times* of 8 September 1969, this innovation for the first time provides that someone acting on behalf of a citizen can penetrate the real motives behind an official decision. A proposal to extend this system to local government, where it is needed to an equal or greater extent, is also being considered.

The value of this development cannot be doubted, and it may be assumed that as the institution becomes more generally known, greater use will be made of it. Nevertheless, it must be reiterated

L

that the Commissioner cannot challenge powers which have been properly exercised, and that, for this purpose, 'properly' means 'within the terms of the grant'. In other words, although the British citizen is at last beginning to possess rights against the executive which have long been enjoyed abroad, the real problem which remains is the extent to which Parliament still delegates, and is prepared to continue to delegate, power to the departments, in a political system which does not enjoy the protection of a written constitution.

X

Home Rule – for Whom?

EVER SINCE Gladstone's conversion to Home Rule in 1886, Home Rule has been recognised as a continuing issue in British politics. Almost inevitably, in consequence, it has failed to secure the consideration which such a major issue deserved. All three parties – Conservative, Liberal, and Labour – have blown hot and cold. They have revived the issue when some group became inconveniently vociferous, or when the progress of a nationalist movement threatened the entrenched position of the parties, only to forget it again once the tide had receded. It was also felt, until recently, that Scotland and Wales, for example, had a good deal to lose by the establishment of a separate political identity, and further, until recently, Scottish and Welsh nationalists have been dismissed in England as amiable middle-class cranks, intent on reviving more obsolescent languages.

Nevertheless, even when the Liberal Party, under Gladstone's tutelage, turned reluctantly towards Home Rule for Ireland, it was recognised that if this case were conceded, there was no logical reason why the same course should not be followed in respect of Scotland and Wales. As early as 1879, in a speech at Dalkeith during his first Midlothian campaign, Gladstone had said: 'If you ask me what I think of Home Rule, I must tell you that I will only answer you when you tell me how Home Rule is related to local government. I am friendly to local government. I am friendly to large local prerogatives. I intensely desire to see Parliament relieved of some portion of its duties. I see the efficiency of Parliament interfered with, not only by obstruction from Irish members, but by the enormous weight that is placed on the time, and shoulders, and minds of those who now represent you. We have got an overweighted Parliament, and if Ireland or any other portion of the country is desirous and able so to arrange its affairs as to take the local portion of some part of its transactions off Parliament, it would liberate and strengthen Parliament for imperial concerns. The Imperial Parliament must be supreme in these three kingdoms, and nothing that creates a doubt on that supremacy can be tolerated by any intelligent or patriotic mind. But subject to that limitation, if we can make arrangements under which Ireland, Scotland, Wales, and portions of England can deal with questions of local and special interest to themselves more efficiently than Parliament now can, that, I say, will be the attainment of great national good.'

Gladstone's pamphlet, *The Irish Question*, published after the general election of 1886, invited Liberals to begin thinking on this very topic, and largely in consequence of this direct encouragement, the Scottish Home Rule Association was founded in 1886 in Edinburgh. The response on both sides of the border was encouraging. Indeed, there were not a few in England who thought that it would be safer to try a measure of devolution in Scotland, rather than support Gladstone's determination to permit Ireland to govern herself.

The alliance between the Liberal Party and the Scottish Home Rulers was close – indeed many Scottish Home Rulers were Liberals, and a number of them were Liberal Members of Parliament. This was not only because the Liberal Party was committed to the grant of Home Rule to Ireland. As in Wales, the bulk of the constituencies returned Whig and Liberal members consistently from 1832 to 1918, and liberalism was the normal allegiance of the Scottish professional classes, and especially the lawyers. So much was this the case, that when the Conservatives were in power, they sometimes found difficulty in filling the Scottish law offices in the government with lawyers of suitable calibre, and their difficulties in making suitable judicial appointments from the ranks of Scottish lawyers who were Conservatives were even greater. Even such a diehard Tory as Lord Halsbury was compelled to look outside the ranks of the Scottish Conservatives for Scottish judges.

In 1889 the Scottish Liberal Association at its annual conference passed a resolution which advocated the establishment of 'Home Rule legislatures' on a federal basis for Scotland, England, Ireland, and Wales, but it coupled with it a proviso embodying the accepted Liberal premise that Irish Home Rule should have priority.

In consequence, the cause of Scottish Home Rule lacked political validity. The Scottish members were Liberals first, and a number of them were Home Rulers afterwards. There was little discussion of the form which it would take, the general assumption being that the Irish model would be followed. The Scottish case was kept alive by occasional resolutions in favour of Scottish Home Rule, which were carried by the Liberal Party whilst it was in office, but nothing followed, as the bitterness of the conflict over Irish Home Rule increased. However, as the Irish Home Rule Bill at last seemed assured of success after the Liberals had curtailed the powers of the House of Lords by the Parliament Act, 1911, the question of Scottish Home Rule began to receive the attention of the government. In particular, Winston Churchill, then Home Secretary, went to work on it. He laid his finger on a problem which has bothered many people since that date. It is not too difficult to contemplate the creation of Parliaments for Ireland, Scotland, and Wales. The problem which appears difficult is England. In a federal system, it would still be overwhelmingly stronger than the other three. On the other hand, it is difficult to think of an English Parliament largely duplicating the work of a federal Parliament. To this one further point may be added. Almost miraculously, the establishment of a separate Parliament and government in Northern Ireland has not involved the adoption of a written constitution for the United Kingdom, but it would be a practical impossibility to establish legislatures in Scotland and Wales without doing so; and when ultimately devolution is faced, as faced it must be, it may well be that it will go a good deal further than Scotland and Wales. Churchill in 1911 showed very considerable insight when, in his report to the Cabinet, he suggested that the United Kingdom should be divided into ten areas, having regard to geographical, racial, and historical considerations, even though he was only thinking of legislatures for three of them.[1]

The result of Churchill's examination of the problem appeared in Asquith's speech, on introducing the Government of Ireland Bill in April 1912, for on that occasion he explained that it was only the first step in a larger and more comprehensive policy, and he added that greater administrative devolution was already overdue. This prompted a group of Scottish Liberal members in 1913 to introduce a Scottish Home Rule Bill, proposing the revival of the Scottish Parliament, but subordinate to Westminster, and a Scottish Privy Council. There was no chance whatever of the bill becoming law, and by this date, with the Irish Question apparently further from solution than ever, and with war clouds spreading over Europe, the government could scarcely be accused of breach

[1] H. J. Hanham, *Scottish Nationalism*, p. 97.

of faith for failing to implement the policy which Asquith had outlined in 1912. Accordingly, Scottish Home Rule remained dormant until 1919, when a Scottish Home Rule Bill was again introduced. The government, however, was now a coalition of Liberals and Conservatives, and the Conservatives were as opposed to Home Rule for Scotland as they had previously been, and still were, to Home Rule for Ireland. The question was referred, together with the general question of devolution, to a Speaker's Conference, whose report, issued in 1920, attracted little attention and was promptly forgotten. The cause of devolution, discarded without a backward look by both Conservatives and Liberals, was taken up, but again not as an urgent question, by the Labour Party. Indeed, the decline in the Labour Party's interest began almost immediately, with the return of the Clydesiders to reinforce their Welsh allies from the coalfields in the steadily increasing numbers of the Parliamentary Labour Party. With the advent of a Labour government to power, it was thought that more immediate and tangible benefits could be secured from it than from local legislatures still to be established. And so, once again schemes of devolution were placed in cold storage until in the sixties both the Scottish and Welsh Nationalists at long last succeeded in returning their first members to Westminster, and votes at successive Scottish and Welsh by-elections showed that both movements were rapidly becoming firmly entrenched in the minds of Scottish and Welsh voters. The Labour government took the hint and set up a Royal Commission to study (once again) the whole question of devolution in the British Isles. Presumably this was intended to be a holding operation, until a general election showed whether the return of Scottish and Welsh Nationalists was a permanent feature of the Westminster scene, or a passing phase.

The most serious criticism which can be made of such procrastination is that it gives force and, ultimately, more general support for the arguments of extremists, who assert that nothing can be won by argument, but only by violence; and they point to Ireland as the supreme example of this. Unfortunately, the history of the struggle for Irish independence, and of the emergence of Ulster, offers support to this view. It also illustrates the maxim that, where the recognition of national claims is ignored or delayed, those who advocate an orderly transition are almost invariably supplanted in popular estimation by those who favour more extreme measures.

It is highly significant that Gwynfor Evans, M.P., president of Plaid Cymru, the Welsh Nationalist Party, giving evidence (in Welsh) before the Royal Commission in September 1969, said that whilst the party was not asking for absolute independence for Wales, they would insist on Commonwealth status, making England and Wales equal partners, in no way subordinate to one another, within a Britannic Confederation. These proposals he would expect to see put into force when the majority of Welsh seats at a general election were won by Welsh Nationalists, whose views would then be reinforced by a referendum of the Welsh people. In similar vein, the Scottish Nationalist Party informed the Commission at Edinburgh, immediately afterwards, that Scotland would make a unilateral declaration of independence as soon as a majority of Nationalist candidates was returned after a general election.

The Irish Home Rule Bill which was introduced in the House of Commons in 1912 was, by modern standards, a limited measure. There was to be established in Dublin a Parliament of two Houses, having control over Irish affairs, but with so many reserved questions, and with the superiority of Westminster so firmly written in, that it would have little more authority than a County Council. Even those Irish groups who accepted it, did so only on the basis that it was a first instalment: but in the six counties of Ulster, it was rejected outright as a threat to be resisted by force, if necessary. In the debate on the committee stage of the bill, in June 1912, voices were already being raised, suggesting the exclusion of Ulster from the bill – a suggestion which Asquith firmly rejected. By the time the Home Rule Bill, with the assistance of the Parliament Act, 1911, was placed on the statute-book in September 1914, both Nationalists and Ulstermen were armed and ready to fight; but since World War II was already in progress, this domestic problem was placed in cold storage, and the operation of the Home Rule Act itself was suspended by the government until twelve months after the end of the war. In his announcement of this postponement, Asquith gave an indication that he had at last yielded to some extent over the question of Ulster. At any rate, he pledged the government to the introduction of an Amending Bill dealing with Ulster before the Home Rule Act should be brought into operation.

By the time the war was over, the initiative in securing Irish independence had passed almost entirely from the hands of the Nationalists into those of Sinn Fein, as the general elections of

December 1918 clearly showed. Further, the opportunities offered by the progressive withdrawal of troops and even police from Ireland, to increase the armies on the Western Front, were eagerly accepted by the I.R.A. to disrupt all public order by direct action, including assassination, the burning of property, and attacks upon trains and post offices. It was in this atmosphere that Lloyd George introduced, in 1920, a new Government of Ireland Bill in place of the still-born, and now almost forgotten, Home Rule Act of 1914. Under the new bill, there were to be two Parliaments in Ireland, one for the six counties in Ulster, and the other for the rest of Ireland, but in addition, there was to be a Council of Ireland, consisting of members nominated by the two Parliaments, 'with a view to the eventual establishment of a Parliament for the whole of Ireland, and to bringing about harmonious action between the Parliaments and governments of southern Ireland and northern Ireland, and to providing for the administration of services which the two Parliaments mutually agree should be administered uniformly throughout the whole of Ireland'. The bill also provided that if the two Parliaments agreed, by absolute majorities, they should have power to replace the two Parliaments by a single Parliament for the whole of Ireland. As in the earlier bill, defence and foreign relations were excluded from the competence of the two Irish Parliaments. The question of customs and excise was to be settled by agreement between the two Irish Parliaments and Westminster, and Ireland was to make a contribution to the imperial expenditure of £18 million per annum.

In 1920 these proposals fell far short of the aspirations of the Nationalists, who promptly rejected them, and after two years of bitter civil war in Ireland, the Free State came into existence, and was ultimately replaced by the Republic. In Ulster, the bill was accepted without great enthusiasm, and the provisions relating to Northern Ireland were the only part of the Government of Ireland Act, 1920, which ever came into operation. This Act, with the Ireland (Confirmation of Agreement) Act, 1925, and the Northern Ireland (Miscellaneous Provisions) Act, 1928 and 1932, and the Northern Ireland Act, 1947, embody the present constitution of Northern Ireland. In the Ireland Act, 1949, recognising the establishment of the Irish Republic as an independent nation, it is provided in Section 1 (2): 'It is hereby declared that Northern Ireland remains part of His Majesty's dominions and of the United Kingdom, and it is hereby affirmed that in no event will

Northern Ireland or any part thereof cease to be part of His Majesty's dominions and of the United Kingdom without the consent of the Parliament of Northern Ireland.'

Since Northern Ireland is part of the United Kingdom, it is neither a Dominion nor a self-governing colony. Its position is analogous to that of a state within the American Union. The Parliament of Northern Ireland comprises the Queen, the Senate, and the House of Commons. The Senate consists of the Lord Mayor of Belfast and the Mayor of Londonderry, together with twenty-four senators elected by the House of Commons for eight years, half of them retiring every four years. The House of Commons comprises fifty-two members, elected on the same franchise as that for the United Kingdom Parliament. The maximum duration of the life of Parliament, as of the United Kingdom Parliament, is five years. It may not alter the constitution which, it has been seen, is based on statutes of the United Kingdom Parliament. Its competence is to make laws for the peace, order, and good government of Northern Ireland. Certain topics are reserved for Westminster, in which, in consequence, twelve representatives of Ulster constituencies continue to sit. Matters excepted from the competence of the Northern Ireland Parliament are matters relating to succession to the Crown, peace and war, defence, foreign and Commonwealth relations, naturalisation and control of aliens, external trade, coinage, wireless telegraphy, patents, and copyright. In addition, certain matters are reserved to the United Kingdom Parliament. These include taxation (including income tax and customs and excise) and postal services. So far as taxation is concerned, United Kingdom taxation in Northern Ireland is appropriated to Northern Ireland, which, in addition, receives a small annual subsidy from Westminster.

If it should be thought that a law passed by the Northern Ireland Parliament exceeds its competence, or conflicts with a law of the United Kingdom Parliament in an area reserved to it, the Governor of Northern Ireland, or the Home Secretary in London, may require the Judicial Committee of the Privy Council to pronounce upon its validity, and occasional cases of this kind have arisen, and have been so dealt with.[1]

The government of Northern Ireland is carried on by a Cabinet, headed by a Prime Minister, and depending on the support of the majority party in the House of Commons. Owing to the special

[1] e.g. *Re a Reference under the Government of Ireland Act 1920* [1936] A.C. 352.

circumstances in which Northern Ireland, as a separate political entity, came into existence, the majority party has always been the Unionist Party, and it would conform more closely to conditions elsewhere if there were a regular alternation of governments. The disturbances of 1969–70 have shown very clearly that some kind of party equilibrium is required to remove the feeling of exclusion which the Nationalists possess. The difficulty is to establish such an equilibrium, in an area in which there is a long legacy of political and religious cleavage, and in which Unionists cling so tenaciously to their separate political identity.

In addition to a legislature, Northern Ireland also possesses a separate judicial system, comprising a High Court and a Court of Appeal. From the Court of Appeal, there is a further appeal to the House of Lords. These courts, unlike their English counterparts, hear cases in which the constitutionality of Northern Irish legislation may be questioned. So far as law in general is concerned, the law of Northern Ireland, being based, as in England, on the Common Law, shows little variation from English law. In the main, Northern Irish courts tend to follow the decisions of English courts, subject to the qualification that they must also apply the provisions of the Northern Irish constitution and the legislation enacted thereunder.

In the fifty years which have elapsed since the establishment of the Northern Irish constitution, there have been until 1969 remarkably few problems arising from the relationship of Northern Ireland to the United Kingdom as a whole. Upon occasion, Labour members of the House of Commons have challenged the right of Ulster to be represented at Westminster, when Ulster has its own Parliament, but such representation is a necessity, so long as the competence of the Northern Irish Parliament is limited, and the Parliament at Westminster has overriding powers. Indeed, the principal difference between the relationship of Ulster to the United Kingdom, and that of a state of the American Union to the United States, is that the position and competence of an American state are defined and governed by a constitution which cannot be changed either by the legislature of the state or by the legislature of the United States, but only by a special constitutional amendment; whilst the position of Ulster can be changed at any time by the legislature at Westminster; although Westminster would depart from all constitutional precedents if it so legislated without first discovering the wishes of the people of Northern Ireland.

The prolonged disturbances in Northern Ireland during 1969 have unfortunately shown that self-government has failed to resolve the deep-rooted antagonism of Protestant and Catholic communities, which is partly the product of Ireland's stormy history, and partly the consequence of partition. But it cannot be assumed that without a Northern Irish constitution, the situation in Ulster would have been better, and on the other hand, the relations between the United Kingdom and the Irish Republic might have been considerably worse.

Indeed, the acute political tensions which have afflicted Northern Ireland since August 1969 have illustrated the very great value to be derived by both Northern Ireland and the United Kingdom from this form of devolution. The problems, unhappily, are Irish problems, but they have not intensified party conflict in Great Britain, as they have so often done in the past. All parties have united in accepting the fact of Northern Irish self-government, and it may be added that the Home Secretary, James Callaghan, acted with complete constitutional propriety in the nature of his intervention. The fact of an overriding United Kingdom responsibility for the maintenance of law and order has been accepted, and assistance in its preservation has been freely given. He was able to act in association with the Northern Ireland government in this, and in other matters, and he was able to offer further assistance in the resolution of the antagonism between the Protestant majority and the Roman Catholic minority. Even in Northern Ireland, his intervention has been recognised as disinterested – in sharp contrast with the Irish view of British intervention prior to 1914. Whatever the outcome of these unhappy disturbances, it can at least be said that the constitutional relationship, based upon a written constitution for Northern Ireland, has proved equal to the strain.

Perhaps the principal reason why this has been the case is that the preservation of the existing state of affairs has been desired on both sides of the Irish Sea. Although Northern Ireland controls its own internal affairs, and although its governments since 1920 have been uniformly Unionist, it has followed the social legislation of England, whether enacted by Labour or Conservative governments, very closely, in response to the pressure in Northern Ireland for uniform standards in social benefits. On the other hand, the pattern of education is different. There are separate arrangements with the voluntary schools, made necessary by religious differences, and Northern Ireland has as yet been spared the interminable wrangles on comprehensive schools.

The 1920 settlement originally contemplated that Northern Ireland would pay a *per capita* 'imperial contribution', retaining the remainder for local administration, taxation being the same as in Great Britain. The sharply rising cost of the social services common to both have made this arrangement unworkable. There is now a common economic policy, and a subsidy is paid to Northern Ireland in respect of its particular problems, e.g. a higher rate of unemployment, and the 'remoteness' of its agricultural industry. As a result of that common policy, Northern Ireland participates in the price support system for agriculture, and in the annual price review, although Northern Ireland has established out of its own revenues advisory and research services. As J. P. Mackintosh, Labour M.P. for Berwick and East Lothian, pointed out in *The Times* of 6 August 1968, one lesson of this form of devolution is that the pressure for common social standards and for economic development leads to the establishment of common policies with Whitehall.

This circumstance, which J. P. Mackintosh stresses, is probably the answer to the claims of the Scottish Nationalists for total independence. Although in October 1969, the Scottish Nationalist Party produced a survey of Scotland's probable economic situation after independence, showing that Scotland would have a surplus on current account of £159 million, and a surplus of £21 million on current and capital accounts combined, these figures seem unduly optimistic, and they were refuted by a Scottish budget prepared by the Treasury on the eve of the Gorbals by-election, at the end of October 1969. The Treasury calculated that Scotland, in 1967–68, had a deficit of £130 million, compared with a surplus for the United Kingdom as a whole, and that there would have been a borrowing requirement of £466 million. Of course there can be (and is) argument about the meaning of these figures, and about Scotland's proportion of the National Debt servicing defence and other matters; but the Northern Irish experience suggests that the balance is tilted against Scotland, and would remain tilted, and that, with a struggling economy, the drift to England would not be reversed, and might even be accelerated. This, of course, does not take into account the possible changes in the economy which an independent Scottish government might introduce; but it is unlikely that these could greatly affect the situation for some time to come. Nor does it take into account the fact that in Scotland today the achievement of self-government is not seen primarily as an economic question, but as a debt due to Scotland's history and past achievement.

Constitutionally, there would be no difficulty whatever in applying the Northern Irish solution to Scotland and Wales, and possibly to other parts of the United Kingdom. Indeed, so far as Scotland and Wales are concerned, it would simply carry further a process of devolution which is already far advanced. A Secretary of State for Scotland has existed since 1885, and as the years have passed, there has been transferred to him practically all the departments of public administration in so far as they relate to Scotland, and since 1939, they have been concentrated in a single building in Edinburgh. So considerably has the work grown in recent years that he is now assisted by three Under-Secretaries, and the staff of the various departments is constantly expanding. It would be a simple and logical step to separate out from this complex administration four main departments of state – Home, Education, Agriculture, and Health – and to place a Minister responsible to a Scottish legislature in charge of each of them. There exists a strong reason why such a change should occur. The constantly expanding activities of the Scottish Office provoke frequent criticism, and sometimes resentment. In the minds of some, it is a kind of faceless juggernaut, remote from, and indifferent to, public opinion. In the minds of others, it is the instrument of English 'imperialism' in Scotland. In fact, the Scottish Office is staffed by Scots, is responsible to Scots, and the legislation which it puts into force is framed by Scots in London. There seems to be no reason whatever why Englishmen should be blamed or, very infrequently, praised, for its existence and application.

One illustration of this attitude towards the Scottish Office is furnished by the Orkney and Shetland Islands, two hardy and self-reliant communities who would provide a further problem of local autonomy, should Scotland become formally responsible for her own destinies again. In both these communities, there are thriving local industries, which are placed in jeopardy by continuing increases in the cost of transport to the mainland. Recently, there have been strong manifestations of resentment in the islands for the neglect from both the Scottish Office and Westminster, from which, it is alleged, they have suffered. Neither Edinburgh nor Westminster has been indifferent to the position of the islanders, but what has been done has been regarded as quite in-adequate. The result has been the birth of a separatist movement, which looks back to the mortgage and later cession of the islands by the King of Norway to Scotland five hundred years ago. Today, there is a reawakened interest in Scandinavian associations, in the history of the Vikings, and in the ancient laws, customs, and lang-uage of the Orkneys. With the example of the fully self-governing Faroe Islands between them and Norway, this development is one that cannot be ignored, although once again it illustrates that, in the context of the states of Western Europe, the resurrection of these long-ignored nationalisms is often a prolonged love affair with the past, in which legendary heroes often take on the characteris-tics of Arthurian Knights. This was very plainly evident in August 1968, when the Orkneys commemorated the five-hundred-years-old pledge of the islands by Christian I of Denmark and Norway.

The autonomy of Scottish administration is being matched today by a similar autonomy in Wales. There is a Secretary of State for Wales, and the various departments are gathered together, as in Scotland, under one roof in Cardiff. There is one important differ-ence. Since Wales has been incorporated into England since the reign of Henry VIII, there is no separate legal system or judiciary, and laws applicable to England automatically extend to Wales also. Once again, as in Scotland, there is growing impatience with control and incessant interference from Whitehall. As in Scotland the extent to which the Welsh control their own affairs is concealed by the absence of a local legislature, to which the heads of the various administrative departments would be responsible.

These are by no means all the constitutional problems which exist within the British Isles. The Isle of Man is not technically a part of the United Kingdom. It was a separate kingdom, of which the Earls of Derby were lords, until it was surrendered to George III in the second half of the eighteenth century. It has its own administration and its own legislative assembly – the House of Keys – and for that reason, it does not send any representatives to Westminster. The Manx, like the inhabitants of the Orkneys and Shetlands, have strong Norse affiliations, and they possess a dis-tinctive language which, after almost being forgotten, is now in com-mon use again. One may, perhaps, notice the anomaly that the Isle of Man has always possessed self-government, whilst Scot-land and Wales have not. Even so, there is today serious dissatisfac-tion in the island about relations with London. It has never been doubted that the Parliament at Westminster has an overriding power to legislate for the Isle of Man, but by custom it has not done so without consultation, and it has been content to leave Manx affairs exclusively to the islanders. In recent years, there has been much irritation, however, arising from the application to the Isle of Man, without consultation, of British Acts governing broadcasting, having as their object the suppression of unauthorised radio stations, one of which was situated in a vessel just off the Manx coast. This episode is regarded as one of a series of interventions from London, by various government departments, which appear to be an inevitable consequence of the assumption of more and more governmental functions by the Welfare State. In September 1968, the disappointment over the refusal of the Postmaster-General to make concessions produced a suggestion that the dispute should be referred to an international court.

The position of the Channel Islands in some ways resembles that of the Isle of Man. Again, forming no part of the United Kingdom, and being originally part of the Duchy of Normandy, they have retained their own distinctive language, customs, and identity for nine centuries. They do not form a single unit, since both Jersey and Guernsey have their own legislatures and administration and even some of the lesser islands, e.g. Alderney, possess a limited degree of autonomy within the islands. So far as the Channel Islands are concerned, there was resentment that the impact of entry into the Common Market upon them was never considered, and also that the Sanctions Order in respect of Rhodesia was applied to them without consultation, but they too have felt the general pressure of the departments in Whitehall.

For some time past talks have been in progress between representatives of the States of Jersey and the Home Office, and the islanders have made it clear that they do not wish to see any modification of a status which they have enjoyed for over seven centuries. At the same time, they wish to have that status embodied in a constitutional document, making a clear division of functions between the United Kingdom and Jersey. For this reason, they have recently strengthened their links with the Isle of Man, which is in a somewhat similar position. Both also have been disturbed by the extension of the activities of the Royal Commission on the Constitution to them, regarding it as quite incompatible with the bilateral talks which they have been carrying on with the Home Office. Further difficulties lie ahead, more especially as the Jersey

Constitutional Association strongly asserts that, as the Channel Islands have never had representation at Westminster, no legislation of the United Kingdom should have any validity there unless it is approved by their assemblies. They point out, moreover, that they are far more capable of managing their own affairs than many overseas territories which have been granted complete independence during the past twenty years. Possibly the suggested applications both of the Isle of Man and of the Channel Islands for separate admission to the United Nations need not be taken seriously, but it is indicative of a growing concern for the preservation of separate identities which have strong roots in history. Where such a separate identity exists within the framework of an existing European state, the determination to preserve it has grown in direct proportion to the progressive efforts of the state to establish uniformity, and causes of friction have been numerous, as a direct product of the continuing control which the state now exercises over almost every aspect of the life of its subjects. Coincidentally, the resentment which this universal control provokes is now concentrated upon a single institution – 'the government' – within which comprehensive term there is included Parliament, the departments of state, their huge and ever-growing army of civil servants, and the nationalised industries. Since the state has eagerly entered more and more fields of social activity, it cannot complain too much at the resentment which its intrusion evokes. On the other hand, a situation in which the separation between government and governed has never been clearer is not a satisfactory one, and it cannot be expected to endure indefinitely, especially in areas in which there is a clearly-defined national consciousness.

The problems of devolution discussed in this chapter are not peculiar to the United Kingdom. Across the Channel, the Liberation Front of Brittany is now an active and powerful organisation, provoking frequent disturbances. It turned General de Gaulle's visit there at the end of January 1969 into a prolonged demonstration for independence, or for greater autonomy. Like Welsh and Scottish nationalism, Breton nationalism is partly compounded of historic pride, partly of resentment that there is such continuous interference from Paris, and partly of the conviction (which may be ill-founded) that Brittany has been neglected in the industrial development which has occurred in recent years. The activities of the Breton nationalists are being watched with close attention in Cornwall, where the Sons of Cornwall, whilst rejecting the violent tactics of their Breton neighbours and kinsfolk, have recently stated Cornwall's case for greater autonomy in plain terms.

The sudden rise to significance of these numerous and localised nationalisms was succinctly explained by Wilfrid Sendall in an article in the *Daily Express* of 22 July 1968:

> 'No matter how efficient government is made, it will not provide a substitute for the emotional deprivation which is at the heart of these nationalistic protests. What people are crying out for is a sense of identity in a community small enough for them to influence, yet large enough to influence the whole state'

in an era in which every trend has been, and continues to be, towards centralised standardisation.

In any scheme of devolution within the British Isles, there remains, as Winston Churchill pointed out in 1911, the problem of England. It would, of course, be possible simply to establish subordinate Parliaments in Scotland and Wales, leaving Westminster as it is. This would be, in effect, to extend the Northern Irish pattern, by the addition of two more Parliaments, and it may be that this plan has the greatest prospect of being put into force. It should be recognised, however, that such limited Home Rule would not now satisfy the aspirations of either Scottish or Welsh Nationalists, and that if it is long delayed, it may prove as unacceptable as the Home Rule Act of 1920 proved to Eire. A criticism of possibly greater force is that it not only denies Home Rule to England, permitting her affairs to be greatly influenced by Welsh, Scots, and Irish, but it fails to take account of the tensions which are progressively building up within England itself, as a consequence of the ineffectiveness of local government, its powerlessness to deal with modern problems – for example, traffic – effectively, and of its almost total dependence for finance upon Whitehall. Since the structure of local government has proved inadequate, and since the local government electorate fails to take it seriously, it has become a common fashion to suggest that regionalism may prove more effective and more popular. It was with this object that the Greater London Council, operating over a wider area, was substituted for the London County Council, and that there was a redistribution of functions between the Council and the councils of London boroughs which had been recreated as larger units of local government.

It is probably too early as yet to pronounce upon the success or

M

failure of this first experiment in regionalism. It has patently provided an organisation in which the problems of the greater London area can be considered as a whole. On the other hand, there have been criticisms that the volume of work to be done by its committees, which must meet for frequent and lengthy sessions in the daytime, excludes exactly those younger and more vigorous men and women who should take an active part in the shaping of policy, since they cannot afford to give the time on a voluntary basis, thus limiting the selection of candidates for election, and at the same time necessarily leaving the formulation of that policy to full-time paid officials of the Council, who alone have time to make a full investigation of the problems awaiting solution. It is significant that four young Conservative councillors, all businessmen who were elected to the first Council, indicated that they were not prepared to stand again for these reasons, although they were satisfied that the Council itself was a valuable development in regional government. The problem is one of effective local government, coupled with greater decentralisation, and it affects the whole of the United Kingdom. It is a quite distinct problem from that of a separate government reflecting nationalist aspirations. It would, for example, exist as much in Scotland, after the establishment of a separate Parliament as before it, and it involves many matters which have no connection at all with any separatist tendencies – for example, communications, unemployment, the location of industry, the construction of airports, and housing. Accordingly, this problem will be considered separately in the next chapter.

XII

The Reorganisation of Local Government

ALTHOUGH THE habit of self-reliant local government has often been stated to be a notable English achievement, in its present shape it is, unlike the English constitution, exclusively the product of legislation, and it is manifestly in an advanced state of decay. Local government elections commonly attract no more than a third of the electorate, and the supply of persons able and willing to undertake the duties of local government councillors is limited. The work, especially of chairmen of committees, can be exacting and time-consuming, and recently a group of energetic young members of the Greater London Council announced that their onerous duties as councillors interfered with their business activities to such an extent that they were not prepared to offer themselves again as candidates. This is the more to be regretted, because the population governed by the Greater London Council exceeds that of the combined populations of Norway and Denmark, and the Council's budget is greater than that of Portugal. In the past, membership of the Council has sometimes been combined with membership of the House of Commons, and more frequently has served as an apprenticeship for national politics, but the indications are that this will be less frequent in the future. Non-availability of the best candidates affects all parties, and is not confined to any social class. Many employers are unco-operative in their response to suggestions that the duties of their employees should be so arranged that they can take part in local government. Quite plainly this unco-operative attitude has been strengthened by the increasing pressures upon commercial and industrial activity, and by the high level of taxation, and the incidence of Selective Employment Tax. Accordingly, the average age of local government councillors tends to be high, and council work tends to be looked on as a suitable activity for those about to retire, or who have recently retired, and for housewives and clergymen. Finally, there is a strongly held conviction that so much local government is now firmly controlled from Whitehall, and that the relations of the Council with Whitehall are so complex that only the Council's permanent officials are able to handle them effectively, so that there is little scope for the initiative of the individual councillor. The demand for greater independence from Whitehall is general, but the prospect of achieving it seems remote, more especially as many local government activities depend upon Whitehall for financial support, which is only granted if what is to be done conforms with departmental specifications. From the centre, local government authorities are seen as the agents through which national policies are executed. This has been particularly evident in recent years in the long struggle between local authorities and the Department of Education over the universal establishment of comprehensive schools. Moreover, in recent years the power to sell council houses to tenants has been removed from local authorities, whilst the central government now decides the rent structure for council houses, and it is the central government again which prevents local authorities from providing mortgages for older houses.

The tradition that English local government is firmly rooted in local life is derived from pre-Conquest England. In later Saxon times, the shire-meeting was a body fully representative of the shire, and through it, the sheriff governed the shire in conformity with long-standing customs, of which the representative freeholders who met in the shire court were the custodians. A very great variety of business was transacted in the shire court, and at a later date, it was found convenient for the Knights of the Shire who were to represent it in Parliament to be selected there. The Normans found the shire assembly of great value for fiscal and judicial purposes, and also as a check upon the power of their feudal barons. The decay of the shire court was gradual, but it was greatly accelerated by the establishment of a national body of Justices of the Peace, who remained the chief administrative officers of the shires until the end of the eighteenth century. They were responsible for the preservation of order, for the apprehension of offenders, and for the trial of them in petty sessions and quarter sessions. In the sixteenth and seventeenth centuries, a considerable volume of other functions was imposed upon them. They administered the poor law, and attempted to enforce the statutes of labourers. Some functions were plainly beyond their capacity, and gradually other boards of administrators came into existence – for example, Commissioners for Turnpikes. The old shire assemblies had disappeared, and as yet, there was no disposition to establish new ones.

Local government in the cities and towns developed upon quite different lines. Those of greatest importance sought to obtain, as early as possible, charters exempting them from feudal jurisdiction, establishing their own separate commission of the peace, together with the control of public order which this implied, and, where the borough returned members to Parliament, the election of borough representatives. During the Middle Ages, many towns were controlled by merchant guilds, but when these decayed in the sixteenth century, many boroughs became close corporations, election being by the members of the corporation. Where the borough returned members to Parliament, membership of the corporation became a financially valuable privilege, and in the eighteenth century a number of corporations regularly offered their right to Parliamentary representation to the highest bidder. Prior to the Reform Bill of 1832 county administration, though inevitably biased because of the class from which Justices of the Peace were drawn, was freer from corruption than the administration of many boroughs, some of which, though they had decayed to vanishing-point, still returned two members to Parliament. Writing in the university session 1887–88, immediately before the Local Government Act of 1888 created county councils, Maitland commented:

'During the last two centuries Parliament has continued to heap work upon the justices. The Commission of the Peace has become the one vigorous and healthy local institution. The old communal courts of the hundred and shire had fallen into utter decay; they had become at best courts for petty debts held by the under-sheriff. A non-representative assembly of freeholders was an antiquated institution quite unsuited to the wants of the time, and no attempt was made to introduce representative government into local affairs. The municipal corporations again were becoming utterly unfit for any governmental work. With the view of getting favourable parliaments the Tudor and Stuart Kings had spoilt the constitution of the boroughs; by their charters they had vested the local government along with the parliamentary franchise in small oligarchical bodies – mayor, aldermen and councillors – who had the right to fill up the vacancies in their own bodies. These bodies became hopelessly corrupt; some belonged to the Crown and returned to parliament the nominees of the ministry; others belonged to great land-owners, Whig or Tory, and returned their candidates; others sold themselves from time to time in open market. The justices, on the other hand, were competent members of the ruling class, and nothing was more natural than that a parliament of land-owners (and remember that in the eighteenth century members of the House of Commons had to be landowners) should trust to them all manner of duties and governmental powers.'[1]

But even as Maitland wrote, the day of the justices, except as magistrates, had already passed, and with a few broad strokes, Maitland outlined the salient features of this great revolution. The Reform Act of 1832 dissociated Parliamentary representation from borough charters. The great Municipal Reform Act of 1835 swept away the old borough constitutions, replacing them by a uniform model, with elected councillors, and with power to grant the same constitution to other towns not hitherto incorporated. The governing body of every borough was given power to make by-laws for the government and good order of the borough, and every borough was required to maintain its own police force, and to make proper provision for the paving and lighting of its streets. Until the Local Government Act of 1888 there were variations in the extent to which boroughs were exempt-ed from the jurisdiction of the county justices. After 1888 these variations were preserved in respect of the new County Councils. But some boroughs and cities were placed outside the government of the county for all purposes, and it therefore happened that county council government was least effective in counties in which the number of county boroughs was large.

Before the end of the nineteenth century, a number of other elective local authorities had been created by statute. Below the county councils, there were urban and rural district councils, for areas too scattered and sparsely populated for incorporation as boroughs. There were Poor Law Unions, with elected Boards of Guardians of the Poor. These were abolished in 1929, and their functions transferred to the local authority. For a time, there were elected School Boards, which were abolished in 1902, when their functions were transferred to the local education authority, i.e. the county or county borough council or, for elementary educa-

[1] *Constitutional History*, pp. 493–4.

tion, the borough council. There were also elected Highway and Sanitary Boards, whose functions were in 1894 transferred to district councils; and finally, Burial Boards, whose functions were taken over at the same time by those shadowy authorities the parish councils, provided they adopted the Burial Acts. If the parish council did not, the urban district council could apply to become the sole burial council. Maitland summed it all up in these words:

'We are becoming a much governed nation, governed by all manner of councils and boards and officers, central and local, high and low, exercising the powers which have been committed to them by modern statutes.'[1]

Once again, however, Maitland was able to discern the line of future development, when he expressed the hope that some future lecturer, explaining English local government, would be able to point to a coherent system of all-purpose authorities. One by one, the special boards have disappeared, and the powers of local authorities have become more comprehensive, as the range of public services which they provide has increased. Coincidentally, the revenues which they derive from local rating have become increasingly inadequate to finance them. One of the major problems, for which no agreed solution yet exists, is the equitable division of taxation between central and local authorities. Subsidies from central government now amount to approximately 40 per cent of the budgets of local authorities.

In spite of the limited rationalisation of local authorities which has been carried out in the past half-century, one of the major difficulties remains the number of local government bodies, all of them (except parish councils) employing full-time staff, coupled with the very great disparities in size and revenue which exist between them. Another difficulty is that many problems, e.g. crime or transport, cannot today be considered by a single authority in isolation from other neighbouring authorities. Transport, in fact, complicates the local authority's problems in a number of ways. It is increasingly common for a businessman to have his place of business in a city, and his home twenty or thirty or more miles away. Today there are businessmen who commute regularly from one major city to another. In these cases, their attachment to the locality in which they may happen to live is slender in the extreme.

Still more recently, a further development has complicated the

[1] *Constitutional History*, p. 501.

pattern of local government. This has been the intrusion of regional boards, which are subordinates of central government departments, and which are not elected, but are responsible to Whitehall. Foremost amongst these are the regional hospital boards set up by the former Ministry of Health, and the local committees established by the Ministry of Agriculture. There are, in addition, numerous commissions for particular activities, e.g. forestry, national parks, and ancient monuments. This tendency to intrude outposts of central government into local affairs depresses the status of local government still further, and emphasises their subordination to policies centrally established.

The existing pattern of local government in the United Kingdom is certainly a bewildering one. In England and Wales, there are at present 58 county councils and 82 county boroughs. Below the county councils there are 270 boroughs, 535 urban district councils, 473 rural district councils, and finally, over 7,500 parish councils. Scotland has 31 county councils and four city councils, 21 large burghs, 176 small burghs, and 198 district councils. In the English counties, populations vary from 27,950 (Rutland) to Lancashire with two-and-a-third million. In Scotland, one large county, Lanarkshire, has a population of almost 600,000, whilst three counties have less than 20,000 inhabitants. Moreover, there is a nationwide tendency for populations to drift from rural counties into the cities, which is counterbalanced to some extent by the movement of persons employed in cities into outer suburbs and adjacent small towns which, for administrative purposes, may be beyond the city limits.

Few would challenge that local government in the United Kingdom is wasteful of resources, and that its efficiency varies very greatly from authority to authority. Three departments – the Home Office, the Department of Education and Science, and Health and Social Security – all consider that the minimum size of a local government unit for the services for which they are responsible should have a population of somewhere between 200,000 and 250,000.[1] In the areas of housing and transport there are far too many authorities, many of them too small to make any effective contribution. All of them require consultation, and their existence is in itself an almost insurmountable barrier to the changes which are already overdue.

The existing system has numerous other failings. There are

[1] J. P. Mackintosh, *The Devolution of Power*, p. 22.

shortages of staff in a number of authorities, and a steady drift towards higher-paid authorities. Again, the work of all councils other than the smallest is divided between committees supervising a particular department – e.g. housing, transport, or health. The work of the committees is conducted in isolation, and sometimes in secrecy, until it is brought before the full council. There can be little question that the committee system in local government has been extended to the point where its inefficiencies are all too obvious. One of the major questions awaiting solution in local government is the reorganisation of the procedure of local government bodies.

In recent years there has not only been continuous public discussion of the problem of reorganisation, but also investigation by committees of different aspects of it. In such discussions, much attention has naturally been given to the size of units, which might be expected to be more satisfactory units than those which now exist, but there has been less consideration of the functions which these units may be expected to discharge, particularly in relation to the central government. Are they to act primarily as outposts of Whitehall? If so, then the difficulties of attracting elected members to local government bodies may be expected to increase, since they will operate merely as a façade behind which a central policy is being carried out. This, in turn, raises the question whether such uniformity is always desirable, or whether it will indefinitely be regarded as acceptable. If, on the other hand, it is desired to give expression to regional, or even larger, variations of pattern, then efficiency must come to terms with local patriotism. From the standpoint of Whitehall, it would all be so much simpler if men and women were simply computers, into whom information could be fed, and from whom the 'right' answer could eventually be obtained. It is because they are so varied in their reactions that the task of government is so complex. Everyone today is involved, whether or not he would choose to be, yet the rapid development of the activities of central government has left the ordinary citizen with the conviction that he is the object of policy, with no part in its formulation, and with little chance of 'contracting out.' It is, therefore, not without importance that there has been in recent years a significant number of those, not exclusively young, who have embraced non-participation in the normal activities of society as a comprehensive creed. It is, in essence, a total rejection of the paternalist philosophy and the minute regulation of the modern state.

Unfortunately, neither the activities of central government, nor the investigations of a variety of committees, limited by their terms of reference, inspire any belief that there is a desire to re-establish local government upon vigorous local support. The drift is steadily towards uniformity and central planning, and starting from the assumption that local government is demonstrably failing to fulfil its existing tasks, it has adopted the policy of creating an increasing number of regional boards, which are simply branches of Whitehall, and the existence of which curtails the freedom of local government bodies. There has also been a marked affection for advisory bodies which, having no backing in popular election, can be ignored if their advice should prove to be at variance with the general lines of policy laid down in Whitehall. Even in spheres which traditionally belong to local government, for example in education and housing, the voice of Whitehall, and of the appropriate Minister, is heard to admonish local authorities to toe the ministerial line, reinforced by threats of legislation, if existing powers fail to produce the required compliance. Such an attitude can scarcely do other than provoke local resentment, nor fail to depress the status of local government still further.

Whilst it would be quite untrue to say that over-centralisation is responsible for the existence of Home Rule movements in Scotland and Wales, and possibly in other parts of the United Kingdom, it is not open to question that it has been in part responsible for the rapid and considerable increase in support which they have received. Nationalism has deeper roots, and evokes stronger loyalties, than regionalism, but it is certainly not accidental that the 'Men of Cornwall', Yorkshiremen, Lancastrians, and Northumbrians today all experience feelings of separate identity which have been dormant since the Industrial Revolution. One natural consequence of the attempt to impose the drabness of uniformity from the centre, is renewed pride in separateness, and any attempt to create a successful pattern of local government must today take notice of it. One of the most interesting features of the United States, so far as the European visitor is concerned, is that its citizens have a dual pride – in the United States itself, and in their own state, even though the majority of the states were created in recent times, possess mainly artificial boundaries, and have been settled without regard to any specific ethnic plan. This pride is directly linked with the vigour of state institutions, and with the fact that state Governors, and Senators and assemblymen, have a definite role to play in political life, and not infrequently pass from state to national office. The American constitution has prevented the national government from draining away the vigour of local institutions.

In a recent study of local government and its reform, entitled *The Devolution of Power*, J. P. Mackintosh, M.P., pointed out and analysed the possible alternatives to the present system. One solution would be to create between thirty and forty city regions, with populations of 250,000 or upwards. Another would be to create between ten and fifteen large regional units (which would include Wales, Scotland, and south-eastern England as single units). In both cases, he contemplates that it would also be necessary to create second-tier units, to which a number of the more localised services could in turn be delegated.

Each solution has advantages and disadvantages. City governments have, on the whole, been more vigorous, and more firmly rooted in popular support, than county councils. Large cities tend to act as magnets for the services of the surrounding country. Moreover, it is significant that central government has seen in city-based units of this size the most convenient instrument for carrying into execution national planning policies, centrally decided. In addition, the division of the United Kingdom into a limited number of areas grouped round one or more large cities would bring to an end the distinction between county and borough which although it has a long history, is no longer appropriate in a highly mobile society, whose social needs continue to increase, without regard to local government boundaries. One has only to think, for example, of the present-day problems of supplying the population and industries of a large city with water, or with adequate communications, to appreciate the strength of this line of argument. It has a logically tidy appearance. Nevertheless, the resistance to the elimination of historic units, with their traditional boundaries, is real and deeply-felt. In part it is based upon the apprehension of country-dwellers that their interests would be subordinated to the inhabitants of cities – an apprehension which could well be translated into reality simply by the preponderance of representation of city populations in local councils.

There are further objections. The forty-two city pattern for Great Britain could only be achieved by gross distortion of the facts of geography. It is certainly not true that the whole of Great Britain is focused on a small number of large cities, and a future in which it was no more than the background of these cities seems bleak in the extreme. There are other difficulties. The regional councils which some Ministries have established for some areas, in which unified planning and development is being undertaken, do not correspond, even broadly, with the enlarged city areas of this proposal, and their existence, then as now, would condition and limit the activities of the authorities of the enlarged cities. Whether, in these circumstances, city government would attract a better type of councillor, or whether the inhabitants of the outlying areas would feel any identity with the inhabitants of the city itself, is at least doubtful. Mackintosh's summing-up of this type of proposal is that it will really bring about very little improvement. Nominated bodies, meeting in private on regional councils, will still carry out the policies of Whitehall, independently of local elected councils, whose efficiency will be determined by the extent to which they carry out central directions. Proposals such as this will not bring about the revitalisation of local government, which is so long overdue.

A strong body of opinion has advocated the establishment of a small number (between fourteen and sixteen) large regions or provinces – a solution which has been pressed by both *The Economist* and *The Observer*. Without entering upon a discussion of the requirements for regional planning for different purposes – e.g. industry, transport, housing, amenities, education, and so forth – it is difficult to state precisely what areas are most suitable, but it may be suggested that they must be large enough, and strong enough, to take over the functions now being exercised by non-elective regional councils. This, in turn, would involve a greater flexibility between Whitehall and the regions than now exists, or is even possible under the present system. Whilst the main principles of policy must always remain with the central government, the formulation of plans in conformity with them would be a function of the regions. Police, transport, education, and agriculture are all matters in which a greater degree of regional autonomy is desirable. If it is thought right that these, and other matters, should be administered regionally (if Wales and Scotland can be regarded for this purpose as regions), it is difficult to see why it should not be appropriate also for large regional areas in England.

It is at this point that one is compelled to consider other factors, which have greatly complicated all discussions of local government reorganisation. At bottom, the question is whether the central government wants vigorous local government or not. Local government in England will never be vigorous unless local councils are convinced that they have the power to decide. If decisions are really made in Whitehall, and the function of councils is to carry them out, then there is little value in being a councillor. It is noticeable (as Mackintosh points out) that the enlarged city solution has been favoured in Whitehall precisely because it would prevent any further devolution of power to local councils, and also because the powers of regional boards would necessarily remain as they are. No opportunity has been lost to pour ridicule upon the conception of 'mini-Parliaments' in the regions, yet Parliaments for Scotland and Wales now appear to be just over the horizon, and the principal question which remains for settlement is the extent of the powers which will be delegated to them. Regionalism is, of course, something quite different from nationalism, and the pattern of a United Kingdom in which extensive 'devolution' of power has occurred need not be a uniform one. Mackintosh has outlined a scheme for democratically elected assemblies, sitting for a fixed term of three years, for mini-regions. Quite clearly, he has been influenced in his formulation of the scheme by the Stormont pattern, and he would sweep away the ineffective committee system, substituting for it an executive which included a Prime Minister and a Cabinet of about eight Ministers. Under such a system Mackintosh believes (and the present writer agrees with him) that local government would at last be given a reason for existence. Further, the experience of other countries in which such a delegation of power exists suggests that provincial assemblies would attract members comparable with those who are returned to Westminster, and that local elections would once again become a matter of concern for the ordinary citizen.

However attractive such proposals might appear to be, they must today be considered in the light of the Maud Report, which appeared in June 1969. In an acute analysis in *The Times*, shortly after its appearance, Mackintosh pointed out that, in spite of the chorus of praise with which its appearance was greeted, the report really made the worst of both worlds, because the commission was handicapped by its terms of reference, since they had been asked to consider local government 'in relation to its *existing* functions,' and accordingly, their recommendations upon the size and character of the local authorities were based upon this limitation. 'Had the terms of reference,' he wrote, 'included functions recently taken away from local government, new tasks allocated to *ad hoc* authorities and any aspects of central government that might be better administered in localities, then the optimum population figures would have been very different and the most desirable structure for a reformed system would have been profoundly altered.'

The report has done lip-service to both schools of thought which have been mentioned above. It proposes the establishment of fifty-eight units, each with a single-tier authority and a population of between 250,000 and 500,000 (the size, it will be noticed, that several government departments cite as the most efficient for their purposes, in so far as these were being discharged by local authorities). Where the population is predominantly rural, these approximate in size to large counties, and they will include all the functions of local government at present discharged by a variety of locally elected bodies, with the reservation that a few, mainly advisory, functions will be reserved to boroughs within their areas. Accordingly, the civic life of many of the lesser towns of England – towns of the size of Stratford-upon-Avon, Abingdon, Boston, Warwick, or Launceston, which have strong links with national history – will for practical purposes disappear. This is a heavy price to pay for an uncertain industrial future.

Above these fifty-eight units of local government, to which should be added the three metropolitan areas of south-east Lancashire and north Cheshire, Merseyside, and the West Midlands, there are proposed eight large indirectly elected regional councils, but it is not altogether easy to see who will be attracted to serve on them, since, as proposed by the report, their function is simply to advise and co-ordinate in an environment which is already littered with a mass of non-elective boards and commissions which are regional or functional projections of Whitehall. The report was careful to exclude the possibility of equipping the provincial boards with additional functions, and it does not discuss in detail their organisation and procedure, regarding these as questions which could be affected by the work of the Crowther Commission on nationalism and devolution.

As seen by the report, the provincial councils are to be bodies elected by and from the ranks of the new, single-tier authorities. Their task, as described by the Local Government Correspondent of *The Times*, is seen as 'setting the strategic framework for the operational authorities,' thereby replacing the present regional economic planning councils, and working in close association with central government, in laying down guide-lines for the sixty-one authorities, in accordance with which the latter could develop their own plans and settle their own priorities. It looks like a bureaucrat's idea of heaven. What is abundantly evident is that at no stage is it proposed that the shadowy provinces will enjoy an independent existence even though their work as a buffer between the new local government units and central government will at times be important and exacting.

The three metropolitan areas would contain twenty district councils -- four for Merseyside, nine in the south-east Lancashire and Cheshire area, and seven in the West Midlands – but elsewhere the councils of the larger cities as they now exist would disappear. This would mean that the vigorous city administrations of cities such as Newcastle, Leeds, Sheffield, Bristol, Nottingham, and Derby would be replaced by ghostly advisory bodies. Obviously the oft-repeated phrase 'local self-government' in the report needs very close examination before it can be accepted.

Not unnaturally, the local authorities who would be adversely affected by the Maud Commission's proposals have reacted sharply against them. Even the cities which, if anyone, would be the beneficiaries of such a change, have looked coldly at them. Elsewhere, opposition and resentment have been more strongly expressed. In the Isle of Wight, for example, memories have been revived of the island's successful resistance to the proposal to subject it to the Hampshire County Council in 1889. This is simply one illustration of an affection for traditional county and local boundaries which has affected the development of the national character, and which cannot be lightly dismissed. A Roses cricket match between Yorkshire and Metropolitan Areas Nos. 22 and 23 somehow fails to stir the imagination.

It is not the purpose of this chapter to examine in detail the proposals contained in the Maud Report. They are the product of much thought, and if adopted, they would reduce the number of local authorities from 1,210 to about seventy. There would be considerable reduction in the numbers of persons permanently engaged in local government, and it is reasonable to suppose that those who remained, and who served the larger units, would be more efficient than many of those who served the large number of smaller units. But the effect of this from the standpoint of democratic control of local government remains doubtful. City councillors know their cities; whether unit councillors will know their units so well is uncertain. If they do not, then more and more of the actual decisions will fail to be made by the permanent officials. In spite of reiteration of the phrase 'revitalisation of local self-government' in the report, it is not at all easy to see how its proposals will give birth to the loyalties without which local self-government cannot exist. One is left with the uneasy conviction that once again a report has reached what, from the standpoint of central government, is the right answer – a streamlined system capable of responding more promptly than the existing units to the directive from Whitehall.

XIII

Trade Unions and the State

THE YEAR 1971 will be an extremely significant one in the history of English trade unionism, for it will be the centenary of the passing of the great Trade Union Act of 1871, an Act which has so decisively influenced the nature of their subsequent development. For the nation as a whole, trade unions have become a stabilising and remarkably conservative element. For millions of workers (whether 'working men' in the old-fashioned sense or not) the union has become the one vigorous institution, directly protecting their personal interests, in a society in which the ineffectiveness of other voluntary organisations in face of the constant inroads of the state is only too apparent. Further, the collective outlook of the unions – especially the big ones – continues to be deeply influenced by their history. For them 'the struggle' is still going on, even though almost all of the objectives for which unions were originally formed have been largely achieved. That struggle, whether still in progress or not, has taught them one great lesson – that power counts for a good deal more than good intentions, and that great power is enjoyed by organised labour.

The modern history of trade unions begins with the repeal of the Combination Laws in 1824 – a decisive change which was primarily due to the enlightened attitude of Huskisson and Sir Robert Peel in Lord Liverpool's government, and the efforts of Joseph Hume and Francis Place for the workers. Trade unionism had been a consequence of the industrial revolution and the growth of the factory system, which in turn had been responsible for the final breakdown of a system of regulating wages and prices by Justices of the Peace which had its origins in the scarcity of labour which followed the Black Death in 1348. Workmen themselves were reluctant to see the old system finally disappear, and there is a petition of labourers, as late as 1796, asking for a further statute to regulate wages and prices. By this time, however, the attempt had been finally abandoned, and the first modern trade unions struggled into existence, at almost the moment when the outbreak of revolution in France, followed by the long-drawn-out war with Revolutionary and Napoleonic France, threatened the national existence. The result was a series of repressive enactments which made combinations of workers either to withhold labour or to alter wages illegal. These greatly inflamed antagonism between employers and workers. There were outbreaks of violence, boycotting and blacklisting, and heavy sentences of imprisonment and transportation for those who defied this harsh code.

With its repeal in 1824, it was hoped that a new chapter in industrial relations had opened, but there followed a wave of strikes for higher wages, which caused the government in the following year to pass a second Act, which, whilst maintaining the principle that combinations of workmen for altering the rate of wages, or lessening the hours of employment, were not punishable under statute or Common Law, nevertheless enumerated a number of acts, and in particular the use of force or threats, for achieving the objects of such a combination, which would constitute punishable offences. Whilst as yet unions enjoyed no legal status, they were no longer illegal, and in the three decades which followed the repeal of the Combination Laws, they grew and prospered, adding to their original objects provision for old age, sickness, loss of employment, and similar occurrences. For these activities unions could obtain registration as Friendly Societies under the Friendly Societies Act of 1846. By 1861 approximately 2,000 such societies had been registered in 405 towns, with an annual income of over £1 million.

There were in the mid-nineteenth century other major developments, one of which was the movement towards the federation of local unions within a particular trade, these having been separate organisations. One of the earliest was the Amalgamated Society of Engineers, and as these great federations progressively came into existence, with the possibility of bringing industries to a halt on the national scale, employers became alarmed, and once again the activities of trade unions were exposed to attack in the courts.

In 1847 Baron Rolfe had decided in *R.* v. *Selsby*[1] that workers who kept within the terms of the Act of 1825 committed no offence when they met together to discuss their contemplated action, but other judges were a good deal less liberal. Already in 1832 Patterson J. had decided that colliers who threatened to strike, unless the

[1] (1847) 5 Cox. 495.

manager discharged seven men, could be convicted of conspiracy,[1] and Lord Chief Justice Campbell in *R. v. Rowlands*, in 1851,[2] also held guilty of criminal conspiracy a body of workers in Wolverhampton who had induced workers either to leave, or to refuse to enter, the service of an employer. Baron Bramwell explained the doctrine of criminal conspiracy in classical terms in *R. v. Druitt*[3] in 1867:

'If any set of men agreed among themselves to coerce the liberty of mind and thought [of another] by compulsion and restraint, they would be guilty of a criminal offence, namely, that of conspiring against the liberty of mind and freedom of will of those towards whom they so conducted themselves.'

The importance of this statement of the law was emphasised by the fact that it was accepted both by the Royal Commission on Trade Unions which reported in 1869, and whose report was the starting-point for the Act of 1871, and by the House of Lords in *Larkin v. Long*.[4] Criminal conspiracy had unhappily taken deep root, and the limitations imposed by the Act of 1825 were now apparent. The minority report observed:

'We find a series of decisions by which the following acts have been held punishable: – Giving an employer notice that his workmen will strike unless he dismisses particular workmen;[5] telling a workman that he will be struck or considered a "black";[6] ordering a picket to shout "ba-ba blacksheep";[7] coercion not extending to abusive language or gestures;[8] and telling a workman that if he goes to work "there will be a row".'[9]

Certainly these decisions appeared to press down the scales firmly against the unionist, but there was another side to the picture. The Royal Commission had been set up by Lord Derby's Conservative government in 1867, largely in consequence of outrages which had taken place during strikes in Sheffield and Manchester. The evidence brought before the commission very clearly

[1] *R. v. Bykerdike* (1832) 1 M. & Rob. 179.
[2] (1851) 5 Cox 436.
[3] (1867) 10 Cox 600–601.
[4] [1915] A.C. 829.
[5] *Walsby v. Anley* (1861) 30 L.J.M.C. 121.
[6] *Perham's Case* (1859) 5 H. & N. 30.
[7] *R. v. Hinchcliffe*, August 1868.
[8] *R. v. Druitt* (1867) 10 Cox 592.
[9] *R. v. Hamilton*, 28 August, 1868.

proved the existence of coercion of a very different character from the examples cited in the report of the minority. In Sheffield the practice of rattening – i.e. of abstracting or spoiling the tools of workmen who failed to comply with orders to strike – was general, whilst at times the violence used extended to explosions, maiming, and even murder. Nevertheless, the commission rightly rejected any assumption that violence was an inherent element in the activities of trade unions. The majority report accepted that trade unions had two main objects: (1) they are friendly or benefit societies, and (2) they are trade societies, whose function is to promote the interests of members, particularly against 'the undue advantage which the command of a large capital is supposed by them to give to the employers of labour'. The commission therefore recommended that there should be a change in the legal status of trade unions. The law must be clarified so that unions could not be regarded as existing for unlawful objects. The right to combine must be fully recognised, and so also must the right of a worker to abstain from joining a union, if he wished. At the same time, the law relating to molestation and obstruction should be retained, but subject to this, no combination for the regulation of the conditions of employment should be illegal merely because it was in restraint of trade.

Gladstone's Liberal government, which had replaced Lord Derby's in December 1868, decided to give effect to all the main recommendations contained in the majority report, and this was achieved in two Acts in 1871. The first provided, as the report had suggested, (1) that the purposes of a trade union should not, merely because they were in restraint of trade, be regarded as criminal, nor should they make void any agreement or trust; (2) that a trade union might register itself, and thereafter, it could vest its property in trustees, capable of suing and being sued on all matters touching the property, right, or claim to property of a union; and (3) that the treasurer and other officials of a registered union should be made liable to account, and persons embezzling the funds or other property of a union should (for the first time) be liable to prosecution. The Act also provided that no trade union was capable of being registered as a company under the Companies Acts, a provision which, though not of great practical importance, emphasised that although unions now enjoyed a limited legal existence, they had no distinct legal personality such as a corporation enjoys.

Much of the good which was achieved by the passage of this

Act was stultified by the passing at the same time of the Criminal Law Amendment Act, 1871, which gave statutory force to the second group of recommendations in the majority report, relating to violence, threats, and molestation. The violence and oppression which had occurred during some of the strikes whilst the commission was actually in session were responsible for the firmness of the Liberal government in passing this Act, but it has been common doctrine with the Webbs and other historians of the trade union movement that it was a deliberate blow aimed to cripple trade union activity. There is, however, another view, which has been concisely expressed by Sir William Holdsworth:[1]

> 'Their criticisms of the Act really amount to a claim to exempt from punishment acts which violated the rights of others, if done in the course of a trade dispute – to a claim, in other words, for a relaxation of the criminal law in circumstances which called for its stiffening. Why the offences described in the Act should be less offensive because committed in the course of a trade dispute it is difficult to see; and it is equally difficult to see why trade unionists should be privileged to do criminal acts, even if they aimed at attaining a laudable object, or why they should take offence at being compelled to keep within the law.'

The view which Holdsworth expresses is without question the view which was adopted by the judges in the years which immediately followed the passing of this Act.

The legislation of 1871 had, from the legal point of view, some other unusual features. The first two sections of the first Act, which legalised trade unions by providing that their purposes were not in restraint of trade, would, if they had done no more, have had the effect that contracts between members and their unions, and between one union and another, would have been legally enforceable. This was desired neither by employers nor by workers, and accordingly Section 4 provided that these contracts were not to be directly enforceable by the courts. This clause was to be productive of much future difficulty, and it also initiated the process by means of which the activities of trade unions were progressively exempted from legal control.

The year following the passing of these two Acts was followed by an unusual number of widespread strikes (including one of agricultural labourers, now organised by Joseph Arch), and the

[1] *History of English Law*, XV, pp. 79–80.

granting of numerous wage increases, and public alarm grew when they spread to the London bakers, to the police, and the stokers of gas companies. The result was a series of repressive decisions in the courts. In the most famous of them, a prosecution arising out of the strike of the gas stokers, *R.* v. *Bunn*,[1] Brett J. directed the jury that an agreement of workmen to control the will of their employers, and an agreement to induce men to break their contracts with the object of securing the reinstatement of a fellow-workman, amounted to criminal conspiracies, even though no violence was used. He added that the agreement to control the will of an employer was 'molestation and obstruction' within the meaning of the Criminal Law Amendment Act, 1871, and after the jury had found the five accused guilty, they were sentenced to a year's imprisonment. The agitation which followed this, and similar trials, eventually induced the Disraeli government in 1875 to pass the Conspiracy and Protection of Property Act. This repealed the Criminal Law Amendment Act of 1871, abolishing the doctrine of criminal conspiracy, but at the same time penalising the wilful and malicious breach of a contract of service by workmen, where the probable consequence was to deprive a town of gas or water, or where the probable consequence was to endanger human life, or to cause serious bodily injury, or serious harm to valuable property. For the wider provisions of the Act of 1871 relating to violence, threats, and molestation, there was substituted a section of much more limited effect, to which there was added a proviso that 'attending at or near the house or place where a person resides or works, or carries on business, or happens to be, or the approach to such a house or place, in order merely to obtain or communicate information shall not be deemed as watching or besetting within the meaning of this section.'

And so, at last, 'peaceful picketing' obtained full statutory protection.

Although the legal conditions under which trade unions operated in the United Kingdom were established in the years 1871–75, there remained a number of battles still to be fought, this time in the civil courts. In *Bowen* v. *Hall*[2] the Court of Appeal decided that where A induced B to break his contract of employment with C, then C had an action against A in respect of the loss he had suffered. This action had nothing to do with the activities of trade

[1] (1872) 12 Cox 316.
[2] (1881) 6 Q.B.D. 333.

unions, but it offered a valuable weapon against them, which employers gratefully accepted. In *Temperton* v. *Russell*[1] the Court of Appeal decided that a combination of persons who knowingly induced others not to enter into a contract with an employer, would commit the tort of civil conspiracy, and would be answerable in damages for the loss. A crop of decisions in the following years firmly established this tort in its application to the activities of trade unions in industrial disputes.

By the end of the nineteenth century, there were other signs that the position of the unions, as established during the period 1871–75, might not be as strong as had been supposed. In *Lyons* v. *Wilkins*[2] the Court of Appeal decided that 'watching or besetting' was unlawful within the meaning of Section 7(4) of the Act of 1875 unless it was 'in order merely to obtain or communicate information', and secondly, that watching or besetting a house or other place where workmen are is unlawful if done in order to compel a master to do, or abstain from doing, what he has a legal right to do or abstain from doing. This decision, which was followed by two others to the same effect in the same year, threw the question of picketing back into the melting-pot; but the greatest blow of all was about to be delivered, in the historic decision of the House of Lords in the *Taff Vale Case*.[3]

In that case, it was decided that a trade union, registered under the Act of 1871, could be made liable for the torts of its officials, when committed in furtherance of a trade dispute. It is at this point that the indecisive attitude of the law towards trade unions becomes painfully apparent. A company or a municipal corporation or a university is necessarily liable for the acts of its employees. This is a simple consequence of the fact that these bodies are in law considered to be separate legal personalities, to whom the acts of their agents, acting within the scope of their authority, must be attributed. But the Act of 1871 had stopped short of conceding legal personality to a trade union. The unions had no desire to assume corporate liability for the acts of their members, and the employers were suspicious of the powers which incorporation would give; so the Act permitted registration, but did not grant legal personality. In the *Taff Vale Case* the House of Lords attempted to supply the deficiency.

[1] [1893] 1 Q.B. 715.
[2] [1899] 1 Ch. 255.
[3] [1901] A.C. 426.

It has long been common to describe this decision as a disaster and so, from the political point of view, it was; but it was also a direct consequence of the confusion of thought which surrounded the legislation of 1871, which the legislature had left the court to clean up. The long and learned judgment of Farwell J. at first instance attempts to resolve this confusion, and attempts to resolve it, not in terms of vague generalities, but in expressions to which a precise legal significance can be attached. The fundamental question to be resolved was whether trade unions were above, or at the very least outside, the law or not. The judgment of Lord Macnaghten (a judge of the very highest eminence) is an object-lesson on the manner with which issues which have been productive of prolonged and bitter controversy are considered in a court of law. He says:

'Parliament has legalised trade unions, whether registered or not. If registered, they enjoy certain advantages. The respondent society[1] is a registered trade union. Subject to such control as an annual general meeting can exercise, the government of the society is in the hands of its executive committee, a small body with vast powers, including an unlimited power of disposition over the funds of the union, except so far as it may be interfered with by the annual general meeting or restricted by the operation of the society's rules, of which in case of doubt the executive committee is the sole authorised interpreter. Counsel for the respondents pointed out, what is true enough, that the funds of the society were contributed for benefit purposes as well as for trade purposes, and warned us that, if those funds were made answerable for the consequences of such acts as those complained of in the present case, the widow and the orphan might suffer in consequence of the ill-advised or illegal action of the executive of the union. At first sight that seems a plausible argument. But the truth is that all the funds of the society, for whatever purposes they may be collected, form a common fund. That, I believe, is the case with most, if not all, trade unions. If you take up the report of the Royal Commission on Trade Unions and turn to the statement accompanying the minority report, you will see that there was nothing on which the advocates of trade unions insisted more strongly or more firmly than on the right of unions to employ the whole of their funds, if they chose, for the purpose of strikes

[1] The Amalgamated Society of Railway Servants.

and in connexion therewith. "At present," say the authors of that statement, "the strength of the union and the confidence of its members simply consists of this, that it can, if so disposed, employ the whole of its funds in the support of the trade ends." [Final (11th) Report, 1869, p. lxi] An enforced separation of the funds of the union would be, they say, "arbitrary interference with the liberty of association", it would "paralyse the efficiency of the institution". The suggestion of such a proposal is "tantamount to a proposal to suppress unionism by statute."

'The substantial question, therefore, as Mr Justice Farwell put it, is this – Has the Legislature authorised the creation of numerous bodies of men capable of owning great wealth and of acting by agents with absolutely no responsibility for the wrongs they may do to other persons by the use of that wealth and the employment of those agents? In my opinion Parliament has done nothing of the kind. I can find nothing in the Acts of 1871 and 1876,[1] or either of them, from beginning to end to warrant such a notion. Nor, indeed, was anything of the kind contemplated by the minority of the members of the Royal Commission on Trade Unions, whose views found acceptance with the Legislature. In paragraph 4 of the minority report they say: "It should be specially provided that, except so far as combinations are thereby exempted from criminal prosecutions, nothing should affect the liability of every person to be sued at law or in equity in respect of any damage which may have been occasioned to any other person, through the act or default of the person so sued." Now, if the liability of every person in this respect was to be preserved, it would seem to follow that it was intended by the strongest advocates of trade unionism that persons should be liable for concerted as well as for individual action. And for this purpose it seems to me that it cannot matter in the least whether persons acting in concert be combined together in a trade union, or collected or united in any other form of association.'

To these, there may be added the observations of Lord Lindley, whose authority upon company and partnership law was unrivalled:

'I entirely repudiate the notion that the effect of the Trade Union Act of 1871 is to legalise trade unions and confer on them

[1] This Act slightly amended the Act of 1871.

rights to acquire and hold property, and at the same time to protect the union from legal proceedings if their managers or agents acting for the whole body violate the rights of other people. For such violation the property of a trade union can unquestionably, in my opinion, be reached by legal proceedings properly framed.'

The *Taff Vale* judgment had only brief validity, so that on the broad question there is little point today in giving it extended consideration. What is still of importance today, however, is the obscurity relating to status which the Act of 1871 created, and the claim to exceptional privilege which was founded upon it, which still persists, and which was extended by the Act of 1906.

The Liberal Party had promised that it would destroy the effect of the *Taff Vale Case* whenever it was returned to power. This occurred at the general election of 1906, but when the leading legally qualified members of the government attempted the task of drafting a bill,[1] a sharp division of opinion was revealed. Asquith, Haldane, and other lawyers wished simply to restrict the operation of the law of agency, so that a claim against union funds could only be admitted if it was clear that the act was authorised by the governing body. There was also a desire to protect the benefits of branches in parts of the country remote from the area in which a dispute had arisen. The result was a bill the effect of which was obscure, even to some of its supporters, and in the debate on the second reading, the possibility of incorporating trade unions was again discussed, but without attracting support from either party. The entire situation changed when the Labour members introduced a bill which was not only clearer, but which went a good deal further than many of the Liberal government had intended. The government nevertheless accepted from it in committee so many amendments, that in its final shape the Act resembled the Labour bill more closely than it resembled the original draft.

The Trade Disputes Act of 1906 overturned a number of established doctrines then existing. Section 1 provided that an act done by a combination of persons which would not be actionable if done without such a combination, *if done in furtherance of a trade dispute*, should not be actionable. This put an end to the doctrine of civil conspiracy, originating in the decision of the Court of

---

[1] The origins of the Trade Disputes Act, 1906, are discussed more fully in Chapter X of the present writer's *A Liberal Attorney-General*.

Appeal in *Temperton* v. *Russell*.[1] Section 2 made a change in the definition of peaceful picketing, by providing:

'It shall be lawful for one or more persons, acting on their own behalf, or on behalf of a trade union or of an individual employer or firm, in contemplation or furtherance of a trade dispute, to attend at or near a house or place where a person resides or works or carries on business or happens to be, if they so attend merely for the purpose of peacefully obtaining or communicating information, or of peacefully persuading any person to work or abstain from working.'

Section 3 made non-actionable, if done in furtherance of a trade dispute, any act inducing a breach of contract of employment or an act which is an interference with the trade, business, or employment of some other person, or with the right of some other person to dispose of his capital or his labour as he wills. Such activities had previously been held actionable in a series of decisions which also had their origin in *Temperton* v. *Russell*.[2]

In the fourth section, the Act of 1906 took yet another major step forward in the process of placing trade unions in a specially privileged position by providing:

'(1) An action against a trade union, whether of workmen or masters, or against any members or officials thereof on behalf of themselves and all other members of the trade union in respect of any tortious act alleged to have been committed by or on behalf of the trade union, shall not be entertained in any court.'[3]

The unusually emphatic language of this section doubtless owes something to the bitter feelings aroused by the *Taff Vale* decision, but the section did much more than overturn it. It conferred immunity upon trade unions for the acts of their agents, *whether done in furtherance of a trade dispute or not*. On this provision, Sir Frederick Pollock commented, shortly after its enactment:

'The legislature has thought fit by the Trade Disputes Act 1906, to confer extraordinary immunities on combinations both of employers and workmen, and to some extent on persons acting

---

[1] [1893] 1 Q.B. 715.
[2] By S.4(2) the trustees of a registered trade union remain liable for a tort touching or concerning the property of the union, unless the tort is committed in furtherance of a trade dispute.
[3] *Vacher* v. *London Society of Compositors* [1913] A.C.107.

in their interests. Legal science has evidently nothing to do with this violent empirical operation on the body politic, and we can only look to jurisdictions beyond the seas for the further judicial consideration of the problems which our courts were endeavouring (it is submitted, not without a reasonable measure of success) to work out on principles of legal justice.'[1]

Sir Frederick Pollock's condemnation was echoed in the delicate irony apparent in a passage of Lord Macnaghten's speech in *Vacher* v. *London Society of Compositors*:[2]

'Some people may think the policy of the Act unwise and even dangerous to the community. Some may think it at variance with principles which have long been held sacred. But a judicial tribunal has nothing to do with policy of any Act which it may be called upon to interpret. That may be a matter for private judgment. The duty of the Court, and its only duty, is to expound the language of the Act in accordance with the settled rules of construction. It is, I apprehend, as unwise as it is unprofitable to cavil at the policy of an Act of Parliament, or to pass a covert censure on the Legislature.'

The irony was the more pointed because in that case, the House of Lords had been compelled to refuse legal redress to a firm of printers who had been libelled by the union, at a time when no trade dispute affecting them existed.

Between legal justice and political expediency there often exists a gulf, which it is not always easy to bridge. There is a deep-rooted conviction among trade unionists that the courts have been in constant alliance with sections of the public hostile to trade unions, and that this has been responsible for a crop of unpalatable and cramping decisions. This suspicion has been responsible for the oft-repeated affirmation that the unions will have 'nothing to do with the law'. In spite of their wide immunities, however, unions exist in a society regulated by law to which, in the last resort, they, as well as everyone else, must conform. It is precisely because the status of trade unions has been, and remains, anomalous in so many respects that awkward problems regularly arise for the courts to solve; and the courts have little by way of analogy to guide them, as they would have if some general regulatory statute, such as the Companies Act, existed. Instead, we have a collection of

---

[1] *Law of Torts*, 8th ed. 1908, p.v.
[2] [1913] A.C. 107.

isolated enactments, often registering no more than a temporary victory for one or other party in an industrial dispute, showing little or no organic coherence, and finally, giving no clues to matters upon which this piecemeal legislation is silent.

These points are well illustrated by two further landmarks in the history of trade unions. The first is the Osborne judgment in 1910,[1] in which the House of Lords decided that it was not within the powers of a registered trade union to apply its funds towards the support of a Member of Parliament. Perusal of the speeches of the Law Lords will show that they were still haunted by the analogy of corporate personality and the law of corporations – from which they derived the doctrine of *ultra vires* which they applied in this case. Once again, legal principles yielded to political expediency, for the Trade Union Act, 1913, provided that a union might establish a separate political fund, provided political purposes had been made expressly part of the objects of the union, but a member could refuse to pay the political levy by giving express notice, without forfeiting his benefits from the union's general funds.

The second illustration is afforded by the decision of Astbury J. upon the legality of the General Strike of 1926 in *National Seamen's and Firemen's Union of Great Britain and Ireland* v. *Reed*.[2] He held that a general strike called by the Trade Union Congress was illegal, so that persons taking part in it were not protected by the same sections of the Trade Disputes Act, 1906, which related to trade disputes. There was no dispute between the Trade Union Congress on the one hand, and the government and the nation on the other. Legal writers have differed sharply in their attitudes to this decision, but it may be suggested that the difficulty arises from the uncertainties of the courts upon the functions of trade unions, arising from the absence of adequate definition of them. Once again, these uncertainties were resolved by two statutes which represented little more than temporary political victories. The Trade Unions and Trade Disputes Act, 1927, declared illegal any strike or lockout if it: (i) had any object other than, or in addition to, the furtherance of a trade dispute within the trade or industry in which the strikers (or employers) are engaged; and (ii) is a strike designed or calculated to coerce the government either directly or by inflicting hardship upon the community.

[1] *Amalgamated Society of Railway Servants* v. *Osborne* [1910] A.C. 87.
[2] [1926] Ch. 536.

It also penalised all those who took part in such a strike, and protected in his union benefits any union member who refused.

The decisive victory of the Labour Party in 1945 was responsible for the passing of the Trade Disputes and Trade Unions Act, 1945, which totally repealed the Act of 1927; but it does not deal with the interesting question whether Astbury J.'s judgment was a correct exposition of the pre-1927 law, and if, therefore, that law is in force today. Accordingly, the Act of 1945 cannot be regarded as the close of this chapter of trade union history.

Trade unions have sometimes profited by the desire of the courts to find company law analogies for the internal proceedings of a union. For example, in *Cotter* v. *National Union of Seamen*[1] the *Rule in Foss* v. *Harbottle* was applied to the affairs of a union. This rule establishes that if an act is within the powers of a corporation, and can be sanctioned by the members in general meeting, the court will not restrain the corporation or the union, because of alleged irregularities, unless the action is brought by the majority of the members and in the name of the corporation itself. As Lord Hanworth put it, in the Court of Appeal, the union is a legal entity which can work through its agents, and which is governed by the code which is contained in its registered rules.

The overriding importance of the rules was emphasised in the well-known case of *Maclean* v. *Workers' Union*.[2] In this case, it was decided that a person who joins an association governed by rules under which he may be expelled, has no legal redress if he is expelled in accordance with the rules, provided that the body invested with the power of expulsion acts in good faith, even though they may be suspected of bias. The judgment of Maugham J. in this case is noteworthy for the elaborate consideration which it gave of the principles applicable to cases of expulsion, and to the contrast between the strict rules of a court of law and the elasticity of domestic tribunals, of which the committee or other body of a trade union, to which the task of considering expulsions is committed, is one. He summed it all up as follows:

'A person who joins an association governed by rules under which he may be expelled . . . . . has, in my judgment, no legal right of redress if he be expelled according to the rules, however

[1] [1929] 2 Ch. 58.
[2] [1929] 1 Ch. 602.

unfair and unjust the rules or the action of the expelling tribunal may be, provided that it acts in good faith. It is impossible to doubt that, if the rules postulate an inquiry, the accused must be given a reasonable opportunity of being heard. The phrase "the principles of natural justice" can only mean in this connection the principles of fair play so deeply rooted in the minds of modern Englishmen that a provision for an inquiry necessarily imports that the accused should be given his chance of defence and explanation.'

Much more was to be heard of the power of expulsion in the forty years that followed, more especially as 'closed shop' tactics might make expulsion equivalent to depriving a worker of his living. This situation had actually arisen in *Bonsor* v. *Musicians' Union*.[1] Mr Bonsor joined the union (a registered trade union) in 1947. In 1949 the union purported to expel him, and the consequences of this wrongful expulsion (as it was established in the action) were described by Upjohn J. as follows:

> 'The plaintiff is aged some fifty years and has all his life been a professional musician. He joined the Musicians' Union through the Liverpool Branch some time before 1947. The Musicians' Union is what is familiarly known as a "closed shop union". That is to say, it is virtually impossible to get employment or engagement as a musician unless the musician is a member of the union. That, indeed, has been strikingly illustrated in this case, for after his expulsion the plaintiff was unable to obtain any employment except at Cheltenham for a short time with a non-union orchestra. He was, apart from that, unable to get any employment and he had to seek his livelihood in entirely different spheres. He was at one time even reduced to accepting employment to remove rust from a Brighton pier, and he is now earning a wage of some £6 a week in some engineering works, whereas formerly, earning his livelihood as a musician, he was earning sums certainly well in excess of £10 a week.'

Mr Bonsor's legal proceedings began in October 1952, and it was not until June 1955 that the House of Lords was able to decide that he was entitled to an injunction, damages, and costs for wrongful expulsion. The difficulty in the case existed, not in respect of the injunction, but in respect of the damages for the financial loss

[1] [1956] A.C. 104.

which Mr Bonsor had suffered. A decision of the Court of Appeal, given in 1915, had held that the Trade Disputes Act, 1906, had made it impossible for an expelled member to sue the union in tort, and the action for damages in contract could not be against the union as such, but only against the individual members, because the trade union was not a legal entity distinct from its members. Once again, therefore, the lack of corporate personality seemed to bar the way to simple justice, but in *Bonsor's Case* the House of Lords overruled the earlier decision of the Court of Appeal, and held the union liable in damages. In the opinion of the Law Lords, it was a legal entity, distinct from its individual members, and capable of suing and being sued in its registered name. Behind these decisions, and the legal problems which they decide, one fact is apparent. Both unions and their members would be on firm ground if the separate legal personality or existence were clearly recognised, and if their procedures concerning membership and expulsion conformed to some generally accepted pattern.

In the period since 1945, with many of the objects for which unions struggled in the early days of their existence won, and with the prospect of regular alternations of power for strong Labour governments, the necessity for defining the role of the trade union movement within a state whose economy is as precariously balanced as that of the United Kingdom has proved to be, has become a matter of pressing importance. Whatever the complexion of the government, the Trade Union Congress has been careful to preserve its separate status and function. Moreover, the Trade Union Congress is not a federation with strong central powers. Its influence is manifested by persuasion and advice. Unions determine their own policies, especially where their own interests are concerned, and in spite of its well-merited reputation for constructive leadership, the Trade Union Congress has found it progressively more difficult to preserve a balance between the policies of the Wilson Labour government and the reactions of the unions to them. Whilst the unions have welcomed the restriction on prices and dividends imposed by the Prices and Incomes Board, their opposition to wages' restraint, imposed by government, in place of freely negotiated wage settlements, has been continuous. Further, union leaders themselves have been faced with problems which so far they have been unable to solve. Foremost among them is the unofficial strike, often engineered from the shop floor, and originating in some purely local grievance. Such strikes can, in a highly integrated economy, have repercussions far beyond the industry directly affected.

It is this problem above all which has led both the Labour and the Conservative parties to the view that there is urgent need for greater legal resolution of trade unions, and for some additional machinery to 'outlaw' unofficial strikes. It was also the primary reason for the establishment of the Royal Commission on Trade Unions and Employers' Associations (the Donovan Commission), whose report appeared in 1968.[1] It surveys the entire field of labour relations, and it naturally discusses at considerable length the remarkable fact that in the United Kingdom collective agreements are not legally enforceable, although the experience of many other Western countries has shown the value of making them enforceable at law. The majority report accepted this basic condition, and were unable to recommend any change. Paragraph 471 of the report says:

'Collective bargaining is not in this country a series of easily distinguishable transactions comparable to the making of a number of contracts by two commercial firms. It is in fact a continuous process in which differences concerning the interpretation of an agreement merge imperceptibly into differences concerning claims to change its effect. Moreover, even at industry level, a great deal of collective bargaining takes place through standing bodies, such as joint industrial councils, and national or regional negotiating boards, and the agreement appears as a "resolution" or "decision" of that body variable at its will, and variable in particular in the light of such difficulties of interpretation as may arise. Such "bargaining" does not fit into the categories of the law of contract.'

This may be true, although a recent writer has very strongly challenged it,[2] but it may be suggested that the process of bargaining here described is not unlike that which occurs in the sphere of international relations, yet in this sphere such bargaining is expected to result in binding agreements. What can happen at the present time is illustrated by the long-drawn-out negotiations at Fords, when in 1955 and 1967 the company and the unions concerned made agreements for regulating the procedure for the

[1] Cmd. 3623.
[2] N. Selwyn, 'Collective Agreements and the Law', *Modern Law Review* (1969), Vol. 32, pp. 377-96.

relations between the company and the unions, and the conditions of employment. The agreements were signed by members of a joint negotiating committee of the companies and by union representatives. In 1969 the company and a majority of the union side of the committee agreed to a number of variations of the conditions of employment, but the unions in the minority dissented and declared an official strike. When the company sought to obtain an injunction against the striking unions, the court held that the collective agreements were not intended to be legally enforceable, but were undertakings binding only in honour.[1] The effect of this absence of enforceability is a factor which foreign investors must necessarily take into account. Very many points for consideration arise from this decision, but it will be sufficient to quote the conclusion of a recent critic:[2]

> 'The system of collective bargaining as practised in this country can only survive if the balance of power is maintained between the parties. The economic forces which operate in a society which is basically capitalistic in structure, can work effectively only if there is equality of bargaining power around the negotiating table, and an adequate supply of weapons in the armoury of both sides. In so far as the *Ford* case has apparently deprived employers of the only alternative remedy that could have been made available, its reasoning must be challenged and its conclusion regretted. There is no particular reason why trade unions should continue to be regarded as the "sacred cows" of our society and be granted immunities additional to the ones they already have. The wisdom of Fords in bringing this action must always be open to doubt, but this should not have prevented them from having the remedy they sought. The law, like the right to strike, must always remain the ultimate deterrent.'

The report of the Donovan Commission was followed by the publication of a Government White Paper, entitled *In Place of Strife,* foreshadowing legislation designed to improve industrial relations, more particularly in relation to strikes and collective bargaining. Following the guide-lines traced by the Royal Commission, the White Paper avoided the issue of the direct enforceability of collective agreements, and concentrated upon establishing a coherent system, with collective agreements concluded both

[1] *Ford Motor Co.* v. *A. E. F.* [1969] 1 W.L.R. 339.
[2] Selwyn, *op. cit.*

at the factory and company level. For these, the White Paper stated, the major responsibility lies with the management. The agreements should be precise, they should establish fair and comprehensive pay structures, encouraging efficiency, by linking pay to production, and looking to the progressive elimination of restrictive practices. The White Paper also stressed that machinery and procedures should be established for the prompt discussion of grievances, dismissals, and redundancies.

To assist in the establishment of such a system, the government proposed to establish a Commission on Industrial Relations; and this, in fact, was the only part of the proposals to be immediately implemented, the first chairman of the commission being George Woodcock, who retired from the Secretaryship of the Trade Union Congress, and took up his appointment as chairman in March 1969. The main function of the commission was stated to be the reform of the system of collective bargaining by way of investigation and advice. A register of collective agreements was also established, registration being for the present purely voluntary. This new departure has attracted considerable criticism, since the commission has no power to enforce its recommendations, and it is yet to be seen how effective its work will be, as an alternative to legally enforceable agreements, to which the trade unions are immovably opposed. The White Paper did, nevertheless, include a proposal that agreements between unions and employers might be legally enforceable, if the parties so wished. In the light of existing attitudes, the prospect of such a wish being manifested appears remote.

The most controversial part of the White Paper, however, was that which foreshadowed the restriction of the right to strike. It proposed that discretionary powers should be given to the Secretary of State when there is unconstitutional action by a union, or where official action by a union is contemplated. To restrain unconstitutional action, a twenty-eight-days' 'cooling off' period was proposed, to allow time for procedures established by agreement to operate, or, when there were no such procedures, for an inquiry to be set up. A strike ballot could be ordered, whenever a strike would present a serious threat to the economy, or to the public interest. Action in defiance of these procedures would render those participating liable to a financial penalty, imposed by a new Industrial Board.

The proposals of the White Paper encountered hostility on all sides, as did the Trade Unions Bill founded on them, which the government introduced and then abandoned in the early summer of 1969, primarily on account of union opposition. Their attitude may perhaps be summed up in the phrase 'the strike, the whole strike, and nothing but the strike', but there were other voices, expressing more rational fears. Enoch Powell for once found himself in substantial agreement with speakers representing large unions in denouncing the White Paper as a further step towards the corporate state; Edward Heath reiterated his view that the rights of all voluntary associations, including trade unions, should be enforced in the courts, and not by yet more administrative tribunals.

Barbara Castle's[1] task in 'selling' the White Paper was not easy; for the reserve powers which it contained were of uncertain extent and, in addition, they recalled to the minds of union members the techniques used in bringing into operation the Prices and Incomes policy, which they had accepted only with extreme reluctance. The motives for both may be understood, but the trade union movement as yet has not accepted the role which a Labour government has designed for it in a planned and regulated society, geared to greater industrial efficiency from which, it is assumed, all blessings will flow in the future. It is possible to discuss almost indefinitely the problem of the trade unions from the standpoints of their relation to law, their role in industry, and their political status; but behind them all is a feeling of unease arising from the position in which they now find themselves. If their immunity from control, either legal or administrative, should no longer be acceptable either to government (whatever its political complexion) or to the general public, what ultimately is the security for the preservation of that great influence upon national policy which they now exercise? Ultimately, this is a constitutional question of very great significance. A study of the experience of other Western countries would suggest that this status is not lost, and union rights are at least as secure, when there is clearer legal definition of them than exists in Britain at present.

[1] Secretary of State for Employment and Productivity in the Labour government.

XIII

The Erosion of Liberty

THE ESSENCE of liberty is absence of control, and in its application to the individual's conduct in society, it contemplates that a person
has a choice, which he is free to exercise, between different courses
of conduct. A society in which such choices are protected is a free
society, and a 'democracy' is often regarded as the society best
adapted for the maintenance of a free society, because in a democracy the ordinary citizen chooses his government, and to some
extent controls its operation. It has been shown in earlier chapters
that in the United Kingdom, the choice today is really between
two groups of political leaders whose programmes do not differ
fundamentally – and which, indeed, may possibly not be capable
of wide variation, since the problems which they are designed to
solve are the same for both. Differences, therefore, are mainly in
emphasis. An increasing number of citizens are members of neither
or – if minor parties are included – none of the political organisations which seek representation in Parliament; and so far as the
ordinary elector is concerned, once he has exercised his vote, and a
government has been returned or placed in office, his participation in government is at an end. Politically, he can be permitted
to go to sleep again for the next five years. This quite artificial
system is often contrasted with those of communist countries in
which a choice between parties is impossible, and in which the
programmes of governments are framed in accordance with
particular doctrines which are nominally accepted by all. Here, it is
apparent, there is a fundamental difference. Freedom of association
and freedom of thought are very closely linked. In Western democracies, both have so far been preserved.

A further point must also be made. Political freedom is not, and
cannot be, absolute. It can only be exercised within the context of
law. Without a legal framework, freedom would degenerate into
anarchy, as indeed it shows some signs of doing in the field of
industrial relations. The existence of freedom for oneself implies a
similar freedom for all other citizens. It is the function of law to

guarantee such equal freedom, to define its extent, and to solve problems which may arise from this delimitation. Nevertheless, the existence of law necessarily limits freedom, albeit in the public interest, and it is also apparent that law can be misapplied and made so oppressive in its operation that freedom is suppressed altogether. This is exactly what happened in Germany during the Nazi régime. It is necessary to make this rather obvious point in order to make it plain that law by itself does not, and cannot, guarantee freedom. Laws may be passed with the object of protecting it, but their effectiveness depends upon the outlook of the judges who enforce them, and of the community in which they operate. It has been the special strength of the British people in the past that they have assumed that freedom was their birthright.

A conditioning factor in the enjoyment of liberty is that attempts to use it for the destruction of liberty cannot be tolerated. This was a problem which it was necessary for democratic societies to face, and to solve, when in the inter-war period Fascist and Nazi and communist organisations all sought to use the apparatus of democratic institutions for the purpose of establishing their own one-party states, claiming at the same time that limitation of their freedom to destroy the democratic state from within was 'undemocratic'. The list of states which became casualties as a consequence of response to this argument was a long one, and the repression of Hungary in 1956, and of Czechoslovakia in 1968 and 1969, offer a grim warning to those who may be tempted to think that the difference between communist and non-communist societies is one of form only, or that a 'People's Democracy' is in any sense democratic. It has sometimes been suggested that in a one-party communist state, the dialogue in which the English political parties continuously indulge is carried on within the party. If this is so, the ordinary citizen has no part in it, and often has no knowledge of it. Once again, the unhappy fate of the Czechs affords a good example from which communist techniques of repression may be studied.

One problem with which British and American governments have been faced in recent years has been the irresponsible advocacy of violence as a means of achieving political ends. The argument which is often used is that 'violence produces results', as contrasted with the apparent ineffectiveness of normal political debate. This is precisely the argument which was used to establish the Fascist régime in Italy, and the Nazi régime in Germany. It is a direct

threat, not only to personal liberty, but also to the secu
state itself. Whilst the suppression of these extravagance
for tact and restraint, there can be no question that they
suppressed. One of the chief functions that a governme
quired to discharge is the preservation of public order. Fa
do so will bring about its collapse sooner than anything els

In spite of the difficult problems which have been discussed in
early chapters, the tone of British public life is still extremely
healthy. The Press is free, and it exercises its freedom to the full;
television and radio share that freedom. If at times they seem to
respond too readily to government hand-outs, that is usually a
consequence of misunderstanding their function, and not of
government pressure. Public discussion of major issues is for the
most part intelligent and restrained, and compares favourably
with the tone of discussion of similar problems abroad. The outstanding characteristics of British society are still coherence, tolerance, and a sense of responsibility. These characteristics are to an
important extent interdependent. Discussions at party conferences
and at the annual trade union conference are constructive and restrained. All seem concerned to make plain their capacity to handle
public affairs. The ordinary citizen has nothing to fear in the
expression of his opinions on political matters, so long as he avoids
defamation and sedition. Both political parties which alternate in
office are firmly committed not only to the preservation of free
institutions, but also to a society in which the citizen enjoys the
fullest opportunity for self-expression. So far as the Liberal Party
is concerned, these principles are traditionally an essential element
in its philosophy. From what quarter, therefore, is the attack on
freedom, which has been frequently mentioned in earlier chapters,
to be apprehended?

To this, there is one obvious answer – the state; but this is not
an altogether satisfactory one, for the state is an abstraction, which
men have invented to describe their collective activities compendiously. One is forced to the conclusion that the present feeling of
insecurity, which is widespread, is the consequence of policies
which men are carrying out – a consequence, moreover, which may
not have been foreseen at the time when those policies were
adopted. This need occasion no surprise. Politics is certainly not
an exact science, and much of it is a record of discarded illusions.
Nineteenth-century Liberal philosophy was founded upon the
assumption that the nature of man was inherently reasonable, and

that educated men, acting in concert, would also act reasonably. Two World Wars have destroyed that illusion. More recently, Labour policies have been founded upon the assumption that the major evils of society stemmed from inequalities of wealth, and the absence of adequate opportunities for the bulk of the population. Today, with inequalities removed almost to vanishing point, that assumption is going the same way as the Liberal illusion.

However the programmes of the principal political parties may be modified in the future, it is highly unlikely that any of them would ever advocate the suppression of freedom. Even in conquered Czechoslovakia, the Soviet Union destroys Czech independence in the name of liberty. Just as all governments are in favour of peace, so also all governments are in favour of liberty, just as all priests are against sin. The difficulty arises from the fact that interpretations of these three highly evocative terms – peace, liberty, and sin – vary so widely. The experience of Eastern Europe since 1945 has shown that, by a mobilisation of the means of communications under the control of an authoritarian government, men can gradually be conditioned into an acceptance of the loss of liberty in return for material benefits, achieved by a common struggle, to achieve programmes centrally determined. In such a context, opposition or criticism from whatever source is regarded as anti-state activity, and is appropriately punished; and the techniques of compulsion are unhesitatingly used to ensure compliance with the overall plan.

Western Europe, and in particular the United Kingdom, has so far found no completely satisfactory solution to the problem of reconciling increasing planning, social welfare, and greater industrial production with personal freedom. Britain has long since abandoned the *laissez-faire* habits of thought of the classical economists, but some of their observations still have relevance. For example, in his *Political Economy*,[1] John Stuart Mill remarks:

> 'A people . . . who look habitually to their government to command or prompt them in all matters of joint concern, who expect to have everything done for them . . . have their faculties only half developed.'

It is difficult to free oneself from the suspicion that the torpor which has overtaken British political life owes something to this source. It is quite certain that a people which fails to show

[1] Book V, Chap. XI, para. 6.

diligence in the protection of its liberty is well on the way to losing it. Far too much has already been surrendered to government, much of it without apparent protest. It would be an odd consequence of so much planning in so many spheres if one product was a race of state serfs. Another may be that planning ultimately brings wide areas of human activity to a halt, for it would be quite wrong to assume that the left hand always knows what the right hand is doing.

Both these points may be illustrated from replies given by Ministers during December 1968; and both incidentally illustrated how much bolder in overriding private rights Ministers have become in the course of a decade. In a debate on the adjournment on 18 December, James Davidson, Liberal M.P. for West Aberdeenshire, raised the question of the future of the Inverarie locomotive works which, he understood, British Rail was proposing to close. This, he pointed out, would cause unemployment in the area, and unless alternative employment were found, this would be directly at variance with the government's development area policy, as outlined in the 1966 White Paper, *Scottish Economy, 1965–1970*. In his reply, W. G. Carmichael, Joint Parliamentary Secretary to the Ministry of Transport, declared that the Opposition were nothing less than hypocritical if they imagined that anyone but British Railways had the right to make this decision. Towards the end of his speech, he added:

'I cannot see how we can avoid leaving a fundamental decision such as this to the managers of British Railways who have a responsibility to balance their books. . . . . . This is not to say that the Government have no concern with the situation. Our first priority is to ensure that British Railways are taking all factors into account in reviewing their workshop organisation. It is of course of crucial importance that they pay full regard to the Government's regional policies and in particular to the need to maintain employment in the development areas.'

So who decides? – British Railways, the government, the regional boards, old Uncle Tom Cobley and all? The one thing that is clear from this reply is that Parliament does not.

A few days later, Roy Mason, then Minister of Power, told the Yorkshire area council of the National Union of Mineworkers that the Select Committee on Nationalised Industries had decided that the original purpose of the nuclear reactor programme – to establish a new low-cost fuel source – was already attained.

'Because of that . . . I have refused an independent inquiry into the costing of fuels. I have refused because I am satisfied that the Select Committee had decided nuclear power was competitive and that any examination would prove that and shatter the morale of the miners. I do not see as objective an examination whose ultimate aim would be to kill coal. As far as that is concerned the miners' morale matters most.'

Rarely have the techniques of public inquiries been so neatly exposed.

Possibly the most remarkable deprivation of freedom, and one which has not infrequently been the prelude to a political crisis, is the control of incomes which the combined efforts of both parties have now achieved. Reference has already been made to the ceremony in Downing Street with the Chancellor's battered dispatch case, with the 'goodies' it is supposed to contain. This is, unfortunately, just one more item of propaganda, for what is really happening is that the Chancellor is about to make a statement, specifying how much of the income which an individual has earned he will permit him to retain during the ensuing year. In this Alice in Wonderland setting, the Chancellor explains whether the national economy is running 'hot' or 'cold', and what measures he proposes to take to deal with it. After this operation, the citizen is expected to register delight if his cigarettes and liquor are left alone for another year (they rarely are), or if the rate of standard income tax is not increased yet again. The power of the state to manipulate personal incomes, it would seem, is now absolute – particularly if devaluations, and the statutory regulations of them through the Prices and Incomes Board, are taken into consideration.

It would also appear that the end is not yet in sight. The policy document of the Labour Party, *Agenda for a Generation*, issued in September 1969, in preparation for the general election, expresses the generally felt need to reform the tax structure, and then adds;

'In this connection we shall also review the role of dividends.

'The "demise" of the shareholder, his insignificance in modern industrial management (except in the case of the financial institutions and a small number of cases where ownership of the shares and membership of the board go hand-in-hand), has raised the question of why he should be entitled to an increasing level of income as the process of capital accumulation in industry proceeds.

'It is time to question his claim and to examine the various proposals for the statutory limitation of dividends.

'We believe this inquiry should be conducted as part of a broad review of company structure which we now intend to undertake.'

So that even by thrift, the citizen is not to be allowed to escape, except by remarkable exertions, from the chains which constrict him. These proposals, if carried out, would strike directly at unit trusts and pensions funds, and they deserve the closest examination in association with the scheme for graduated state pensions. From them a pattern emerged; and it is not one which is favourable to personal freedom.

The fact that all governments since 1945 have connived at or stimulated inflation, although in varying degrees, has placed additional fetters upon the citizen, by increasing the capital cost of houses, motor cars (now an essential element in transport), and many other things to which, when purchased on the instalment plan, a high rate of interest is attached. On some houses now being purchased the mortgage will endure until well into the twenty-first century – by which time, no doubt, the house will be due (or even overdue) for demolition. For many citizens upon regular wages or salaries there is today little prospect of escaping from long-term financial commitments, appreciably before the age of retirement. These fetters are the price which must be paid for a welfare state and a planned economy.

Today, it cannot be questioned that some degree of control is needed in wide areas of social activity, or that planning is an essential and continuing element in it. Transport must be planned, both nationally and regionally, if it is to serve the needs of the fifty million people who are crowded into Britain. Industry must be planned in much the same way, if they are to make the best use of resources, both in men and materials. So also must housing, hospitals, and many other things. But every time a planning decision is made, it has replaced an individual decision, and for that reason, wherever it is possible to lleave a course of action open to the locality, or even to an individual, this must be done, if freedom is to be more than an empty word. To give a specific example, planning under the Housing Acts has been pushed to such lengths that the most trifling matters are subject to it, and in this sphere, it has long been apparent that overplanning has produced delay and inefficiency, which in turn brings planning into disrepute.

Removal of the power of decision is apt to affect different groups of the community in different ways. In the businessman it provokes a mood of angry frustration. In the established middle-class citizen, it may produce a philosophy of withdrawal, which has already greatly weakened the fabric of voluntary association with which the United Kingdom has been so well served in the past. Among the young, and especially among students, it has created a mood of violent protest. It is born of scepticism concerning the good faith of politicians, of contempt for established institutions, and of a state in which education, careers, pensions, and many other things are served in neatly-wrapped packages prepared by others, by whom the decisions have been made. This attitude was plainly visible in the demonstrations of French students during May 1968. It has been equally evident amongst American and British students. It is a significant reminder that governments which attempt to decide everything end by deciding nothing. They ultimately accomplish their own destruction. It may also be added that talk of 'involvement' and 'participation' by politicians, even if taken at its face value, is not an acceptable substitute for the capacity to manage one's own affairs, and is not so regarded by the young.

During the past decade, policy-making at the centre has developed new and bolder techniques, involving the use of delicately balanced compulsive methods. Objectives are disclosed to those to whom the policy is addressed, and discussion is invited. This is followed by a statement of policy, in the form of a memorandum or circular, and action to implement it is invited. If, after an interval, such action is not forthcoming, then compulsion may follow, either by legislation or by the exercise of 'reserve powers'. The former technique is being employed to establish a national system of comprehensive schools; the latter was to have been introduced into the compulsive machinery of the Industrial Relations Bill which was abandoned in the summer of 1969. The Prices and Incomes Act, 1966, establishes a statutory board, appointed by the Minister, to control prices, wages, and dividends, but its policy and administration are in the hands of the Minister, and, in this case, are enforceable in the courts. A recent writer has pointed out that, theoretically, workers may expose themselves to a criminal prosecution for asking for a wage increase, although as yet none has been.

Whilst it is not suggested that action in some or all these spheres is undesirable, two conclusions are inescapable. The first is that matters formerly the subject of individual decision or joint negotiation are now determined from above, in accordance with a predetermined policy. The second is that, even where the policy is embodied in general terms in legislation, its detailed application is the province of the appropriate department. The question which is not yet settled is: how far is this substitution of departmental judgment for that of the individual going to be pressed, in a country which sets no constitutional limits to the extent of departmental takeovers?

It is consciousness of this fundamental weakness in the British system which has led writers in recent years increasingly to consider the desirability of enacting a 'Bill of Rights'. It is some evidence of the widespread feeling of insecurity which the citizens of many countries feel in face of apparently all-powerful executives that the last decade has produced a crop of such bills, notable examples being the Universal Declaration of Human Rights, the European Declaration of Human Rights, the Canadian Bill of Rights, 1960, and a number of others. A New Zealand bill, based on that of Canada, was drafted, but was not presented to Parliament, although the matter is still under consideration. Such modern bills, in their preambles, normally contain an emphatic affirmation of the dignity of the human person, the equality of all races, and the determination to preserve freedom, based on respect for moral and spiritual values, the freedoms of others, and the rule of law. Looked at from this standpoint, recent developments in the United Kingdom are not altogether reassuring. As Louis Heren pointed out in the last of a series of striking articles in *The Times*[1] under the collective and apt title *Britain on the Brink*, 'The time is surely long overdue to reassert the rights and liberties of the citizen in relation to Parliament, the executive and the bureaucracy.'

As Washington correspondent, Heren naturally drew attention to the great part which the Bill of Rights, embodied in the American constitution, had played in the development of American political life, but he pointed out two important facts in connection with that bill. The first is that some of the provisions impose limitations upon federal and state governments – provisions which at present would have no direct application in Britain, though if Scotland, Wales, and possibly English provinces achieved some

[1] 21 December 1968.

measure of autonomy, they might have. The second is that Declarations of Rights are useless so long as Parliament by legislation (or by ministerial order, derived from legislation) can abrogate or abridge them at any time. Even if this difficulty were overcome, it would still be necessary for the courts to possess the power, which they do not have at present, to pronounce null and void legislation which conflicted with such a bill. This means that a Bill of Rights must be embodied in a written constitution which Parliament could not change at will. To this, Louis Heren rather sadly concluded, neither major party was likely to give its support, since its present freedom of action would thereby be curtailed. Nevertheless, Heren strongly reaffirmed his belief that only by taking such a step could the United Kingdom begin to set its house in order.

'It might make government a little more complicated ... but Britain is not run for the benefit of Parliament or the bureaucracy. Britain's role, beyond survival and a renewal of the public confidence in her political system, is the improvement of the human condition, and I can see no better way of resuming progress towards that objective than restating the inalienable rights of her people.'

There are many who would agree with him, and who share his conviction that far too much has been lost by negligence or lack of understanding. During two long and exhausting World Wars, powers were willingly surrendered to the executive, and the country became accustomed to a system in which executive action was normal. Since 1945, both Parliament and public have apparently been content to permit this system, in essentials, to endure, thereby invalidating one of Bagehot's well-known aphorisms that although the English were, in the political sphere, unrivalled for stupidity, such stupidity is the strongest defence of free institutions.

Perhaps this chapter may end with a brief reference to another oft-quoted writer. Gibbon, in analysing the causes of the decay of the Roman imperial system of government, pointed out that the interest of the Romans in their political institutions vanished when they were no longer involved in them, but that coincidentally restraints upon their behaviour vanished, and gave place to a universal licentiousness. Is it perhaps only a coincidence that the disillusionment of the British with their political institutions has coincided with a general, if at times uneasy, acceptance of the permissive society? If the experience of the Roman Empire has any validity at the present day, the abdication from responsibility arising from public indifference to political action, combined with the subversion of previously accepted moral standards, will accelerate the crumbling of authority at all levels. This process, which remained unchecked in Rome, was a major factor in the final collapse. There is also another common factor. Rome remained to the end essentially a state based upon a single city, and she never solved the problems created by a great aggregation of people within city limits. Western civilisation today is overwhelmingly an urban civilisation, and its problems are an increasing preoccupation. They are not only material problems, but also problems of adjustment to the constantly changing conditions of city life. It is here that a general sense of civic responsibility must be reawakened, and local initiative fostered, if these problems are to be solved. To take only one example, some American cities have initiated courageous experiments designed to overcome the alienation between youthful gangs and the police. In Philadelphia, mobile police have been partnered in night patrols by gang-members, who have taken a share in the duties of the patrol. Opinion on both sides has indicated that there has been a considerable growth in understanding during the experiment. It does not follow that such experiments would always be successful, or that they should be generally tried. They are inescapably matters for local discussion and decision. It would not be difficult to give other illustrations of matters in which only local knowledge and opinion can hope to be successful, and in which central direction can even be obstructive. Freedom to decide and vigorous local institutions are closely linked, as indeed the past history of Great Britain has consistently shown.

XIV

Public Opinion

IN ASSESSING the extent to which public opinion either influences or assists the formation of government policy, it should be appreciated that there is a two-way traffic between government and public, and that public opinion itself is influenced, to an extent which is variable and which is difficult to determine, by the actions of government. Long ago Macchiavelli, in discussing the extent to which a ruler should deliberately use duplicity as an instrument of policy, pointed out that the wise ruler, though he would not hesitate to lie or to break faith, would not do so more than was necessary, since if he did so, he would forfeit public confidence, and his efficiency would be reduced. Today, the phrase 'credibility gap' is used to describe a statesman or a government whose performance in this respect falls short of Macchiavelli's standards.

It is not by direct exhortation, however, that governments today mainly exercise their chief influence. The general tendency to discount most expressions of opinion by persons in office can be explained, partly by the fact that today members of the public are so constantly exhorted, in the Press, at meetings, and by television, radio, advertisements, and other media, that they have developed a technique of resistance to it. The television set can be switched off when a politician appears, and there is no need to go to meetings. Even the loudspeaker which stridently exhorts one to vote at election times can be ignored.

If these direct appeals to public opinion are of diminishing value, there are others with greater persuasive power. In the nineteenth century, it was frequently said that the opinion which made and unmade governments was formed in the clubs. This has certainly not been true since 1914, but there exists nevertheless a 'climate of opinion' to which governments are not indifferent, and which they take pains to cultivate, by a variety of means. This is the function of 'public relations officers', employed by individual politicians and by government departments. Not only are the staffs of these officers growing in number, but there is a growing

practice, which though understandable is one which needs scrutiny, to appoint active party men to them on a temporary basis.
Whilst the desire to present the case of the government of the day
in the most favourable light is fully comprehensible, the confusion
of civil service and party functions is open to criticism, and has
also provoked some restlessness in the civil service itself. In
October 1969, for example, it was stated that apart from political
appointments in the Prime Minister's Press Secretariat, six of the
thirty-one principal posts of chief information officer had been
filled in the two years previously by men who had been brought in
from outside. The preparation of press hand-outs is only one of
their functions, although it is the most obvious. Hints and carefully calculated 'breaches of confidence' can be useful in forming
'lobby opinion' and, in times of political tension, of influencing
opinion, not only of the public, but in the House of Commons.
Besides the public relations officer himself, there exists a body of
well-wishers and 'well-informed spokesmen', expert, semi-expert,
or merely self-assertive, who interpret 'opinion in Whitehall', 'what the government is thinking', or 'what the Prime
Minister wants' on television and radio, and in the Press, commenting on the action rather like the chorus in a Greek play.
The cumulative effect of all this industry over a period can be considerable.

Governments have at their disposal many other devices for influencing public opinion. One of them, upon which all governments rely to an increasing extent, is the technique of inquiry.
Their influence is primarily exercised in selecting a topic for inquiry at all. This at once marks it as a matter in which government
is interested, and often releases a flood of speculation and discussion. After a suitable interval, the government can then set up a
committee to investigate the problem – an operation which calls
for the exercise of considerable skill. This is manifested in two
ways: first, by the definition of the scope of the inquiry; and
secondly, by the selection of the members of the committee. For
example, as J. P. Mackintosh pointed out, the Maud Inquiry
into local government was limited to an inquiry into the way it
functions. It was not free to consider how other functions, and
particularly local functions not carried out by local government
authorities, could be transferred to a reorganised system of local
government. Others have pointed out that the report did not consider, because the committee were not asked to consider, how the

P

efficiency of local government would be affected by the substitution of new methods and sources of local taxation for a rating system which practically everyone regards as obsolete, inefficient, and inequitable. Inclusion of these two factors would probably have resulted in the production of a substantially different report.

The method of selection of committees of inquiry, which have proliferated since the war, deserves more attention than it has yet received. Should committees be composed of experts or of enthusiastic amateurs, or of a mixture of the two? A glance at the membership of some recent committees suggests that they are usually mixed. In such a case, the experts start with an initial advantage. They are familiar with the background of the problem to be investigated, and almost invariably, their views are well known to the department beforehand. It is therefore neither unfair nor derogatory to suggest that once the composition of a committee is settled, and the departmental view upon the problem is known, the upshot of its deliberations can often be predicted with reasonable accuracy. Accordingly, a harmonious progression may be discerned – public discussion, committee, report, government paper founded upon it, and ultimately, an Act of Parliament; all of them being valuable stages in a 'guided' democracy.

It is not suggested that the process is anything but a valuable one, or that the integrity of committee members is in any way impugned. Much that is useful may, and does, arise in preliminary discussion, and in the evidence given before the committee; and if members of the public fail to take full advantage of these opportunities, they cannot complain too loudly afterwards. What is suggested is that behind these operations is a guiding hand, or a collection of them, delicately steering the operation towards some desired conclusion. One can imagine, for example, the dismay of government if the Maud Commission had produced a report that, after studying alternative solutions, all of which had disadvantages, had reluctantly come to the conclusion that the system of local government was so deeply rooted in tradition and sentiment that, with certain modifications, it could be adapted to modern needs. Although in the past some committees have reached conclusions of this kind, this is not the modern manner. If a committee is set up, then something is going to be changed.

In face of so much manipulation, one might possibly wonder whether public opinion can exist at all; yet there are occasions when it manifests itself in no uncertain fashion, and politicians are compelled to take account of it. One outstanding occasion was in 1935, when the predominantly Conservative National Government had accepted Italy's invasion of Abyssinia, in disregard of her obligations as a member of the League of Nations, apparently without any expression of dissent. This produced a general expression of disagreement which brought about a change in emphasis in Britain's policy at the League Council. Sir Samuel Hoare, in an impressive speech, gave plain indications that Britain would support the League in a determined effort to check Italy's invasion. This was not without influence in producing a healthy majority for the government at a general election held shortly afterwards. With the election safely behind it, the government returned to its former attitude of disinterest, culminating in the notorious Hoare–Laval proposals for a partition of Abyssinia. Once again an angry public opinion manifested itself, and with very great reluctance Baldwin was compelled to accept Hoare's resignation. When the echoes had died away once more, Hoare returned to the Cabinet again, this time as Home Secretary. The episode is instructive in exposing the limited extent to which a plainly manifested expression of public opinion can markedly change the direction of a settled government policy.

It is only occasionally that public opinion expresses itself so clearly upon a major political question. Many of the classic political conflicts in our modern political history have found opinion sharply, and often surprisingly evenly, divided. Irish Home Rule, 'tariff reform', even the House of Lords' veto in 1910, and more recently Suez and Vietnam, have all been made the more difficult because opinion was divided; usually on party lines. This greatly aids the party in office, since it is then possible to represent conflicting opinion as party inspired, and it can then be dealt with in orthodox party fashion. This may not be the case in the future. The great 'moratorium' on Vietnam in the United States in October 1969, an even larger one shortly afterwards, and other similar demonstrations elsewhere, indicate that electorates today can be roused to peaceful demonstrations of great magnitude with which politicians in future must reckon. Unhappily, they are yet another sign of the public's lack of interest in the normal processes of party conflict. Moreover, such demonstrations are by no means always, as politicians would have us believe, the product of 'subversive' influences. The technique is by no means novel. The Chartists were familiar with the monster petition and the peaceful mass demonstration in an age when those who participated in them had not yet obtained the vote. For them, as presumably for modern demonstrators, it was seen as an experiment in 'direct democracy'. Unfortunately, it is not difficult to deflect these towards less meritorious objects, as Hitler, Mussolini, and the rulers of Red China have demonstrated. 'Direct democracy' can lead directly either to mob rule or dictatorship. In any event, it is hardly conceivable that it could produce a coherent outlook upon many of the perplexing issues of the present day, however clearly it may express popular feeling on one specific and simply formulated question.

In all probability, the Press is still the most powerful influence in forming opinion, nowithstanding the direct impact of television upon mass audiences, and also notwithstanding the limitations under which it works, and of which it sometimes complains. Of these, the principal one is the Official Secrets Act, which protects so much official material from disclosure. Opinions may vary upon the necessity for some exercises of government privilege under the Act, but in general it is exercised with restraint. Under governments of a more dictatorial temper, it could prove a major fetter upon the spread of information. Other limiting conditions arise from the law of libel, the law of contempt of court, Parliamentary privilege, and the rule, strongly reaffirmed in the Vassall case in 1963, that a journalist enjoys no privilege in the collection of information, so that if a court, or a tribunal with statutory powers, requires a journalist to disclose his sources of information, he must disclose them, or be imprisoned for contempt. Even within these limits, journalists enjoy a wide freedom to operate, and the British Press compares favourably, from the standpoint of news, opinions, and responsibility, with that of any other free country. Ever since Milton wrote *The Areopagitica* a free Press has been regarded as the birthright of a free people, and it may be affirmed that on the day when its freedom is threatened, the drift towards authoritarianism will be far-advanced. The words of Junius are as true today as when he wrote them two hundred years ago: 'Let it be impressed upon your minds, let it be instilled into your children, that the liberty of the Press is the palladium of all the civil, political and religious rights of an Englishman.' Junius wrote at a time when the encroachments of the executive had provoked intense resentment, which his outspoken, and sometimes malicious, journalism did a good deal to bring into disrepute, but the danger is recurrent. Lord Pearce told the Press Council at the end of

October 1969, shortly after his appointment as chairman of that body, that anything which curbed a free Press is a danger to democracy, and he added that press freedom could be eroded in many little ways, including Acts of Parliament which apparently had no connection with the Press at all.

In recent years, tension between Press and governments, both Conservative and Labour, has sometimes been sharp and prolonged. For some time during the Wilson administration, the premier complained that he was being portrayed unfairly both in the Press and on television, and there were the usual veiled hints that if there was not a change in attitude, 'something' might have to be done. Politicians have always complained in these terms, and in the nineteenth century some of them, even the most powerful, took steps to ensure that some parts of the Press at least were responsive to their influence. Palmerston was notorious for his press contacts, which were often a source of irritation to his fellow-Ministers, and at the same period, and later, *The Times,* especially under Delane, was assumed, both in the United Kingdom and abroad, to have very special contacts with government leaders. Anyone who reads the proceedings of the Parnell Commission cannot fail to be impressed by the close link which evidently existed between *The Times* and the Conservative government, and more recently the association between Geoffrey Dawson and the Baldwin and Chamberlain governments, both at the time of Edward VIII's abdication and of Munich, was apparent. Nowadays this link no longer exists, and the Press as a whole suffers from the excessive secrecy with which much governmental activity is surrounded. The Press has a major public role to play, which is not adequately performed if it is to be simply the recipient of departmental hand-outs. It has countered this to a considerable extent by developing new, and keen, methods of investigation. It is hardly surprising, therefore, that tension between government and the Press recurs. But there can be no doubt that such techniques are necessary.

Moreover, in spite of the new duties now committed to Members of Parliament in sifting complaints of maladministration for the consideration of the Parliamentary Commissioner, it is still the case that the Press is by far the most formidable, and effective, medium for the ventilation of grievances. Even today, when *The Times* can no longer be regarded as possessing a close association with government, a letter to *The Times* is often a matter of serious concern to government, if it exposes some piece of official incompetence. There are, however, other and more powerful weapons. The publicity which the Press devoted to the Crichel Down affair was ultimately the most powerful factor in inducing an obstinate government department to rectify a notable piece of maladministration. An even more notable achievement was the decisive victory of the Press in bringing to a halt the imbecilities perpetrated by the Land Commission. The initiative in this campaign was taken by the *Daily Express,* whose 'black file' of monstrous impositions, often upon people of very limited means, eventually roused the remainder of the Press to a searching investigation, which, in spite of the feeble explanations of Kenneth Robinson, then Minister of Planning, revealed many glaring injustices and ultimately brought about a halt in the persecution initiated by the Land Commission. The entire episode was an object lesson in modern misgovernment. Legislation was rushed through Parliament before its possible effects had been studied, numerous and very substantial acts of oppression ensued in exactly the way that a number of experts – land agents and others – had foreseen; these were at first dismissed as trifling, or quite exceptional; but when the revelations in the Press were ultimately taken up by members of all parties in the House of Commons, it was plainly apparent that the Land Commission had received instructions to go slow; and eventually, the worst evils arising from this legislation were hastily mitigated by Sections 43–49 of the Finance Act, 1969 – an Act which has no logical connection with the Land Commission Act, 1967, which was the starting-point of these injustices, and which urgently needs further amendment. For example, no betterment levy is payable by a local authority which sells for private development, although a private owner whose land may adjoin the council's must pay. But even more inequitable is the fact that the Land Commission may compulsorily purchase the land of a private owner; it may then mulct him of 40 per cent of the price as 'betterment levy' and may then sell the land to a private developer. One is unfortunately left with the clear impression that if the Press had not been so persistent in their exposure of the evils which this legislation inflicted, the major one would still be unredressed today. For the rest, all it can do is to remain watchful for possible abuses which, it may be pointed out, are beyond the purview of the Parliamentary Commissioner, since they are perpetrated under the authority of statute. It may also be added that, whilst the betterment levy imposed by the Land Commission

Act, 1967, was alleged to be a levy to tax property speculators, it would appear to have largely failed in achieving its objective. In the two years between 6 April 1967, when this Act became law, and April 1969, the commission collected, at very considerable expense, approximately £8 million in levies, most of it from persons of very limited means, owning houses on small plots of land. A thoughtful leading article in *The Times* of 15 March 1969 pointed out that there was nothing which the Land Commission could do which local authorities and central departments could not do better between them. The case for the abolition of this pointless experiment in bureaucracy is strong, and the fact that this is now generally understood is due in no small measure to the vigilance of the Press in scrutinising its unhappy existence.

The excesses of the Land Commission are only one of the objects of interest to the national Press. Many newspapers have instituted departments for the investigation of grievances reported to them by readers. By no means all relate to government departments, although it is not without interest that a substantial number do, and that the reactions of departments to press inquiries seem to be a good deal quicker than they do to those of the Parliamentary Commissioner. The common feature of large numbers of these complaints is that private citizens feel the weight of bureaucracy pressing down upon them, and that only the Press can secure any effective redress. Newspapers which receive their complaints can best judge how wide the feeling is, and on it they doubtless base their own assessments of the state of public opinion.

So long as the Press retains its present freedom, it can be predicted with reasonable certainty that tension between government and Press will be frequent. Government plans and interferes. Those affected by the planning resist, whether they are trade unionists, governors of grammar schools, teachers, or businessmen, and the Press reports and comments on this resistance. In a discussion of this problem in the *Sunday Telegraph* of 28 May 1969, Peregrine Worsthorne remarked: 'Planning today involves doing things which hurt the many as well as the few. In this new context, it is surely very doubtful whether central government can ever be strong enough, in a free society, to do all the things it needs to do if planning is not to cause more chaos than it cures.'

The operative phrase in these observations is 'in a free society'. If society were not free, then opposition would be greatly reduced, and less concerted. It is the function of the Press in a free society to ensure that opposition receives at least as much publicity as the plan. After all, planning is what you impose on others. Misgovernment is what others impose on you.

Some people have suggested that the British Press cannot really be regarded as free, because the greater part of it has fallen under the control of a few great newspaper proprietors. However regrettable the limited ownership of the Press may be, it is unfortunately merely one aspect of a general drift towards giant combines in all branches of industrial life, and it has been made inevitable by sharply rising costs of production. The primary purpose of a newspaper combine is to earn profits, and this largely determines the form and content of newspapers. For the same reason, policy must remain in the hands of the professionals – of the editor and his staff. The recent history of the British Press has shown that a newspaper which ignores this major fact of life cannot hope to survive. The great majority of readers are influenced primarily by form and presentation. They often have a particular attachment to features far removed from politics – for example, a racing tipster or a fashion writer. In the inter-war period, the number of people who bought the *Evening Standard* for the Low Cartoon was extremely large, even though these cartoons were unvaryingly hostile to the causes which Lord Beaverbrook, the *Evening Standard*'s proprietor, promoted. Many readers of the *Daily Mirror* buy it for its strip cartoons. A surprisingly large number of newspaper readers remain in ignorance of the policy of the newspaper of their choice, and many, though they may be aware of it, disagree with it. Highly sophisticated journalists are aware of these things, and adapt their presentation to them. They are well aware that carefully staged newspaper campaigns can badly misfire, and even public opinion polls can be misleading.

Compared with the continuing power of the Press, that of television and radio is intermittent and uncertain in impact. There are several reasons for this. One is that the impact of sight and sound, though possibly more direct than that of the written word, is less clearly defined. The drift of a leading article, especially if it is short and clear, can be assessed as a whole. The drift of a commentator upon the news is less apparent. Moreover, although there are exceptions, news commentators on radio and television compare most unfavourably, from the standpoint of insight and independence of view, with leading journalists, and they lack the vigour and independence of their American counterparts. Their sources of information are obviously more limited, and they suffer from the absence of any real competition. B.B.C. and Independent Television, in their newscasts, usually report the same things in much the same way. Both seem unduly addicted to the collection of inane comments from passers-by who, by no stretch of the imagination, can be regarded as contributing anything of value to the matter which is being reported. They are even less illuminating than the emotions of a footballer after a near-miss, painfully 'talked through' by some sports commentator for the fifth or sixth time shortly before Saturday midnight.

Recording and commenting on the news is by no means the only function of radio and television in the formation of public opinion. Talks, interviews, discussions, and many other techniques exist, and opinion may vary upon the extent of their impact. One of the very real difficulties of these two media is, however, a proper assessment of the audience to be interested. A discussion which may be full of interest for a retired bank manager in Surbiton may be totally devoid of appeal for a miner in Middlesbrough. Newspapers have adjusted themselves to this, although with some sacrifice in tone. Radio and television would appear to be still experimenting. One important gap in television's approach to public opinion, which to an important degree affects the nature of its activities, is the absence of facilities for televising Parliamentary proceedings. As long ago as 1959 Robin Day suggested that there should be edited late-night reports of them, but ten years later, nothing has been done to make this suggestion effective, even though a House of Commons Select Committee reported in 1965 in favour of televising edited extracts. It is true that in November 1966, the government proposed to the Commons that a closed-circuit experiment should be made on the lines suggested by the Select Committee, but this was rejected on a free vote, by a majority of one. Exactly three years later, when the same question was again put to the House of Commons, the majority against television was larger. Yet it may be suggested that nothing would do more to bring home to the public at large the nature and importance of Parliamentary activities than such a development. As Robin Day asked, in a contribution to *The Times* of 11 November 1969: 'How can Parliament expect to maintain its prestige and authority as the nation's prime forum of debate if it continues to shut itself off from the nation's prime medium of mass communication?'

This time, it is not the government, but the House of Commons itself, which is reluctant to bring its activities in this form before the public. This is not a new attitude. The House of Commons was for centuries opposed to the publication of reports of its proceedings. The Long Parliament prohibited any member from publishing or permitting the publication of anything spoken in the House, and although in 1680, the House ordered that accounts of votes and proceedings were to be printed under the direction of the Speaker, opposition to the publication of debates (which was regarded as an invasion of Parliamentary privilege) was maintained throughout the eighteenth century. As a result, until 1771, accounts of debates appeared in quarterly or monthly journals with false names attributed to the speakers. Sometimes the names were classical Roman, and the proceedings were assumed to take place in the Roman Senate. From 1771 onwards, notes of debates began to appear in daily newspapers, sometimes accompanied by pointed, and not infrequently offensive, criticism. The result was a succession of attacks by the House of Commons upon printers, who were arrested for breach of privilege. The printers in turn were protected by the city magistrates who, as the dispute developed, were eventually committed to the Tower on the Speaker's order. In face of mounting public opinion, however, the House was compelled to abate its pretensions, and thereafter it no longer attempted to interfere with the reporting of debates – although even today, this activity technically occurs only by sufferance of the House, and not of right. The distinction is no longer of importance, since today, there exists in *Hansard* an official report of the debates, published under the authority of the House itself. If in the future (however remote) Parliamentary proceedings are opened to radio and television, it is essential that editorial freedom is preserved as tenaciously as it is in the United States, or in the Press of both nations.

It is not only in respect of proceedings in Parliament that politicians have been unco-operative or obstructive to television. The proposal to televise the Rochdale by-election in 1958 was opposed by both major parties, and the proposal, made in 1962, to televise party conferences, was tepidly received. Both are now covered, but Denis Ferman, Managing Director of Granada Television, stated in January 1969 that audiences for party conferences are so small that they show that even people who are interested in politics are not interested in the present politics, and he added that party political broadcasts only survive because there is no escape from them, short of ceasing to watch. He continued that over the past ten years there has been nothing to choose between the two major parties in their attitude to television, and even today Independent Television contractors have not been able to secure an accredited lobby representative for their own company in Westminster, no matter how great the volume of their political programming. His penetrating survey of the relation between politics and television ended with a plea that the rules governing political balance 'should be revised to free television from its subservience to the two-party machine'. The present situation, coupled with occasional faint suggestions of control, either direct or indirect, is not satisfactory. Its existence offers an explanation why television in the United Kingdom has failed to a significant degree to have the same impact in the political sphere that it has in the United States.

Press, television, and radio record and comment at frequent intervals upon public opinion polls, which at times are regarded as having a major significance, especially in relation to general elections. Nevertheless, their value is limited, and their limitations were well discussed by Ian Lloyd, M.P., in a contribution to *The Times* of 10 November 1969. The answer to a direct question which way a person will vote is likely to produce a reasonably accurate answer which is of value in testing the variations in party allegiance. Less concrete questions, for example upon standards of living or the Common Market, may produce answers which are substantially valueless, because the person addressed may be ignorant of the factors which should affect his opinion. Ian Lloyd's thoughtful conclusion is that although the public opinion poll has established itself as a method of testing opinion, and thereby giving a warning to government, it cannot be either a substitute for governmental decision, or even a decisive factor in making it. A government makes policy decisions in the light of the evidence available to it. The function of the public opinion poll should be to warn government of the extent to which its decisions are understood and approved by the public at large.

One organisation or group of organisations which has greatly declined in its impact upon public opinion during the past half-century is the Church – or the Churches. Even so late as the abdication of Edward VIII, the Church, in the very different manifestations of Bishop Blunt of Bradford and Archbishop Lang, was assumed to have played a considerable part in bringing about the dénouement. Indeed, for one brief moment, one might conceivably have seen them, like the two clergymen in *Richard III*, as 'two props of virtue for a Christian prince'. (Edward VIII abdicated in favour of his brother, George VI, in December 1936 and, as Duke of Windsor, later married Mrs Wallis Warfield.) Apart from such episodes, of primary significance to the Royal Family, the Church today plays little part in public affairs, and its internal stresses give the impression of intellectual confusion, which the pronouncements of some of its leaders do nothing to dispel. In a society predominantly secular, and apparently addicted to permissiveness, it has failed to give the necessary leadership. If one looks more widely afield, one finds today that little remains of the legendary 'nonconformist conscience', which in the nineteenth century was assumed to have influenced the policies of the Liberal Party. The old antagonism between 'church' and 'chapel' has been replaced by indifference.

It would be reassuring to believe that as the influence of the Churches has declined, it has been replaced by that of the universities. This would be too facile an assumption. It was sometimes thought in the nineteenth century that much government policy was debated, and at times decided, in the Common Rooms of Oxford and Cambridge. Under Jowett, the influence of Balliol was very great, as the memoirs of Jowett's pupils bear witness. During the inter-war period, the influence of Balliol was to a certain extent replaced by that of All Souls at Oxford and Trinity at Cambridge. After all, senior civil servants and political leaders alike had been very largely educated at the same schools and colleges, and at a later stage, they again shared membership of the Athenaeum. It was a pleasant world in which there were common backgrounds, common habits of thought, and common prejudices, and although it was already passing away by 1939, it had an important share in the determination of policy down to that date.

The rise of the Labour Party, and its brief spells of office between 1918 and 1939, brought other influences to the fore, notably that of Laski and his circle at the London School of Economics. Under the energetic directorship of Sir William Beveridge (as he then was) the school had a unique place in the formulation of progressive social policies, which were the intellectual foundation for the work of the strong Labour government which was swept to power in 1945.

The very great expansion in university education in the United Kingdom, which has occurred in the past two decades, together with the more comprehensive activities of government, have

brought about many important changes in the relation of the
universities to the state. The assumption of ultimate control of
them by the Department of Education and Science has limited
their freedom, and in the long run will adversely affect their status
and function. They are in process of being integrated into the
national plan. Their problems are now major news items, and their
activities are the subject of frequent questions and occasional
debates in the House of Commons. They conform to 'guide lines';
they receive frequent directions; their relations with their students,
especially in respect of 'student participation', are the subject of
frequent official exhortation. In a speech at Exeter University in
November 1969, H. S. Ferns, Professor of Political Science at
Birmingham University, discussed these developments at length.
He emphasised that university liberty in Britain was being eroded
by pressure, by the need to yield to the demands of politicians, to
concede to civil servants, and to meet the criticisms of other public
bodies, and he added that universities were being forced to act in
accordance with the ideas of politicians, civil servants, and businessmen concerning how they organise themselves, how they spend
their resources, and how they deploy their time. The main reason
for this fundamental change has been the direct and almost complete dependence upon the state for financial aid, which has been
accompanied by an agreement to keep fees charged to students
almost static, and which has also been accompanied by a failure to
take into account, when assessing university finance, the result of
the research which the universities carry out. Although there are
plainly manifested objectives in this assumption of control which
must give rise to disquiet, this interest and supervision is not
wholly bad. British universities, other than Oxford and Cambridge, were neglected far too long, and their potentialities remained largely unrecognised. In addition, they were starved for
money needed for expansion. Today, they are a major commitment,
making steadily increasing inroads on the public purse. They have
found some difficulty in adapting themselves to a society which is
itself in a state of very rapid change, and whose standards are
utterly different from those of thirty years ago.

Professor Max Beloff, in a contribution to the *Sunday Telegraph*
of 19 January 1969, in which he explained the underlying reasons
for the decision of a very widely representative group to found an
independent university, mentioned some of the main problems
which remain unsolved. These, it should be added, are also

found today in other Western societies, and particularly in the United States. Unless they are solved, and quickly, universities will be in danger of entering a lengthy twilight period of planned stagnation.

Everyone with lengthy experience is aware of the difficulty of persuading scholars of the first rank to accept election as Vice-Chancellors or, more recently, as Heads of Departments. In the summer of 1969, there were in the United States many vacant headships of universities and colleges, with no immediate prospect of filling them with suitable applicants. In one university, of small size, there were sixteen vacant headships of department, and an impressive list of senior professors who had refused to allow themselves to be nominated. The United Kingdom is today seeing something of the same reluctance. In Professor Beloff's words:

'Because growth has meant an increasing element of bureaucracy, men of scientific or scholarly vision have on the whole preferred to concentrate upon their own specialisms, and to avoid wider responsibilities. Vice-Chancellorships have not attracted, as they did in the early days of Redbrick, men of sharply-defined views and clear-cut personalities, but smooth administrators, respectful of other administrators, and happy enough to work in harmony with the bureaucracy of the state.'

Therein lies a major danger for the future. As yet the transition is incomplete, and there are a few notable exceptions, but the tendency is marked. Yet a further step on the downward path of full departmental control was taken with the publication of the report of the Parliamentary Select Committee's proposals for the reform of academic administration in October 1969. On this, the *Sunday Telegraph* of 19 October aptly commented in its leading article;

'The chief and most offensive of these was that a Government Commission should be established to guide and instruct Vice-Chancellors and Senates on how they should conduct their affairs, particularly in relation to student discipline. That such an idea should emerge from an all-party committee proves how wise were the doubts of those who objected in the transfer of responsibility for the Universities from the Treasury to the Department of Education and Science.'

It also proves how much tolerance can be secured from Parliament for the progressive establishment of the corporate state.

Once again, the problem is a complex one. Expansion and change involve a more professional attitude to university administration than has been welcomed in the past, more especially as a weak administration can prejudice a university when 'the cake' of university finance is sliced. Moreover, there has been a clear indication from all the departments of state of a desire to associate university departments, research teams, and individual members of staff of all the universities with the new tasks which the departments have undertaken. It is in this way that the opinions of university men, although not university opinion collectively, permeate government today. It has even led, in particular instances, to interchanges between the staffs of government departments and the staffs of universities for limited periods.

In this environment, the province of the old-fashioned pressure group is today a very limited one. They have never developed in the United Kingdom on the scale that they have in the United States. The chief strength of the older pressure groups was in the educated middle class, with a sense of public duty, sufficient leisure in which to make their activities meaningful, and sufficient financial independence to permit the group to make an effective contribution to national discussion. Conditions have moved steadily against groups of this type since 1945. This is possibly one reason why the new type of pressure group concentrates upon public demonstrations. Another is that the very comprehensiveness of the governmental machine appears to demonstrate the ineffectiveness of persuasion, and leads more active or dedicated idealists, especially among the young, to a total rejection of the society in which they feel enmeshed, and to advocacy of 'direct action', often with no clear idea either of what direct action involves, or what kind of a society would emerge, assuming it were successful.

Distinct from pressure groups, whether old or new, are the organised groups which represent substantial interests and professions. The Bar Council and the Law Society, though primarily interested in the organisation of the legal profession, and with the administration of justice, are today, almost against themselves, compelled to extend their horizons, and to put forward pronouncements upon questions of general concern. The General Medical Council finds itself in a somewhat similar position, and many occupations, professional or commercial, have their appropriate organisations, with similar outlooks. Of more direct general significance, so far as policy-making is concerned, are the trade unions and that complex of interests compendiously described as 'the City', with which there can be linked the Confederation of British Industries. The attitude of both is of major importance in the determination of government policy, especially in the economic sphere. It would need a substantial treatise to describe fully how, and on what topics, the influence of these interested groups is exercised, but it may be said generally that whenever a bill affecting them, or on which they may be expected to have firmly held views, is under consideration, the appropriate department of state will have initiated consultations at a very early stage, and that the shape of the bill may be very substantially modified as a result. Such consultations frequently continue during the entire period that the bill is before Parliament, and it is the close contact between the departments and the representatives of the appropriate interests which makes for the efficiency of a department, and which makes much of what it does more tolerable than it would otherwise have been. It is not difficult to think of occasions when this contact has been weak, or where the advice of the appropriate groups has been neglected, with the result that legislation has had to be abandoned, or has required amendment shortly after its passage, or has provoked widespread resentment. An outstanding illustration of this was the abandonment of one entire section of the government's proposed legislation upon industrial relations in the summer of 1969, in face of the unrelenting hostility of the unions. This episode is nevertheless instructive, in that it emphasises the forces within society which limit the exercise of governmental power. In effect, the trade union movement preferred to maintain its freedom of control in the industrial sphere, rather than accept integration within the quasi-corporate pattern which the government had planned for industry.

XV

Is There an Answer?

IN THE preceding chapters, the political institutions of the United Kingdom have been examined, and an attempt has been made to distinguish what actually happens from the fictions with which it is customary to surround governmental action. It remains to define some of the principal problems, and to suggest what steps can be taken to solve them.

Since the United Kingdom has never possessed a written constitution, and since most of the more important parts of it do not rest on law at all, but upon conventions, it follows that the constitution is no more than what those who operate it say that it is. It can be, and is, changed, not only by legislation, but by different interpretations of the importance of a particular convention, and by changes in the relations of one part of government to another. For example, the almost dictatorial position of the Cabinet is based upon tolerance of its activities, both by Parliament and public. That tolerance is largely due to the fact that what is taking place is not clearly apparent until some appreciable time later.

At every stage of the political process, action is disguised by fictions. The fiction of ministerial responsibility to Parliament suggests that Ministers are in some sense the servants of Parliament, and ultimately of the public. In fact, they are the masters of Parliament and quite free from any direct responsibility to the public except when there is a general election. It is true that public opinion in Parliament, in the Press, in the trade unions, or in other places, may influence what Ministers propose to do, and indeed such agencies affect in varying degrees political action everywhere. The United Kingdom differs from communist countries in the circumstance that the organs which express public opinion are free. If ever there came a time when they were government-controlled, then one safeguard of democratic government would be in process of disappearing. Nevertheless, in spite of criticism in the Press and elsewhere of the use, and occasional misuse, of ever-increasing powers, Prime Ministers and their colleagues have only occasionally shown restiveness, and although they are constantly watchful of their public image, the means which they adopt to maintain or improve it are in general quite legitimate. On the other hand, the observations of two cabinet Ministers, Crossman and Wedgwood Benn, which were mentioned in the first chapter, indicate that there is at least some need for watchfulness on this point.

The progressive and unceasing accumulation of power at the centre, coupled with the lack of responsibility for its exercise, has been in large measure responsible for the alienation of very large bodies of people from the processes of government, and it has led some writers to describe Britain today as being in a pre-Fascist condition, comparing it with the condition of the Weimar Republic shortly before Hitler came to power. Without pressing the analogy too far, one may perhaps mention the increasing tendency in the Germany of 1930–33 to outflank the Reichstag, and to rule by decree; the progressive amalgamation of business enterprises into great combines, with government approval, producing a mood of hopelessness in the small businessman; an egalitarian philosophy, involving the ultimate destruction of the middle class; and finally, a steady and apparently deliberate relinquishment of moral standards, both in public and private life, under the banner of 'progress'.

It is a pattern which is recurrent in the modern history of Europe, and very frequently these symptoms have indicated the imminence of revolutionary change. In the United Kingdom, the principal obstacles to such a change at the present time are the political stability of the ordinary citizen, and the vigilance of a free Press. The political parties, by their neglect of elementary precautions, and their preoccupation with the preservation of their unique irresponsibility when in office, have failed to evolve a single legal constitutional safeguard against a takeover bid. All that would be necessary would be an Act of Parliament, which need comprise only one clause, conferring a general legislative power upon the Cabinet. The transition would be swift, legal, and complete, and if the party in power were resolved upon such a step, there exists no constitutional machinery which would halt or even considerably delay it. At present, the prospect of such a development seems remote, because both the major parties habitually act in accordance with their clearly understood consensus, and also because, both by tradition and by belief, they accept as the fundamental basis for their activities that the processes of political action in the United Kingdom require wide consultation, incessant public criticism, and also the periodic general election as a method of determining which of them will enjoy power during the ensuing period. If ever a firmly disciplined party came into existence, rejecting these basic assumptions, these conventions would prove as flexible as others have done in the past.

To what extent the present situation is due to conscious design, or can be attributed to the general tendency inherent in all modern systems of government to extend their competence in pursuit of some comprehensive social ideal, must remain an open question. What is quite clear is that the British system has proved exceptionally adaptable to the emergence of a strong executive, unfettered by constitutional rules. To some extent, this development has even occurred with general approbation. Two long and perilous World Wars demonstrated the need for the widest powers. Afterwards, with the natural reluctance to abandon such powers, there was coupled the need for other powers, first to ensure recovery and then to satisfy the far-reaching aspirations which those wars had generated. Had they not occurred, the quasi-dictatorship of the Cabinet would have taken a good deal longer to establish. There has been a continuing demand that government should 'get something done', and at times in the inter-war years it could be suggested, with some show of reason, that not nearly enough was being attempted. Today, two general attitudes co-exist. The first is the assumption that the state should ultimately originate or control every major social or industrial activity, and as a corollary, that the state should be blamed if what is attempted by the state proves to be misconceived, or oppressive, or simply fails in its objective. Side by side with this attitude is another, which cannot be reconciled with it, that all these changes can occur without adversely affecting the status of the individual, to any considerable degree. Unfortunately, the changes which have already occurred have adversely affected his position, and will do so still more in the future. At the present time we are appreciating, to an increasing degree, that the strong tide towards collectivism which today is dominant can not only bring about the achievement of ends which at an earlier date were thought to be unrealisable – for example, a free national health service and a national system of graduated pensions on retirement or disablement – but it can also go some way towards reducing the status of the individual to one of dependence on the state. So also can the now plainly apparent policy of government to establish a national plan, in the pursuit of greater efficiency, into which all industrial activity must be fitted.

In this environment, the importance of a Press which is free from government control, and which reserves to itself the right to assess and criticise government action, is much greater than it has been before. Authoritarian governments thrive on secrecy, and it is their habit to seek to muzzle the Press on the ground that its 'irresponsible' criticism is detrimental to the public interest.

Two other general observations may be made. In 1780, the House of Commons, elected upon a corrupt and unrepresentative franchise, nevertheless passed the famous resolution, proposed by George Dunning, that 'the power of the crown has increased, is increasing, and ought to be diminished'. The passing of a similar resolution today in respect of the executive would seem to be overdue, yet the House of Commons has not attempted it, for the simple reason that party discipline makes any such resolution unthinkable. Therein may be found one of the major differences between the eighteenth-century constitution and that of today.

A second general point may be made. It is difficult to observe without anxiety the present predilection of government for the cult of bigness and uniformity. Both are illustrated in the educational sphere by the compulsory introduction of comprehensive schools. In industry, they are exemplified by the unceasing progress of mergers and takeovers. These have been encouraged by the Wilson government since a few large enterprises are more readily integrated into the national economic plan than many small ones with widely differing outlooks. Once again, this development is in harmony with similar developments elsewhere; and it becomes possible for government to treat with industry more effectively than if such giant organisations had not been created. But there are manifest dangers. In the first place, a whole class, which is both thrifty and industrious, is gradually being ground out of existence. In the second, the existence of a few vast enterprises, in which management is divorced from substantial ownership, brings the corporate state several degrees nearer. To those with lengthy memories, it recalls the unhappy experiences of the Weimar Republic – and its aftermath.

This, in its turn, prompts a further reflection. Though the British electorate may at times appear to show a lack of political insight, in contrast with the electorates of other Western nations, its stability is not open to doubt. Although enthusiasm for the Parliamentary system has noticeably waned, it is still prepared to do its duty at the polls, when summoned at four- or five-year intervals. Its underlying attitude seems to be that, although it is only languidly interested in the professions of either party, and although it has a deep-rooted belief that an over-long enjoyment of power corrupts, the dominant party is entitled to a period of roughly six to ten years to develop its policies, after which, it is time for the others to have a try. In view of the noticeable lack of success of some governments since 1945 on a number of issues, disbelief in their professions is now general. In politics, as elsewhere, success is the touchstone by which leaders are judged. Here again, there are dangers, for it is the recurrence of failures in leadership which has been largely responsible for the mood of cynicism in which the electorate surveys the political scene; but failure and cynicism have not infrequently been responsible for the abandonment of democratic constitutions. The failure of successive French governments during the brief life of the Fourth Republic was directly responsible for the acceptance of General de Gaulle as a father-figure. An unusually lengthy leading article in *The Times* during 1968 under the title *The Danger to Britain* stressed this point, adding that the failure of the Weimar Republic to check inflation or to prevent financial collapse led directly to the rise to power of the Nazis. Although the situation today is not so critical as it was when the leader was written, the arguments then put forward are still valid, as also are those of two equally important leading articles entitled *The British Constitution* and *A Free Constitution* which appeared in September and November 1968.

The theme of both was the fragility of British public institutions, and the ease with which they could be employed to destroy what remains of freedom. In the first, the writer stated:

'The potential power of the state to oppress its own citizens is greater now than it has ever been in the past and is still growing rapidly. It is no longer reasonable to assume that we can do without formal safeguards, particularly as the international situation has again become more threatening. British liberty may be perfectly safe in time of peace but may not be so safe if there were a prolonged local war in Europe or the Middle East. These contingencies cannot be ruled out.

'The two main acts which might be passed by a right-wing or a left-wing party which wanted to establish one-party rule would be to govern by decree and to expand the life of Parliament. These were in fact the acts quite legitimately taken during the last war, and the combination of emergency legislation with the suspension of general elections created the effective equivalent of a one-party state under the Coalition Government. Similar actions might again be taken, using war not so much as a reason but rather as a pretext.'

To this it may be added that war is only one pretext. A grave economic emergency is another.

The article then pointed out that the House of Lords would be powerless to prevent these developments. Whilst it is still law that the House of Lords has an absolute veto on proposals to extend the life of the House of Commons, it is open to a government to swamp a hostile majority by lavish creations of life peers. Equally, although the monarchy is the traditional guardian of the constitution, the recent revolutions in Greece (and, it may be added, Mussolini's assumption of dictatorial powers in Italy) show that the monarchy by itself is powerless. Accordingly the article advocated (1) that the area of the written constitution should be extended; (2) that there should be national assemblies for Scotland and Wales, and regional assemblies in England; and (3) a stronger second chamber. Although this article did not develop the theme, it is implicit in these proposals, if the situation is to be improved, that national and regional assemblies should have distinct spheres of action, protected by a written constitution. Finally, there was cautiously suggested the creation of a Supreme Court, with power to decide constitutional questions.

The second leading article was prompted by the establishment of the Royal Commission to examine the constitution of the United Kingdom. It emphasised that the primary constitutional problem was the ever-growing power of government, and unceasing bureaucratic intervention in people's lives. This, it was careful to point out, has made possible the development of the Welfare State, with regrettable invasion of individual liberty. Further, it was not a peculiarly British problem. The increasing power of government is a universal phenomenon in the twentieth century, extending to the United States on the one hand, and to the Soviet Union on the other.

Everywhere, this extension has provoked resentment, and has stressed the remoteness of central government from the people to whom its activities are directed. 'The result of all these developments is that there is a powerful nationalist feeling in Scotland and Wales and a strong resentment of London in the rest of the country. There is now no major provincial city in which criticism of the remoteness and arrogance of London does not meet with warm applause. In this view, whether it is applied to politics or to business, Bristol and Newcastle, Birmingham and Manchester, think as one.'

The danger-signals are there for all to see, and governments will only ignore them, and continue towards policies of centralisation, whether open or disguised, at the cost of continuous and increasing friction. This second article therefore returned to the theme of national and regional assemblies, with competences properly safeguarded, and a second chamber with effective powers.

'The new constitution . . . might provide that Great Britain should be governed for all local purposes in three nations, Scotland, Wales and Northern Ireland, and in the seven regions of England herself. The governments of these nations and regions would be elected governments with very substantial powers and substantial finances. Their leading men would have to be paid salaries as large as those of our present Ministers and would certainly be too busy to seek simultaneous election to the House of Commons. If the Ministers of these authorities were to have *ex-officio* positions in the second chamber for their term of office, they could provide by a process of indirect election a large segment of the membership of a new revising chamber. They could have a fixed proportion of the membership of the new House and the first appointments and life peers might make up the rest.'

The article concluded with a strong plea for the enactment of a bill of rights for citizens – a plea which is in itself an admission of the extent to which, in the twentieth century, the traditional protection accorded by the Common Law has been abridged, and in numerous instances abrogated, by administrative action.

It is already evident that there is a strong body of opinion which believes changes no less radical than those discussed in these two leading articles are overdue. J. P. Mackintosh, M.P., outlined a rather similar development in *The Devolution of Power*, and on the other side of the House of Commons, Quintin Hogg, both in public speeches and in his pamphlet *New Charter : Some Proposals for Constitutional Reform,* has discussed the problem of constitutional reform in much the same way. He has suggested that an early opportunity should be taken to call a constitutional conference, because political institutions are in danger of collapse. Government has become virtually an elective dictatorship, and Parliament is grappling inadequately with too great a volume of projected legislation. His proposals for constitutional reform are those discussed by the leading articles in *The Times*, and by J. P. Mackintosh. They are:

1. The establishment of unicameral regional (or in the case of Scotland and Wales, national) legislatures, with Ministers on the Parliamentary model, and with regional sources of taxation.

2. A Bill of Rights which, except in time of emergency, would limit the power of Parliament to trespass upon the province of regional legislatures. Here, once again, one can see the value of the experience already gained of the relationship between Northern Ireland and Westminster.

3. The establishment of the right of the judiciary to pronounce upon the constitutionality of laws passed by Parliament. Today the United Kingdom is almost the only nation in which the judiciary does not possess such a power. The reason, as was pointed out in earlier chapters, is historical. Ironically, it stems from the victory of Parliament over the Crown in the seventeenth century.

4. Consideration should be given to the possibility of fixed-term Parliaments (thus removing the Prime Minister's power to demand a dissolution at any time); or alternatively, to the possibility that one-fifth of the Members of Parliament should retire annually, in a Parliament of nominally unlimited duration.

Quintin Hogg has spoken several times in the past two years in elaboration of these proposals. In a speech at Blackpool in October 1968, he said:

'Parliament is now an elective dictatorship. Its constitutional legislative powers are admittedly unlimited. Its legislation cannot be questioned in any court. Originally conceived as a brake on the executive, these powers are now controlled by the executive in the shape of a monolithic Cabinet. The party system makes the supremacy of a government like the present automatic and almost unquestioned.'

That supremacy, it may be added, is day by day removing from the ordinary citizen his right to decide matters of importance for himself, and is progressively reducing him to a semi-servile status. It is at least ironic that Crossman who, as was pointed out in the first chapter, was in October 1968 pleading for increased participation by ordinary citizens in government, was in October 1969 introducing into Parliament an elaborate and partly incomprehensible pension scheme without any consultation of the electorate, in a Parliament which had reached the last year of its life; a pensions scheme, moreover, which removes from the ordinary citizen the right to make his own arrangements for his retirement.

Whatever the Royal Commission on the Constitution may report, there is urgent need for a new approach to the constitutional question, preferably by way of the conference which Hogg has suggested. This was the method chosen when constitutions were being devised by the older Dominions, and again in the thirties for India. A conference not only permits the representation of a wide variety of interests. It permits the proceedings to occur in the full light of publicity, and public discussion. What the United Kingdom has regarded as the right procedure for over four hundred millions of people in four continents cannot be wrong for the United Kingdom.

There is another circumstance which must be weighed. The establishment of a separate, written constitution for Northern Ireland was regarded as something quite exceptional, leaving the constitutional structure of the United Kingdom otherwise unchanged, and one consequence has been that the constitutional relationship of Northern Ireland to the rest of the United Kingdom remained largely unexplained until the disturbances in the autumn of 1969. The establishment of similar constitutions for Scotland and Wales could not be similarly ignored, and it is quite clear that new constitutional machinery would need to be established to deal with three self-governing units. Similarly, effective regional governments, as distinct from the sham structure contained in the Maud Report, and not unnaturally favoured in Whitehall, would also require the creation of such machinery.

If the suggestions for constitutional change which are now

frequently made, and which show striking similarities, are to be pursued, certain general questions must first be discussed.

It has been pointed out earlier that the United Kingdom alone of modern nations has no written constitution, and that, in respect of very large areas of government, it possesses no constitution at all, in the sense of legally enforceable rules. Paradoxically, this has sometimes been erected into an argument against change. The habits and usages which masquerade as constitutional rules have been said to be so intricate, and so much a part of the national consciousness, that it would be impossible to codify them. Sometimes, too, it has been said that cabinet government is incompatible with a written constitution. In one sense this is true, in that a written constitution alone will set limits to incessant encroachments of modern British Cabinets. From any other point of view, the assertion is plainly false. Canada, the Union of South Africa, Australia, New Zealand, India, and many other Commonwealth nations have cabinet governments, functioning under written constitutions, which were either made in England, or which were devised under British influence.

Further, it must be recognised that embodying the essential terms of a constitutional compact in a written document does not put an end to constitutional development, nor does it prevent the development of constitutional conventions. The difference is to be found in the fact that under a written constitution such developments occur within a framework which preserves certain fundamental rights which the constitution guarantees. This is the situation in the United States. In the United Kingdom there is no such protection, and its absence was not recognised as a weakness until there was added to the omnicompetence of Parliament the dictatorship of the Cabinet, and the all-embracing activities of the bureaucracy which it has created.

It is also essential to realise that the enactment of a constitution implies a great deal more than passing an Act of Parliament. This, in fact, has been one of the chief weaknesses of the British system. Legislators have looked on constitutional change as exactly the same as any other legislative operation. There is nothing in constitutional theory or in human experience to justify such an assumption. The fundamental terms under which we all live together in a single political community are matters quite different in essence from a bill to amend the Companies Act, or even a bill to amend the criminal law. It should be beyond the competence of legislators appointed for a single Parliament to change them. This issue has been treated far too casually in the past, and a situation so completely at variance with that of any other civilised community should not be allowed to continue.

A constitutional law is a fundamental law, which necessarily governs and limits the operation of government. It is for this reason that it is universally recognised in the United States that the constitution possesses a special sanctity, and that it has a superior validity to all other legislation. It can be changed only by the operation of special machinery, involving not only Congress, but the legislatures of every state, three-fourths of whom must consent to the change. In the consideration of constitutional changes in the United Kingdom, there must be consideration of the principle, although the methods by which a formal constitution can be changed naturally vary from country to country. The United Kingdom today, however, cannot escape from the dilemma presented by Parliamentary sovereignty on the one hand, and the demand for national and regional existence on the other. Devolution, implying that powers granted can be recalled or modified at the will of Westminster alone, is not a substitute, and no useful purpose is served at the present time by pretending that it is. On the other hand, governmental power can be shared in a variety of ways. It is not necessary, for example, that regional powers should be co-extensive with national powers. The constitution of the Soviet Union distinguishes between the powers of distinct national groups (including those of Great Russia) and those of the regions.

The question of a Bill of Rights, such as that which is embodied in the American constitution, is again one in which it is necessary to define clearly what is being done, and how such a bill can guarantee those freedoms which today are under continuous threat.

The classic exposition of the basic British freedoms is to be found in Dicey's *Law of the Constitution*, and their nature is discussed in general terms in Chapter IV. Dicey thought (as did everyone else when Dicey wrote) that British freedoms were more secure than those elsewhere because they were Common Law rights, whilst abroad (i.e. on the continent) they were less secure because constitutions could be suspended. For example, he says:

'The matter to be noted is, – that where the right to individual freedom is a result deduced from the principles of the constitution, the idea readily occurs that the right is capable of being suspended or taken away. When, on the other hand, the right to individual freedom is part of the constitution because it is inherent in the ordinary law of the land, the right is one which can hardly be destroyed without a thorough revolution in the institutions and manners of the nation.'[1]

For reasons not apparent Dicey, throughout this interesting chapter, contrasts the position in England with that of Belgium. What he says is not true, and never has been true, of the United States, where the idea has certainly not readily occurred that constitutional rights could be suspended, and where, incidentally, many Americans thought, at the time of the Revolution, that Common Law rights had been denied them. Dicey extricates himself from this difficulty by remarking consolingly on the previous page that 'the rule of law is as marked a feature of the United States as of England', so all is well again. Constitutions, he implies, may be saved by respect for the rule of law, which, he appears to suggest, is not so marked a feature of those unhappy peoples who live on the continent.

The second part of Dicey's conclusions, quoted above, is also quite erroneous, as the experience of the last thirty years has shown. Rights are not violently overturned. They are quietly and insidiously eroded – so quietly, that the extent of the inroad is apparent only at a later date. Thirty years ago, A. P. Herbert wrote a witty essay entitled 'Is Magna Carta Law?'. The question is worthy of serious consideration. Since no court can challenge the validity of any Act of Parliament, it follows that it has no legal power to hold invalid the provision of any Act which may violate basic freedoms.

This is really the crux of the problem. There is no difficulty in enacting a Bill of Rights. Any government might be willing to enact one; but the rights which it purported to guarantee could be abridged at any time by other legislation, passed in the same way, or even by departmental legislation possessing statutory force, and which the courts would be powerless to question. If it should be suggested that such a situation could not occur, it is sufficient to remember that this is exactly what has occurred, and although in many instances, the object could be regarded as worthy, or even necessary, in the national interest, it does not follow that it will always be so in the future. How serious such a possibility might be is

[1] 10th ed., p. 201.

explained in the clearest possible terms by that great judge Lord Shaw in his speech in *R. v. Halliday, Ex parte Zadig*,[1] when discussing the extent of the powers conferred by Parliament upon the executive, under which Defence of the Realm Regulations were made, permitting the detention of persons without trial. This was in wartime, and many of the regulations, including the one under which such detention was possible, were repealed very shortly after the war ended. The point of importance, however, is that Parliament had power to make such delegations, that the delegations could and did abridge fundamental rights (for the appellant in this case was a British citizen, albeit a naturalised one), and the courts – even the House of Lords as final court of appeal – had no power to do anything about it. The grant and extent of powers such as these would only be contemplated in an emergency – but there may be different views upon what constitutes an emergency.

This, moreover, is by no means the only danger. A more constant threat, and a more insidious one, is the legislation which is passed for an apparently socially valuable purpose, but which incidentally includes yet another abridgement of liberty and yet another infringement of personal rights. For example, the Trade Descriptions Act, 1968, section 28, confers very wide powers upon an officer of a local weights and measures authority or of a government department, to enter premises, seize goods and documents, and require a shopkeeper to break open any container. Unlike his American counterpart, the British shopkeeper has no constitutional protection against such activities. Instances of this kind in modern legislation could be multiplied almost indefinitely.

It is therefore quite futile, and also misleading, to enact a Bill of Rights unless it is also embodied in a constitution which can only be modified by some special procedure, other than ordinary legislation. It is also essential that some court, or system of courts, should be given the power to pronounce legislation, both Parliamentary and departmental, void, if it trespasses upon the constitutional rights embodied in the bill. Further, it is quite misleading to suggest that social conditions are changing so quickly that the enactment of a Bill of Rights in such a form would be an obstacle to progress. The United Kingdom has adhered to an International Bill of Rights and also to a European Bill of Rights. Such adherence must have been intended to mean something,

[1] [1917] A.C. 260.

even though the existence of the legislative sovereignty of Parliament makes rights guaranteed by these documents somewhat shadowy for British citizens.

It will be apparent that under a constitution framed in the way that has been advocated above, there will have been a division between central government on the one hand, and the governments of regions on the other. Upon the extent of such a division, there may be many varying views, and there are, in existing constitutions, many differing solutions. Canada, the United States, and Australia have all given different answers to the questions of division, and in South Africa, there is the interesting situation of a sovereign Parliament and subordinate provincial councils. The powers of the latter are, however, not sufficiently extensive to satisfy the aspirations of Scotland and Wales, and they do not compare in extent with those of Northern Ireland. Entrenched local constitutions, with a reserve of powers for the central government, are both possible and desirable.

Such a development would relieve both Westminster and Whitehall of a load which is already far too heavy, but it would still leave central government with a considerable, and ever-increasing, volume of work. The history of successful federations is the history of the steady extension of the activities of central government. This, in the United States, is today a growing cause of anxiety, but it is part of the universal drift towards increasing state activity, and it is a good deal better than the British position; for, as has already been mentioned, state governments and even city governments have a vitality of their own, which is lacking in Britain.

It is not necessary at this stage to analyse in detail the structure of central government. In general, it would remain much as it is today, and for better or worse, it would still be dominated by the party system. Nevertheless, one or two general suggestions may be made. One possible reason for the decline in reputation of Parliament is that there are too many legislators. For a population of approximately 50 million, we have 630 members of the House of Commons, and approximately 1,100 nominal members of the House of Lords. The United States manages for a population of 200 million, and worldwide responsibilities, with 430 Congressmen and a Senate of just over a hundred. At a generous estimate, the House of Commons could manage with 400 members, and a second chamber of a hundred or a hundred and fifty members would be ample. But in any reformation of the structure of Parliament, the second chamber should be completely separated from the peerage, and definite functions should be assigned to it. Since it is also contemplated that a constitutional court, or system of courts, should be established, the functions of the House of Lords as a final court of appeal should also be abolished. In the composition of such a senate, there could be the Ministers of the national and regional assemblies, as *The Times* leader-writer suggested, the balance being made up of persons elected by the House of Commons.

Constitutional amendments would require the assent of both Houses, and if they disagreed, there could be a joint session of the two Houses to resolve matters. They would also require the assent of any national or provincial assembly whose area would be affected by the proposed amendment.

In an earlier chapter, emphasis has been placed upon the importance of the Press in informing, and also in moulding, public opinion. Since British subjects have been talking for centuries about the excellence of the British constitution without knowing what it was, it would seem appropriate that at this extremely critical stage in British history, the Press should now draw attention to the deficiencies of the system under which people live, and to the possibility of its improvement.

Select Bibliography

[NOTE: The literature on the politics, government, and public law of the United Kingdom is vast, especially if biographies and similar works are included. The selection given below is intended as an aid to further reading.]

Allen, Sir Carleton Kemp, *Law and Orders*, 3rd ed., 1965
    Law in the Making, 7th ed., 1964
Allen, V. L., *Trade Unions and the Government*, 1960
Angell, Norman, *The Press and the Organisation of Society*, 1933
Anstey, Edgar, *Committees*, 1962
Asquith, H. H., *Fifty Years of Parliament*, 1926
    Memories and Recollections, 1928
Bagehot, Walter, *The English Constitution*
Bailey, Sydney D. (*Editor*), *The Future of the House of Lords*, 1954
    British Parliamentary Democracy, 1959
Beer, S. H., *Treasury Control*, 1957
    Modern British Politics, 1965
Beloff, Max, *The American Federal Government*, 1959
Berkeley, Humphry, *The Power of the Prime Ministe.*, 1968
Beveridge, Lord, *Power and Influence*, 1953
Birch, A. H., *Representative and Responsible Government*, 1964
Brasher, N. H., *Studies in British Government*, 1965
Bridges, Sir E., *Treasury Control*, 1950
    The Treasury, 1964
Brogan, D. W., *The American Political System*, 1943
Bromhead, P. A., *The House of Lords and Contemporary Politics*, 1958
Brown, L. N. and Garner, J. F., *French Administrative Law*, 1967
Bryce, Lord, *Modern Democracies*, 1921
Butler, D. G., *The Electoral System in Great Britain since 1918*, 2nd ed., 1963
Butt, Ronald, *The Power of Parliament*, 1970
Campbell, G. A., *The Civil Service in Britain*, 1955
Campion, Lord, *British Government since 1918*, 1950
Carter, B. E., *The Office of Prime Minister*, 1958

Chapman, Brian, *The Profession of Government*, 1959
    British Government Observed, 1963
Chester, D. N. and Willson, F. M. G., *The Organisation of British Central Government, 1914–1956*, 1957
Cole, G. D. H., *British Working Class Politics, 1832–1914*, 1941
Crick, Bernard, *The Reform of Parliament*, 1964
Cripps, Sir Stafford (and others), *Problems of a Socialist Government*, 1933
Critchley, J. A., *The Civil Service Today*, 1951
Denning, Alfred, Lord, *Freedom Under the Law*, 1949
De Smith, Stanley A., *Judicial Review of Administrative Action*, 1959
Dicey, A. V., *The Law of the Constitution*, 10th ed., 1959
    Law and Public Opinion in England, 2nd ed., 1962
Dunmill, Frank, *The Civil Service*, 1956
Eckstein, H., *Pressure Group Politics*, 1960
Emden, Cecil S., *Selected Speeches on the Constitution*, 1939
    The People and the Constitution, 2nd ed., 1956
Finer, Herman, *The British Civil Service*, 1937
Freeman, E. A., *The Growth of the English Constitution*, 1884
Garner, J. F., *Administrative Law*, 2nd ed., 1967
Gilmour, Ian, *The Body Politic*, 1969
Ginsberg, Maurice, *Law and Opinion in England in the Twentieth Century*, 1959
Gladden, E. N., *Civil Service or Bureaucracy?*, 1956
Greaves, H. R. C., *The British Constitution*, 3rd ed., 1955
Griffiths, J. A. G., *Central Departments and Local Authorities*, 1966
Griffiths, J. A. G. and Street, H., *Principles of Administrative Law*, 3rd ed., 1969
Guttsman, W. L., *The British Political Élite*, 1963
Hallam, Henry and de Lolme, J. L., *The Constitutional History of England*
Hamson, C. J., *Executive Discretion and Judicial Control*, 1954
Hanham, H. J., *Scottish Nationalism*, 1969
Hanson, A. H. and Wiseman, H. V., *Parliament at Work*, 1962
Harvey, J. and Bather, L., *The British Constitution*, 1963
Heuston, R. F. V., *Essays in Constitutional Law*, 2nd ed., 1964
Hewart, Lord, *The New Despotism*, 1929
Hill, A. and Whichelow, A., *What's Wrong with Parliament?*, 1964
Hood-Phillips, O., *Constitutional and Administrative Law*, 3rd ed., 1962
Hughes, Emrys, *Parliament and Mumbo-Jumbo*, 1966
Jennings, Sir Ivor, *The British Constitution*, 1950
    Parliament, 1957
    Cabinet Government, 1959
    The Law and the Constitution, 1959
Keeton, G. W., *The Passing of Parliament*, 2nd ed., 1954

Keir, J. C., *The Constitutional History of Modern Britain*, 3rd ed., 1946
Keith, A. Berridale, *The British Cabinet System*, 2nd ed., 1952
Kelly, Sir David, *The Ruling Few*, 1952
Kelsall, R. R., *Higher Civil Servants in Britain*, 1955
Kersell, J. E., *Parliamentary Supervision of Delegated Legislation*, 1960
King, Cecil, *The Future of the Press*, 1967
Laski, Harold J., *Parliamentary Government in England*, 1938
Lawson, F. H. and Bentley, D. J., *Constitutional and Administrative Law*, 1961
Lindsay, A. D., Lord, *The Essentials of Democracy*, 2nd ed., 1948
Lowell, A. L., *Public Opinion and Popular Government*, 1914
Macdonald, J. F., *The State and the Trade Unions*, 1960
McKenzie, Robert, *British Political Parties*, 2nd ed., 1963
Mackintosh, John P., *The British Cabinet*, 1962
    The Devolution of Power, 1968
Maitland, F. W., *The Constitutional History of England*, 1908
Menhennet, H. L. and Palmer, J., *Parliament in Perspective*, 1967
Mill, John Stuart, *On Liberty*, 1859
    On Representative Government, 1861
Moodie, G. E., *The Government of Great Britain*, 1964
Morley, John, *The Life of Gladstone*, 1905
Morrison, Herbert, *Government and Parliament*, 2nd ed., 1959
Muir, Ramsay, *How Britain is Governed*, 1930
Newton, A. P., *Federal and Unified Constitutions*, 1923
Nicolson, Nigel, *People and Parliament*, 1958
Parkinson, C. Northcote, *Parkinson's Law*, 1958
Paton, H. J., *The Claim of Scotland*, 1968
Quekett, Sir A. S., *The Constitution of Northern Ireland*, 1933
Richards, P. G., *Honourable Member*, 1959
    Patronage in British Government, 1963
Ridges, E. W., *Constitutional Law*, 8th ed., 1950
Robson, W. A., *Justice and Administrative Law*, 3rd ed., 1951
    The British System of Government, 1959
    Local Government in Crisis, 1966
Schwartz, Bernard, *American Constitutional Law*, 1955
    An Introduction to American Administrative Law, 2nd ed., 1962
Sieghart, M. A., *Government by Decree*, 1950
Stankiewicz, W. J. (and others), *Crisis in British Government*, 1967
Strauss, G., *The Ruling Servants*, 1961
Taswell-Langmead, T. P., *English Constitutional History*, 11th ed., 1960
Thomas, Harford, *The Press and the People*, 1962
Thomas, Hugh, *The Establishment*, 1959
    The Crisis in the Civil Service, 1968
Thomas, I. B., *The Party System in Great Britain*, 1953
Utley, T. E., *Occasion for Ombudsman*, 1961

Wade, H. W. R., *Towards Administrative Justice*, 1963

Warren, George (*Editor*), *The Federal Administrative Procedure Act and Administrative Agencies*, 1947

Wheare, Sir Kenneth C., *The Civil Service and the Constitution*, 1954
Government by Committee, 1955
Modern Constitutions, 1951

Williams, Francis-, Lord, *Press, Parliament and People*, 1948

Wilson, Norman, *The British System of Government*, 1963

Wiseman, H. W., *Parliament and the Executive*, 1966

Young, Roland, *The British Parliament*, 1962

Index

Printed in Great Britain by
Cox & Wyman Limited
London, Fakenham and Reading